610.92

IN THE FRONT LINE

IN THE FRONT LINE

A Doctor in War and Peace

Alec Glen

BIRLINN

First published in 2013 by
Birlinn Limited
West Newington House
10 Newington Road
Edinburgh
EH9 1QS

www.birlinn.co.uk

ISBN: 978 1 78027 130 9

British Library Cataloguing-in-Publication Data
A catalogue record for this book is available from the
British Library

Contents

Plates

Maps

The Story of the Manuscript

This book was written primarily for Alec Glen's children and grand-children between 1965 and 1970.

His two sons, my brother Iain and I, had both left home and were busy with work and young families at this time. When either of us looked in to see the folks at home we found Alec busy on an old portable typewriter, something new for him. To our enquiries, we were both given the reply, 'I am writing about my experiences. You will see it when it's finished.'

Rather surprisingly, neither of us was shown a draft typescript, and when we asked about progress, we were told, 'I am still working on it.' Later we heard that one or other of his friends had it to read.

I do remember that my brother persuaded him to see Richard Attenborough's film *Oh What a Lovely War*, which was released in 1969. We liked it as a film, but it was not a favourite with Alec, who said, 'It was not like that at all.' Looking back on this now I am inclined to think that he thought it might be better that we read his story when we were a bit older and hopefully wiser.

The manuscript disappeared from our thoughts until 1984 when our mother died, twelve years after her husband. The much-annotated manuscript in its black binder was there with my father's papers, along with a caricature of him drawn by Osborne Mavor in Mesopotamia. The manuscript was copied, and we, and later, the next generation, read it. Although the memoir made an impression on us, we knew that it was a very personal account and not a history of the period.

The original manuscript was worn and the copy never very clear and we realised that it could easily become impossible to read. With the pos-sibility of renewed interest in World War I as its centenary approached, my brother and I agreed that if it was ever to be published, now was the time. I telephoned Birlinn and received an encouraging response. Three chapters of faded typescript were sent to Birlinn in 2011.

When we were considering an approach to a publisher with these memoirs, we asked ourselves why they might be of interest to present-day readers. There have been a number of accounts of the campaigns in Gallipoli and Mesopotamia. What could this book add to the understanding of these events?

This is not an account of strategies or campaign politics, nor is it a day-by-day diary of life at the front line; rather it is a very personal reflection on those days in which details flood back of remembered voices: some of them heroes, some unknown and some recognised leaders.

This is the work of a man with a clear view of right and wrong who displays the classic characteristics of the Scot; thrawn, determined if he thought he was right, yet sensitive to what others were thinking and feeling. The memories of highly charged and stressful situations are recalled with remarkable clarity.

The manuscript was converted to electronic form later in 2011, and after minor corrections and editing we bound up an edition for family members to read. Some friends read it also and made favourable comments.

We were greatly encouraged by an email from Dr Iain Macintyre of the Scottish Society of the History of Medicine, who had been contacted by Birlinn for an opinion. He liked the story and suggested that we apply to the Society for grant support towards publication. We were delighted when in August 2012 we agreed a contract with Birlinn for publication, supported by the grant and a contribution from ourselves.

For the published edition explanatory footnotes for the modern reader have been added to the occasional notes which Alec himself made on the text.

Alastair Glen, June 2013.

Acknowledgements

Thanks are due to Hugh Andrew of Birlinn for taking on publication of this book, with particular thanks to Tom Johnstone, managing editor at Birlinn. Tom's advice, care and can-do approach have been enormously helpful in making the work ready for publication.

Crucial at an early stage were the encouraging comments made by Dr Iain Macintyre of the Scottish Society of the History of Medicine, which led to a grant towards publication provided by the Guthrie Trust.

Acknowledgement is made with thanks to the family of the late Osborne Mavor (James Bridie) for permission to include several extracts from Mavor's writing and plays. A special thanks goes to James Mavor for giving permission to include a 1917 caricature of Alec Glen drawn by Osborne Mavor in wartime Persia.

Alec Glen's family were encouraging throughout and it is a pleasure to recall the enthusiastic contributions made by the late professor Iain Glen, Alec's oldest son, who died in February 2013. He saw the book through as far as the formal agreement to publish, and made working on it a happy memory.

The author left no dedication for the book but the reader can guess who he thought were the many worthy characters in his story.

Preface

I have written this book primarily for my children and grandchildren to read.

A very large proportion of my generation between the ages of twenty and thirty-five died in the First World War. The tragedy was not only in their numbers. It was the best and most generous-hearted men who died. The medical officers in the front line knew this better than anyone else. Sometimes they survived longer in a battalion than any of the combatant officers.

Were these great wars unnecessary, as many of the younger generation are inclined to think today? I do not feel competent to answer that question and am content to leave it to future historians. I can say, however, that when we resisted the German warlords in the First World War we *thought* that we were fighting something evil. Nietzsche had taught them that self-reliance, the will for mastery and the cult of personal distinction were the noblest of all the virtues. Humility, compassion, self-sacrifice, as inculcated by Christianity, were virtues of the poor, the oppressed and the suffering. The pursuit of happiness was the ignoble idea of the common herd of mankind. The German warlords had developed a proud consciousness of their own superiority and a lofty acceptance of the self-sacrifice of others. This is what we were fighting against in the First World War. It is not surprising that it was the most terrible of all wars. In the Second World War we all *knew* that we were fighting against something evil and that made it more understandable.

The second part of this book deals with the aftermath of these two great world wars. During these fifty years we have missed very badly the men who died, and perhaps also we have missed their unborn children. If they had been alive and had been our leaders I think that we might have made a much better job of the years between the wars and since the second war. The men who have ruled us during these years have been mostly unimaginative, ungenerous and not very courageous.

Grievous as these great wars have been, there has been something on the credit side in the great advances in technology which accompanied them. The masses of the people in this country are enormously better-off than they were before 1914. Morally and spiritually, however, meantime at any rate, I do not think that they are as good as their fathers. Perhaps they are too well-off just now. I am not without hope, however, that there will be a reaction and that we will move on from Vanity Fair to better things.

Although written in the form of an autobiography, this is really the story of these last fifty extraordinary years as seen through a physician's eyes.

BOOK ONE

I

Schooldays

I was born in Glasgow in 1890 in a house which is just a few yards from the one in which I have now lived for over thirty years. My father was the younger son of an Ayrshire farmer. He was brought up in a farm and had his early education in a small country school and in Kilmarnock Academy. He came to Glasgow as a young man and worked at first in the offices of the old Caledonian Railway. Later he was offered a post in a paint-manufacturing business, which he accepted, and remained there all his life, being finally Managing Director. My mother's name was Sarah Munro. Her father, Augustus Munro, was the son of a soldier and was born in Fort Augustus in Invernesshire, hence his name. He also came to Glasgow as a young man, and got work in the shipyards which at that time were growing very rapidly. My mother told me the following story about her family.

My mother's grandfather, my great-grandfather, was ploughing in his father's farm near Culloden Moor when he turned up a sword[1] with his plough. The old women in the neighbourhood said that this meant he was bound to be a soldier. Sure enough, according to my mother's story he was lifted by the press-gang along with his two horses the following year and taken into the army. He fought throughout the Peninsular War and at Waterloo.

1. This rusty old sword lay in a cupboard in my old home for many years. I gave it to John S. Clarke who was a patient of mine in Govan. When I visited him I was astonished to find his home full of all kinds of antique weapons. When I showed him the sword later, he became quite excited and said that it was undoubtedly a sword which had belonged to one of Cumberland's officers. The scabbard had been slashed, no doubt in battle. He polished the old sword up and made a mahogany case for it. I wrote a letter giving its history which he included in the case. Clarke was a remarkable man. At that time he was a Glasgow town councillor, but he later became a Labour M.P. He told me that he was brought up in a circus, where he fed the lions as a boy. The sword went shortly after I gave it to Clarke to an exhibition of Prince Charles' relics, and afterwards was put in Fort George Museum, but I have not seen it since.

He married late in life when he returned home and was a Warrant Officer at Fort Augustus. He had seven sons and swore, because of the privations he had suffered in war, that none of his sons would become a soldier. One of his sons, however, Andrew, ran away and joined the army at Inverness. My great-grandmother, however, went to Inverness and bought him out. He ran away again and she bought him out again. He ran away for the third time, and this time he was left alone. Eventually he became a Colonel in the Royal Artillery.[2]

After he returned and his wife had died he came to live with my mother who was his niece, as he had no family. I think the house in the south side of Glasgow in which I was born was bought by him. In some of my earliest memories I can see him working in the garden there. Sometimes, I suppose when my younger brother and I were making ourselves a bit of a nuisance, he would make us stand at attention and then have us march about giving orders in a loud stern voice. I can remember that we liked this, and often asked him to drill us. My father once told me that he took Colonel Munro to a church in the neighbourhood to inspect a Boys Brigade. At his first command, 'Shun!' one of the boys got such a fright that he fell over backwards with a loud clatter.

When I was about five years old I went to a private school a short distance from my house. My older sister had already been there for a few years and there were more girls than boys at the school. I never liked the school very much. For the first few days I had to be taken by my mother, otherwise I refused to go. The school was run by a very prim, middle-aged spinster. She used to stand at the door and kiss each one of us as we left for home. I don't think I liked her very much, and I always dodged under her arm and ran away instead of kissing her. I think perhaps she did not like me much either. I never learned much at that school. I can distinctly remember doing addition in arithmetic and putting down at the foot of the column any number that came into my head. I had no idea how to do it. I do not think the teaching can have been very good.

2. My great-grandfather must have been lifted by the press-gang about 1808 or 1810. That was about sixty years after Culloden and the government was still trying to 'pacify' the Highlands in this way. These press-gang enlistments were still being carried out forty years after this, during the Highland clearances. The effect of this kind of treatment on the character and outlook of the people of the Scottish Highlands has never been fully appreciated by the British people.

At the beginning of the next session we went to another school, Bellahouston Academy. This was a large school in the south side of Glasgow, near our home, which originally had been a boarding school but shortly before had become a secondary day school, having been taken over by the Govan School Board. Most of the boys in the district went there, as transport to the schools in the city was difficult. There were only horse trams which were few and slow, and came only to Ibrox which was some distance away.

I got on much better at this school, and found I could keep my place quite easily. Unfortunately about a year after I went there I developed a stammer in my speech, which in many ways made my life miserable throughout my schooldays. I distinctly remember the day when I first began to have this speech difficulty. The teacher had put a ring of figures on the blackboard and we were supposed to multiply each figure by two. When it came to my turn, for some reason I could not get out the word 'two' and remained silent. As this had not happened to me before and as it looked as if I had not prepared my multiplication table, I was given a stroke of the strap on my hand. The following day the same thing happened again and I was strapped again. The teacher must have realised the next time it happened that something was wrong, because she passed me over and never asked me to do it again. Looking back on it I am not sure that this was wise. She also excused me reading, and I gladly accepted this. I think I would have been better to have persevered.

I continued at that school until I went to the University. In spite of my speech handicap I got on quite well with my school work. I never tried very much to excel. I am sure I had at that time what is now called an inferiority complex. My brother Augustus, or Gus, as he was called, who was two years younger than myself, did very well at school. In his final year at school he won the dux gold medal and the athletic championship in the same year. This was a feat which I do not think has ever been repeated at that school.

My father was a religious man but not a narrow-minded one. We had family worship on Sunday mornings only. On Sunday evenings, for many years, we had readings out of Bunyan's *Pilgrim's Progress*. We read out of a large illustrated volume. The illustrations, I think, made the story particularly vivid for us. I remember many of the pictures still today. We had to read a portion in turn and I had to read my portion with the rest. I am sure this exercise was good for me and gradually gave me more confidence in speaking and reading. I can still remember large portions of the book by heart. I often read it still.

My father was an elder in the church, and for a while was a Sunday School teacher and Sunday School superintendent. He started a branch of the Y.M.C.A. in Govan and actually opened the first Y.M.C.A. premises in Govan and paid the rent himself. Later the Y.M.C.A. had a large institute at Govan Cross.

—

We walked every Sunday from our house in Dumbreck to St Mary's Free Church at Govan Cross. It was nearly two miles, quite a distance for us when we were young. When we were almost halfway to the church we often met a family going the same way. There were three girls and a boy in that family. One of these girls later became my wife.

The minister was Dr Robert Howie, 'Brimstone Bob', as he was called in Govan. I don't remember much about his preaching, I was too young at the time; but I believe it must have been pretty hot stuff. Dr Howie had a large family, most of whom were grown up at the time I knew him. I remember well when his wife died, and he shortly afterwards married a younger woman. There was an enlarged photograph of him in our sitting-room, and after he married my mother took it down and hid it away.

One advantage of having so far to go to church was that we did not go again in the evening, but as children we went to Sunday School in a church nearer home. This was Sherbrooke United Free Church, now Sherbrooke Church of Scotland. I went to Sunday School there in 1896 or 97, shortly after it was opened. I still go to this church.

My father was a keen naturalist and geologist. He was a member of the Glasgow Geological Society and attended their meetings regularly.

When we were quite young, a large private estate near our house was presented to the Glasgow Corporation by the owner. It was called Bellahouston Park. Our house faced into the park and was quite near one of the entrances. Several times in the week at least, my brother and I and sometimes our sisters had a walk in the park with my father. He had a walk himself every morning before breakfast and we sometimes accompanied him then. There was another and very much larger and more ancient estate belonging to the Maxwell family about a mile away, which was also open on most days, and we often went there if we had more time. If the weather was at all fair we went winter and summer.

The routine was that my father, as we went along, pointed to a tree or a shrub or a flower or a bird, and we had to give its name and answer questions about it. We had turn about of questions, and usually kept a score of our correct answers. This was a fine experience for us, and we soon could recognise all the common trees, even in winter without their leaves. The birds were also of great interest to us, and we saw a surprising variety of animals also, especially in the early morning. We saw field mice, rabbits, moles, hedgehogs, hares, roe deer and even a badger.

We tried several times to keep hedgehogs in our garden but they always disappeared. I think they were able to climb the walls. We did not examine birds' nests in the park, although we knew where many of them were, but on country walks we were allowed to inspect the nests, though we never took any eggs.

My father also was very good at finding birds' nests, as he had been brought up in the country. I remember one day walking along a country lane with a thick hedge on either side. My father walked along the middle of the lane and my brother and I peered into the hedges on either side. Every now and then my father would point from the middle of the road and say 'There is a nest in there.' Sure enough, we always found an occupied nest, sometimes after considerable searching in the place where he had indicated.

We were greatly mystified as to how he did it. He did not tell us at that time how it was done, but told us to use our powers of observation. He later told us the secret. He said that it was obvious that boys went along that road every day to school, and he just looked for their footmarks in the verge at the side of the road. There was usually a well-marked track made by the boys' feet when they inspected the nest each day.

In later years I often told that story to medical students to illustrate the value of observation. I told them that the attitude of the patient in bed, the articles on the table at the side of the bed, the size and shape and surface of the patient's hands, all these were valuable clues as to the nature of the patient's disease and the way that he should be treated. The students always seemed to be impressed with the story about the birds' nests, and I think it helped to make them better observers.

5

For most of my youth we had a small house at Saltcoats on the Ayr-shire coast. We went there frequently at weekends throughout the year and also at the New Year and Easter holidays. My brother and I fished for saithe and small fish off the rocks and from the old harbour. At weekends we went on expeditions with my father. We found some very complete fossilised trees at low water and spent a long time chipping away the sandstone to expose them properly so that they could be inspected by the Geological Society. We also found some very good specimens of flint arrowheads and implements on the beach at Stevenston.

Later on the weekend house was moved to Prestwick. In August, however, we had our real holidays on the Island of Arran. My father's mother's name was MacKinnon and she came from the south end of Arran. Arran had a great attraction for my father besides having family connections. It is a paradise for naturalists, geologists, botanists and marine biologists. It has some of the oldest rocks in the world, the old red sandstone, exposed round its beaches. In addition there was, in later years, geologically speaking, volcanic eruption of igneous rocks in the centre of the island which form the remarkable granite peaks of Arran, similar in many ways to the Cuillins of Skye. In several parts the new rock up-ended the old rocks and made it very easy to examine the different layers. I believe that the geologists say it is the best island in the world for the study of geology.

We had many long walks, particularly round the shores of the island where the rocks are exposed, while my father chipped the rocks with his hammer and gathered specimens, and we learned the names of the different rocks and the history of their origin. On a tributary of the Lagg Burn near the south end, we discovered a very interesting collection of fossil shells and fish which is still visited by geologists. Perhaps due to the variety of rocks in the soil, the flora and marine ecology of Arran are particularly rich and varied and were also a great source of interest to us.

Getting ready to go to Arran was always a great thrill. We often left from Saltcoats where we had been for July. There were various hampers to be packed with linen, cutlery, clothes etc. and there was always a large box of provisions. There were few stores in Arran in those days, and although we sometimes stayed at Brodick, Lamlash and

Whiting Bay, we were usually at the south and west side of the island where stores were more difficult to get. We always had a furnished house, and our housemaid went with us. These were wonderful girls who nearly always came from Lewis or the outer isles. Some of them stayed with us for many years and became part of the family. They were paid I think about £1 per month.

My mother was a very gentle type of woman who never scolded us much, although I have no doubt we often deserved it. On the whole I think we behaved fairly well. If we got into any bad scrapes we were referred to my father and we did not like that. My father usually stayed with us on holiday for a fortnight in Arran and travelled daily for the rest of the month. One year we stayed at Whiting Bay for two months and he travelled for six weeks. This meant getting up very early in the morning. In those days, however, the service by train and boat from Glasgow was actually better than it is today.

My brother and I later became keen fishermen and fished most of the small streams, sometimes getting sea trout out of the most unlikely places. We also walked long distances over the moor to fish in the small lochs or tarns. I remember one fishing story at Kildonan in the south end of the island. There was a small stream alongside the old manse where we were staying. An elderly man, Captain Mackinnon, who was a cousin of my father and captain of the lifeboat which was then stationed there, lived in a small house nearby. We asked him if there were any trout in the stream. His answer was rather remarkable. He said, pointing to a pool. 'There are three nice trout in that pool, several in the pool above it and there is a good fellow in the pool just opposite my house.' We thanked him for his information. We always hoped that he was not disappointed later if he came to take them out and found them gone.

II

Medical Student at Glasgow

One day, as I was nearing the end of my schooldays, the headmaster of Bellahouston Academy, Duncan McGillivray, sent for three of us in the senior class and asked if we would like to be chartered accountants. None of us had thought much about that idea, but we accepted gladly the prospect of a forenoon off work to go into town and be interviewed by a large firm of chartered accountants. At the end of the interview we were told that the firm would be pleased to accept all three of us as apprentices. My two companions accepted but I said, I think to their surprise, that I did not wish to become a chartered accountant. Both my fellow students who were accepted that day, William Miller and Herbert Craig, did very well and eventually occupied a high position in their profession. William Miller became secretary of the Burmah Oil Company, and Herbert Craig managing director of a large Midland coal and oil combine.

My father had said to me at one time that he would like my brother and I to enter one of the professions. He said that he thought it was becoming impossible to get on in business without doing things which he would rather not have done. He thought that in a profession we would be working independently and could keep our own standard of conduct. I said that I would like to be a doctor, but it was decided that I would take an Arts degree first.

I matriculated at the University of Glasgow in September 1907 when I was aged 17. When I matriculated I stated that I was going to take an Arts course, but after speaking to some other students who were taking Medicine and finding that they were starting with subjects like Zoology I decided to change and enrolled in Zoology and Chemistry instead. The Registrar was not very pleased at my change of faculty, but after a little persuasion he agreed to it. There were only ninety medical students that year so there was no great difficulty. This would have been a very different matter today, but in those days one took more or less the class one fancied.

I loved the Zoology class and was fascinated by Professor Graham Kerr's lectures. I took notes but they were unnecessary as I remembered quite easily everything he said. The Chemistry class was a very different matter. Professor Ferguson, or 'Soda', as he was called was at that time an old man with a long grey beard which waggled every time he spoke. There were about 200 students, half of whom were science students or arts students. We could hardly hear anything he said for the noise in the classroom. He performed chemical reactions in large conical glasses instead of test tubes. When he poured one glass into the other the movement was accompanied by loud gurgling noises produced by the students.

My previous education had been classical and I had never had any chemistry, so that the whole thing was a mystery to me. Previously also I had never, I am afraid, done much homework. I had got on well enough with what I had been taught at school and had never got down seriously to study at home. I now had a recommended text book but I could not make much of it. There were four class examinations in the winter session. I got 'under 30%' for the first two examinations. When 'Soda' told us after the second examination that anyone who got less than 50% in the four tests would not get his class ticket and would require to resit the class I realised that I would have to start working and make a serious attempt to understand the subject. I had no help or tuition, but I managed to get over 70% in the third test and over 80% in the final examination and got my ticket. I had learned one valuable lesson. In a Scottish university at that time one had to teach one's self, with an occasional lecture from a professor. Botany and Physics followed in the summer session, but by that time I had mastered the technique and had no serious difficulty with class or profession-examinations.

The next stage was Practical Anatomy. This included a complete dissection of the human cadaver by each individual student. There were plenty of available unclaimed bodies in those days, and the first view of the dissecting room was a bit of a shocker to an innocent youth. There were probably twenty or thirty bodies lying in rows in various attitudes and stages of mutilation. There was a strong odour of formalin preservative.

Eight students were allocated to each cadaver: two had arms, two had legs, two had thorax and abdomen and two had head and neck. One could take as long as one liked over the work, but we usually worked two to three hours daily. There were fat and thin and old and young cadavers. One was lucky to get a thin one. They were easier to work with and not so disagreeable. We had to spend eighteen months to two years at this work.

Although we joked about it, this gross display of what death was like had an effect, I think, on most of us. It was really difficult at first to believe that these cadavers had recently been living, probably with thoughts and emotions like ourselves. The effect it had on me was that I immediately began to doubt all that I had so far believed about the future life after death. In a few weeks I imagined that I had become a 'materialist'. I didn't believe in any of the 'Christian myths' that I had been brought up on.

I read widely in my spare time. There were no cinemas and shows in those days, and on Saturday nights we used to walk into town, about two miles, to the nearest corporation lending library for books. In addition to my studies I read such books as Darwin's *Origin of the Species*, Herschel's *Riddle of the Universe*. I also read widely in philosophy, and for the first time regretted that I had not taken my father's advice to take an Arts degree before starting medicine. I did not tell my parents anything about my loss of faith in the religion which I had been taught, but I was quite sure that I was right in my new conviction.

This state of my mind and thoughts continued for a long time and I felt strangely miserable. I suppose it was my period in the wilderness, and I spent many months there. Gradually, however, my mood began to change. Perhaps it was because I had plenty to do to occupy my mind otherwise, and university life was full of interest. I began to frequent the students' union more to drink beer with the boys and argue about all sorts of things. My name was posted up in the Anatomy lecture room along with a number of other students as having too few attendances, with a warning that if I did not attend more regularly I would not get my class ticket. I thought that these anatomy lectures, especially those by the Professor's assistants, were extremely boring. I always seem to have had a much better visual than auditory memory, and I found I could learn much more easily from my dissections and diagrams than I could from listening to these lectures.

For the first year of my anatomy studies we had Professor John Cleland. He was a very large stout man with an enormous head which was covered with grey hair and curls. His hair always seemed greasy, like his jacket, as if he had wiped his fingers on it after being in the dissecting room. He walked with a tottering gait as if he was just about to fall. He was not a bad lecturer and told stories which helped to relieve the monotony. For many years before he retired he was subject to seizures of *petit mal* or minor epilepsy. He would be in the middle of his lecture and suddenly his head began to nod. Perhaps some student had annoyed him. The janitor, who always stood just out of sight behind the lecture-room door, would rush in and place a chair behind the Professor, who would sit down heavily on it. For a few minutes he was apparently semi-conscious and had great many facial and bodily contortions. He never fell off his chair.

While he was in the fit there was pandemonium in the class room. We were scared however to move out of our seats, because he was liable to come round suddenly and point to any student who was misbehaving himself and ask him a question in the subject on which he had just been lecturing. We had an idea, no doubt mistaken, that Professor Cleland always remembered anyone he caught on those occasions, and that it did not help much when it came to examination time. Professor Cleland retired after our first year and we had Professor Thomas Bryce. He was a very able man but not so interesting a lecturer as Cleland.

However, to get back to my story, I found one day on reading Thomas Carlyle's *Sartor Resartus* that he seemed to understand my mood at that time. Carlyle's hero, Professor Teufelsdrockh, gradually loses faith in everything he has been told. He loses all faith in religion. He finally reaches a point where the only things he believes are the things he knows for certain about himself, the fact that he is alive now and will die some day. He thinks there is no hope for the world or for anyone in it. He decides, however, to defy fate and make the best of the world as he finds it. This Carlyle calls the 'Everlasting No'.

After reaching this point, however, Teufelsdrockh began gradually to realise that there were other things in the world, besides material things, which he experienced himself and knew to be true. There were things like friendship, love, faithfulness and duty which he could not deny. He began to think less about himself. To quote Teufelsdrockh: 'With other eyes, too, could I now look upon my fellow man; with infinite love, an infinite pity. Poor wandering wayward man: art thou not tried and beaten with stripes even as I am? . . . The poor Earth with her poor joys was now my needy mother, not my cruel stepdame: man, with his so mad wants and so mean endeavours, had become the dearer to me; and even for his suffering and his sins I now first name him Brother'. This stage in Teufelsdrockh's story Carlyle calls the 'Everlasting Yea'.

———

Not very long after this period I started my clinical work in hospital. Instead of studying cadavers we were studying live men, women and children, all of whom were suffering and needed sympathy and under-standing. These people were just like myself, but they had many more difficulties and troubles than I had. I realised that I had a vocation now, and that my immediate duty was to work hard at my profession so that I would be able to help them. In fact I found myself too busy to continue to bother about the 'ultimate realities'.

For some time my father had been trying to persuade me to join the Church, but I always managed to put it off as I did not wish to hurt his feelings. However, I thought it was not right to deceive him any longer, and I told him one day that I did not think I would ever be able to join the Christian Church. I did not believe most of the doctrines of the Church. I did not believe the miracles that were recorded and there were a great many other things I could not accept as being true.

My father was very sympathetic and we talked over these things on a number of occasions. After a while he asked me if I would go and see our minister and talk over these things with him. I said that I did not think that would be much good, but I rather liked our minister at that time, the Rev. W. Macintosh Mackay, and I finally agreed that I would go and see him.

He received me very kindly and after a little while he asked me to tell him what I really did believe. I said that I believed in God, or at least that there was a power in the world that continually worked on the side of goodness and truth. I told him that I also believed that there was a great deal of evil in the world and that there was a continuous struggle going on between the good and the evil. I said that I wanted to be on God's side in this struggle. I could not say that I believed in the divinity of Christ or in his resurrection, but I realised that there was more godliness in Christ than in any other human person. I said also that I saw God in Nature and in the beauty of the world, and that I saw Him also in the love and kindness of many human beings.

To my great surprise Macintosh Mackay said that he would accept me as a member of the Church with these beliefs, and so I became a member of the Church. For a long time I was not sure that I had done right and wondered whether I was a bit of a fraud. I have an idea that ministers of religion are stricter in these matters today than they used to be, and I am not sure that I would have been accepted today. As the years have gone on, my beliefs have gradually tended towards more acceptance of Christian faith and ideology, but I have never been able to accept all the doctrines of the Church.

Macintosh Mackay was a remarkable man in many ways. He had a beautiful voice and was a great preacher, but he was a very absent-minded man. Fortunately for him he had a wonderful wife. She was a very able and attractive woman and a sister of Professor Moffat, who made a new translation of the *New Testament* which is still used and quoted. Mackintosh Mackay later received a D.D. degree and became, I think, Moderator of the Church of Scotland.

Many stories are told of his absent-mindedness. He is said to have met a nursemaid with a baby in a pram. When the maid smiled at him he stopped and said, 'What a lovely baby!' The maid replied, 'Yes, Mr Mackay, he is a lovely baby. He is your own baby.' He was sometimes seen to get on to a tramcar and put his hat on the box in the vestibule, thinking that he was going into a house. When he went to preach at a distance it is said that he sometimes had to get out at a station where the train stopped to telephone his wife to find out where he was going.

Everyone in his congregation could tell many of these stories and I could tell many more myself, but he was a very kindly and sincere man and was greatly loved by all. One rather different incident occurs to me. When he was a somewhat older man he was at the Church Assembly in Edinburgh one year when the weather was very warm. He was very fond of bathing and he went down to Portobello and had a swim in the sea. One his way home to Glasgow he developed an abdominal pain which continued to get worse during the evening. Mrs Mackay wanted to call in a doctor, but he had not seen a doctor for many years and said that he did not believe in doctors.

Towards the morning he seemed to be very ill and Mrs Mackay said that it might be a good thing if he had a talk with Dr Glen about it. He said, 'All right, I will see him.' It was the first time I had seen him professionally, but he was operated on within an hour or two for strangulated hernia, just in time, and made a good recovery.

At his final illness many years later, Mrs Mackay was an invalid and had had one leg amputated, so Dr Mackay had to go to hospital and be nursed. I remember seeing him in hospital. He had no idea where he was and talked quite happily and contentedly on other subjects. He never mentioned his own illness.

—

Life at the University in these pre-1914 years was very pleasant. There was no great rush to pass professional examinations. There were several 'chronic' medical students who had been attending classes for as long as 15 or 20 years. They had a very pleasant life and were often very capable people who took a prominent part in the life of the University. Their chief trouble, perhaps, was that they had too much money.

I joined the Officers Training Corps in my first year at the University and had a fortnight each year in camp with some of the best students of these times. We got to know one another well at these camps, and it was there that I first got to know men like Walter Elliot, Osborne Mavor and many others who made history in later years, and many other exceptional men like G. Buchan Smith who would have made history if they had survived the first great European war. We had camps at Stobs, Carnoustie, Folkestone and Gailes. We attended the Coronation parade of George V in Windsor Park in 1912 and afterwards went on to camp near Folkestone for a fortnight along with Edinburgh University O.T.C.

In the years before the First War we had regular Army officers attached to our O.T.C. units who trained and lectured to us specifically about the war which they appeared to assume was almost certain to come. One of them, Captain A.N.E. Browne, who was our adjutant for some years, was a great favourite with us. He had lost most of one arm in the South African War and had a hook fixed on his arm instead with which he could do all manner of things. We called him 'Captain Hook'. When he left us finally at Folkestone we paraded in his honour and marched at attention all the way to the station, about two miles, to see him off.

One other incident remains in my memory about the camp at Folkestone. We were having a field day, and I was sent forward as a scout party vanguard in charge of two other cadets. My patrol on that day lost contact with the main body. Strictly speaking we did not lose our way, but after a while we found ourselves on the beach. It was a lovely day and we could see no sign of our comrades or the so-called enemy. We had a bathe and then went into a small hotel and had some lunch and spent the afternoon on the shore. We thought it wise not to turn up too soon and arrived back at camp about 7 p.m.

The officer then in charge of my company (B Company) was Captain Bowman. At that time he was an assistant to the Professor of Logic in Glasgow. He was captured by the Germans in the First War and was a prisoner for several years. After the war he went to Princeton University in America and later returned to Glasgow, where he became a famous Professor of Moral Philosophy. I reported to Captain Bowman and said that we had lost contact. He said 'Did you try to get contact again?' I said that we had looked for the unit for a long time but that they must have gone in a different direction. Bowman said 'I am very sorry. You will have had nothing to eat,' and gave orders to the Cookhouse that we should get some supper.

We had expected at the very least to have got some sort of punishment or reprimand, but Bowman was a man who always acted in this way. He expected everyone to tell him the truth. I felt very miserable about this incident at the time and vowed that I would always tell him the strict truth in future. Bowman was a shy kind of man, but he made a very fine officer and B Company was a good company.

I sat my second Professional examination in Anatomy, Physiology and Materia Medica in March 1910. Osborne Mavor, who had started two years before me, was still struggling with his Anatomy at that time. He was in the same batch with me for his oral examination. We usually waited in the lecture room on those occasions till we were called in individually for our oral. I was feeling rather nervous, but Mavor started drawing cartoons on the blackboard of Professor Cleland and Professor Bryce and various other notables. Then we started a sing-song and the janitor came from the examination room to tell us to stop the noise. When we asked Mavor afterwards how he had got on at his oral he said that Professor Bryce had asked him when he went in if he considered that he really knew his subject. Mavor truthfully answered 'No'. Professor Bryce then proceeded to give him a

15

short demonstration all to himself on a specimen of the human heart.

Mavor was ploughed that day for the third time. He afterwards wrote a small poem in the *G.U.M.* (*Glasgow University Magazine*) one verse of which ran as follows:

> Professor Bryce, Professor Bryce,
> You've ploughed me twice,
> Let twice suffice.

He passed at his fifth attempt. Many years later when we were colleagues in hospital I told him that one of my sons had been ploughed in Anatomy. He said 'Good man. No self-respecting man should pass in Anatomy at his first attempt.'

I think Mavor must have started working seriously after he got through Anatomy, because he passed his final in the same year as myself. I was frequently in the same clinical class as Mavor after this. One morning in Professor Samson Gemmell's clinic, Mavor and Walter Elliot arrived about an hour late. As they rather shamefacedly joined us in the ward, Samson Gemmell looked up and said in his drawling nasal voice, 'Here they come, dragging their weary feet after a mis-spent night.'

Mavor, who was standing next to me round the bed, told me shortly afterwards, 'We have been up since 4 a.m. We were at the Gonachan for the weekend and tried to take a short cut over the Campsies and lost our way in a mist.' The Gonachan was an old house on the banks of the Gonachan burn, a tributary of the Endrick at Fintry. I don't know who paid the rent but I spent several weekends there myself as a student. There were beds and blankets and several sets of kilts which we put on on arrival. We washed in the river. The first time you were at the Gonachan you were taken up the river in a follow-the-leader game. At one point you had to climb round a cliff with a large pool below. If you did not know where to feel for a crack in the rock where you could get a grip, you were almost certain to fall into the pool. This was considered to be your initiation.

We worked fairly hard these days but we had lots of fun. I managed to get through my examinations most of the time. I never distinguished myself at the theoretical work but I did well at clinical work, with one exception which I will describe later, and gained several clinical prizes and a medal in clinical medicine.

I sat my Final Professional Examination in the autumn of 1912 and failed in Midwifery. This was the first time I had failed in a Professional Examination and I was much upset at first. It happened in this way. I passed apparently well in Medicine and Surgery, and was given separate passes in these subjects which I would not have been given had I been borderline. I got a first class certificate in the Midwifery written class examination a few weeks before I sat the Professional exam. I think in fact I was fourth or fifth in the class. I thought I had done a reasonably good written paper, but when I came to my oral Professor Cameron handed me a pessary and a model of the female pelvis and said, 'Let me see how you would insert the pessary.' I inserted it upside-down. I knew immediately that I had done it incorrectly and tried to reapply it, but this was a fatal mistake. Cameron looked at the outside examiner and said to me, 'That will do.'

It was my own fault. I had neglected my clinical midwifery and especially clinical gynaecology. I felt somewhat shy and embarrassed in examining women in that intimate way. I had only attended gynaecological dispensary on about two occasions. It was quite easy to get an attendance ticket in these dispensaries. The teachers were too busy with the practical work to trouble about the students' attendances, and one had only to enrol in the class and call at the end of the session for one's ticket, and I had not attended. I had never applied a pessary myself in the living subject, though this was an extremely common manipulation in those days. I knew my subject well theoretically and I vaguely thought it would be time enough after I qualified to do the practical work.

By this time I had made up my mind I wanted to be a physician and I was not really interested in gynaecology. I had not liked Professor Cameron's lectures. He told a lot of lewd coarse stories which I did not appreciate very much. I thought that they were funny enough but rather out of place.

There is no doubt that in all this I did Professor Murdoch Cameron an injustice. He was a great man in many ways. He has been given the credit throughout the world of introducing the modern operation of Caesarean Section. In 1891 he wrote, 'I think the time has come when the lives of mother and child alike may be saved, and I prefer to think that an infant come to maturity is destined for something greater than to have its glimmering life extinguished by an accoucheur[3] skilled in the use of the dreadful perforator.'[4]

Glasgow in Cameron's day and in my own was full of women with rickets and deformed pelvises, and at that time destruction of the child was a very common operation in order to save the life of the mother. Unfortunately Caesarean Section has to be performed in the early stage of labour, or preferably before labour has started at all. If Caesarean Section is left too late and the head is too large to come through the bony pelvis and at the same time the mother is becoming exhausted, perforation has still to be performed. I have seen it done myself and hated to see it. I have never actually done it myself, although in my early years in general practice I attended more than 1,500 confinements. Fortunately, with more careful prenatal examination, there is now practically never any necessity for this procedure.

When I got over the shock of my failure I realised that I had been at fault, and made up my mind that I would really make a study of practical obstetrics and gynaecology. I joined all the clinics I could and attended the maternity hospital for experience whenever possible. I told some of my teachers my story and they were somewhat amused, but they gave me every help, and after six months doing nothing else I became quite expert at gynaecology and obstetrics.

I was not asked to take any more maternity cases in the district and I was glad of that. I had not liked my previous experience. The women whom we attended in the poorer districts of Glasgow in those days lived in incredibly miserable conditions. The houses were mostly quite primitive, almost devoid of furniture and often very dirty. As students we had occasionally to go out and buy clothes for the baby. Lice and fleas were everywhere. I remember attending the wife of a carter who at that time only earned 18 shillings per week. The only water obtainable was from a pump in the back-court. This was in the centre of Glasgow in the year 1913. It was a very different matter attending a confinement in the spotless conditions of the maternity hospital. I remember being thrilled when I saw a young woman whom I had attended in hospital having her first baby put in her arms.

3. Male midwife.
4. An instrument used to abort and remove a baby from the womb by boring a hole in its skull.

I still get something of that feeling when I see a woman with a baby in her arms. I began to understand women much better. I talked to them about their troubles and their home affairs. Instead of finding them embarrassed I found them extremely practical, sensible and grateful. In their view I was only a doctor and a very useful person when required. I am sure that that winter's work was a very valuable experience for me. I have always had confidence since then talking to and in treating women, and seem to get their confidence in return.

About six months later when it came near the time for my repeat Professional Examination I suddenly realised that I had not done any systematic reading of my text books. When I did get down to it, however, I found that the reading and revision of my books was quite easy. I got Murdoch Cameron again in my oral. I got nervous and stammered a little when he asked me some questions. He then asked me if I played the fiddle. I suppose it was kindly meant and he thought that perhaps music might help my speech. However, I got suddenly annoyed and stammered out, 'I don't see what that question has got to do with obstetrics.'

He looked at me coldly and then at the external examiner and said again, as he had said in my previous interview, 'That will do, Mr Glen.' I got a sudden sinking feeling and thought I was ploughed for the second time. However, I wasn't and graduated in Medicine a few days later. Walter Elliot was in the same batch with me that day at my oral examination and graduated at the same time. Osborne Mavor graduated six months later.

III

Hospital Life

I started work in the Western Infirmary as a resident physician to Dr William MacLennan in March 1913. I had been booked to start with him in the previous autumn if I had not failed in my Final, but he was good enough to take me the following year. It was a very busy life. He was a very popular teacher. We had about 60 medical students.

MacLennan was also, for his day, a fairly advanced clinical biochemist. In those days any biochemistry was done in the ward test-room. There was no hospital biochemist. After working all day in the wards doing medical reports etc. I was often up till long after midnight working in the test-room. The Superintendent of the hospital called MacLennan's test-room the 'stink-room' and closed the door every time he found it open. One morning the ward maid found me asleep in a chair at 7 a.m. I was as much surprised as she was. One might be inclined to think, judging from what we see on the television screen today, that indoor hospital work is chiefly concerned with interesting situations associated with a lot of fun and games. Actually it is really very hard work and the working hours are very long, so long in fact that I am sure no other profession or trade would put up with them.

◆

Many incidents that occurred there are very clear in my memory. On my first receiving night[5] after I started work, a young well-developed woman in her early twenties was brought in unconscious. She had gone unconscious quite suddenly when going about her usual duties. She was completely paralysed down one side of her body and was breathing stertorously, i.e. very loudly. The pupils of her eyes were unequal in size. I diagnosed a cerebral haemorrhage. Although I must have read it in my books, I had never quite realised that such a thing could happen to young healthy people like this.

5. Period, usually 24 hours, when a hospital admits all the emergency patients in its specialty to one ward.

I telephoned my chief and thought that he would come up to hospital to see her. He said to me, 'Do you think that she is going to live?'

I replied, 'No, I am afraid she is dying.'

He said, 'You will just have to look after her yourself, Glen. You can do as much as I could do.'

A few days later, a woman who was to be transferred the following morning to a surgical ward for an operation for gall-stones died quite suddenly in the ward. I telephoned my chief to tell him about it, and all he said was, 'Thank God'. I suppose he meant that it was better she should die in bed than on the operating table.

I began to understand what the practice of medicine really meant. There were a great many disappointments and tragedies, and in those days not so much to be happy about.

There were, however, lighter moments. We were able to get out of hospital on certain days if our work was up to date. A minimum number of residents, however, had to be on duty all the time, and on Sunday afternoons things occasionally got a bit quiet. John Teggart, who was always up to tricks of some sort, invented a game of 'follow my leader'. Hospital was a fine place for such a game. There were great spaces in the cellars of the hospital full of hot pipes and all manner of things where one could be hidden for weeks. There were the attics; there were the nurses' and sisters' quarters. We did not dare to venture far into these in those days.

There was also an underground passage to the mortuary, which was set apart from the hospital, so that patients who died could be removed there without being seen by all the patients and staff. We went along that passage one Sunday and arrived in the mortuary. There were three or four inmates of the mortuary, but what was more interesting to John Teggart was that there were several men leaning on the wall outside, in what was one of the main thoroughfares of the city. We could see their legs through a grating. John signalled for silence and began to moan heavily. Then he murmured, 'They think I am deed and I am no deed. Oh! Oh!' and more groans. There was immediately much excitement outside. The men peered through the grating but could see nothing because it was quite dark inside. I am not sure whether they had even realised previously that they were standing outside a mortuary.

We hurried off to the residents' quarters by the underground passage and sat quietly looking as innocent as possible. Very soon there was considerable excitement at the gate and the head porter came along and told us that some men had heard sounds coming from the mortuary, and would we come along to see if by any chance there was anyone alive there. We of course hurried along with him and carefully examined all the bodies and declared them all thoroughly dead.

There was much mystification when we came away, but the fireman who was on duty that day was overheard to say that he thought 'Some of they young doctors had been up to some mischief.' Of that small party that day John Teggart and Teddy Maitland died in the war a year or two later.

One receiving day in the medical wards I had been very busy and had admitted eight new cases of pneumonia. At that time pneumonia was a very prevalent and terrible disease, and was admitted to the general hospitals as well as to the fever hospitals. The acute stage lasted for 7 to 9 days and ended with a crisis, when the temperature suddenly dropped and the patient began to recover. During the fever period they were very delirious and noisy and liable to fall out of bed. Quite a large proportion did not recover, many of them men in the prime of life.

Later in the evening when I visited the ward there were about a dozen wildly delirious male patients. There were only two nurses on duty, a staff nurse and a probationer. The staff nurse had gone crazy with overwork and anxiety. She was weeping and shouted at me, 'If any more patients come into this ward I will murder them!' I beat a hasty retreat and got the night sister. We took the staff nurse off duty and put two others in her place.

At that time there was only a night and a day shift. Night nurses had, I think, to work 13 hours, 7 p.m. to 8 a.m. Pay for a probationer was £10 a year with deductions for books etc. Staff nurses got £30 to £40 and sisters £50 to £80. Resident doctors got no pay. We were supposed to be gaining experience.

After six months I transferred to the surgical side of the hospital under Duncan Macartney. He was a big strong man with a beard who came from Girvan in Ayrshire. His ancestors, I believe, had been fishermen.

The first morning I arrived on the corridor I had to give seven or eight prolonged anaesthetics for major surgical operations. At that time there were no specialist anaesthetists as there are now who do nothing else but give anaesthetics and are specially trained and very skilled at their work. The anaesthetics we gave were often chloroform and open ether, much more dangerous methods than are used today. Under Sir William Macewen we had a very good training but very little practical experience. That morning I got through successfully and gave little cause of anxiety, and Macartney was kind enough to give me a word of appreciation afterwards.

These were the early days of recognition and appreciation of acute appendicitis, and we had several young children brought in too late who died from peritonitis. I remember that Macartney, in spite of his rather gruff manner, was very upset about these children.

One morning a woman arrived from Girvan to see the chief with a story of having vomited for about 24 hours. Macartney examined her and seemed puzzled about her. He said she should be admitted and kept under observation. She was a stout woman and difficult to examine, but a few hours later when I saw her again she complained of some tenderness when I palpated her groin. On feeling more carefully I made out a small round hard knob about the size of a marble. I suspected a strangulated hernia and telephoned to Macartney. I was fortunate to get him at his lunch. When he heard my story he exclaimed, 'Good God, at my age! I will be up in ten minutes.'

He operated and found, as we suspected, a small strangulated hernia. The bowel was black but not gangrenous and she made a good recovery. Another few hours and it would almost certainly have been fatal.

We made mistakes and learned from them. Unfortunately, in medicine, mistakes may cost lives. One night I was called down to the receiving room, or outdoor casualty department as it is usually called today, and found a man in a wildly excited state. He was smelling of drink and would give no account of himself, but was striking out at everyone who came near him. I was very unwilling to admit him because it was very unfair to the nursing staff and to the other patients. However, I felt that there was something wrong that I did not understand, and with the help of porters I gave him a sedative injection and went upstairs to make my apologies to the staff.

He quietened down after a bit and I got to bed about 2 a.m. An hour or two later I was wakened in my room, which was in the same corridor as the ward, by the nurse on duty, who said that she had taken this man's temperature and it was 108°. This was an almost unheard-of temperature and I said to the nurse, being only half awake, 'Don't be daft. There is something wrong with your thermometer. Away and take it again.'

She went off somewhat in a huff, I think, and I fell asleep again. Probably about an hour later I was wakened again with a loud banging on my door. 'Maybe you will believe me now. That man is up and trying to jump through one of the windows.' I found him half out of a broken window being held by several convalescent operation cases.

We got him to bed and shortly afterwards he became unconscious and died an hour or two later. He had unequal pupils and I thought he had had a cerebral haemorrhage. There was no history of accident and no evidence of serious injury on his head or body. At Post Mortem he was found to have a fractured skull. The injury and associated haemorrhage had interfered with the temperature-regulating centre in the brain.

We got his story the following day. He had fallen over the gallery of a theatre down among the seats below and had got up and walked away. Some instinct must have taken him to the Infirmary, where he apparently arrived under his own steam. A decompression operation on the skull done in time might possibly have saved this man.

I made another similar mistake when I let an old, very dirty, drunk woman go home after stitching a wound in her head. She was found dead in the morning, no doubt with a fractured skull. The Superintendent of the hospital, Colonel Macintosh, sent for me to his office and said it was lucky for me that nobody seemed to be the least interested in her, otherwise there might have been a fatal accident enquiry and I would have had a bad time.

One day a notice was posted in the residents' quarters in the Western Infirmary: 'The Royal Infirmary Resident Staff, invite the Resident Staff of the Western Infirmary to a symposium at 6.30 p.m. on … Carriages at 12 midnight prompt.' We all went, except one man who was receiving surgeon that night. It happened to be Sir William Macewen's unit.

When we arrived at the Royal Infirmary we found a table laid out in the out-patients department, well away from the wards. The porters were acting as waiters. The decorations were a row of beer bottles four deep down the centre of the table. Walter Elliot and O.H. Mavor were residents in the Royal Infirmary at that time. Walter Elliot took the chair. After the main part of the dinner was over, Walter started to make a speech which seemed to me to continue all the rest of the evening, with intervals during which Mavor entertained us with songs at the piano, 'The Ballad of John Glaister' etc., in which we joined in the choruses. It was a most enjoyable evening. At 12 midnight prompt we were assisted by the porters into four or five horse-drawn cabs which had arrived at the gate, and returned to the Western Infirmary singing joyfully all the way.

We had settled down to have another sing-song round a bottle of whisky which someone had produced, when Macewen's resident arrived to say that Sir William had arrived himself to do an emergency operation and he must have one of us as anaesthetist, as he himself had to assist at the operation. It was a strangulated umbilical hernia in a stout woman over middle age, a difficult and dangerous anaesthetic to give in those days. It was a grim prospect, and to make it grimmer it was unanimously decided by the other residents that I would have to undertake the job.

When I got up to Macewen's operating theatre the patient was already on the table. The great Macewen was standing waiting impatiently, ready to begin. I washed up and donned a gown and started. The patient was already cyanosed[6] before I started the anaesthetic, and she seemed to get bluer and bluer as I continued, but miraculously continued to breathe steadily.

This is often a long and tedious operation, and towards the end of it the anaesthetic must be very deep to enable the surgeon to draw the abdominal walls together. As I pushed the chloroform and ether she seemed to get almost black, but Macewen never spoke a word to me even when he had finished and I stopped the anaesthetic. I might never have existed so far as he was concerned. This was quite typical of Macewen, though I think he must have smelled the beer on my breath that night.

6. Turning blue due to lack of oxygen in the blood.

IV

Ship's Surgeon, War and Kitchener's Army

My year at the Western Infirmary came to an end in March 1914. I would have liked, and in fact had arranged, to spend six months in Bellshill Maternity Hospital because I had become interested in that kind of work, but it was not to be. My oldest sister had become engaged to be married to a man who had gone out to Canada for an appointment in insurance. She wanted to go out that spring to be married in Montreal. I agreed to go as surgeon on a ship to Montreal to represent the family at the wedding.

I sailed as ship's surgeon on the Allan liner, the *Corsican*, early in April. My sister had booked a passage on the same ship. The *Corsican* was a ship about 8,000 tons which carried 1,500 passengers, most of them third-class emigrant passengers from Eastern Europe. Most of the third-class accommodation was arranged in the large holds of the ship, which were crowded with tiers of bunks, about 4–6 bunks above one another. So far as I can remember, men and women were in separate holds. They were mostly Russian and Polish peasants who had never seen a ship before. My sister was one of the few Saloon passengers.

We went into a very severe storm shortly after leaving the Clyde, and practically all the passengers on the ship, including myself, became sea-sick. The next few days were pandemonium. There were a great many accidents from people falling out of bunks and tumbling down stairs. One of the men had a fractured skull and remained unconscious until we got to Canada. We had several broken limbs.

The only hospital accommodation was a small unfurnished saloon over the stern of the ship which could accommodate six patients. I think it was intended to be an isolation hospital. The stern of the ship went up and down about 30 feet with every wave, and the propellor came out of the water with a shuddering vibration. I was sick every time I went up to see my patients. In the middle of the storm one of the Russian emigrants gave birth to a baby.

As I was trying to get out of my bunk on the third or fourth morning after we sailed, the ship gave an extra lurch and I rolled over into the corner of my cabin. I had great difficulty getting on my feet again, and when I did I sent for the Chief Steward. He had told me a few days before that he was my chief assistant, and certainly he had been very helpful to me in many ways. When he came along I said to him, 'You told me you were my chief assistant. Well, carry on now. You will require to take over – I'm done.'

He replied, 'You're not done. I have been watching you. All you require is some food.'

He took me along to his office and gave me a glass three-quarters full of neat whisky. He said that he was my doctor now and that he would wait and see me finish it. I did so with difficulty, and then on his advice I staggered along to the dining saloon and went through the full menu. I felt much better and had no more sea-sickness.

When we arrived at Father Point in the Gulf of St Lawrence, the ship stopped and a French doctor came aboard about 5 a.m. to inspect the ship for infectious disease. I met him as he came aboard, and told him that so far as I was aware there was no infectious disease; but that we had had a rough passage, many of the emigrants were still sick and I had difficulty in keeping up with the work.

'Parade the ship,' he replied. That meant that everyone had to parade on deck to be inspected. He was within his rights in asking for this, but I thought it an extraordinary request under the circumstances and at that time in the morning. I went up to the bridge to report to Captain Hall. 'Tell the Chief Steward what he says,' was his response.

By that time, however, the Chief Steward had got hold of the French doctor, and I found him down in my cabin inspecting my log book. He had half a dozen tins of cigarettes and a box of cigars in front of him. He then announced, 'I have inspected your log doctor. Everything seems to be in order. We will call off the inspection.'

I was not very impressed with the whole procedure, but there were probably some mitigating circumstances. We were the first ship to come up the river that year after a prolonged winter, and no doubt the doctor was very short of cigarettes.

Actually we had passed a Donaldson liner a few hours earlier. There is always a race to be the first ship up the St Lawrence after the winter, but the Donaldson ship had gone too close inshore to avoid the heavy ice with which the river was jammed and had run aground. We were the first ship to arrive at Montreal that year, and the Captain got the customary umbrella and top hat from the Mayor.

I noticed that when the French doctor came aboard at Father Point, the full passenger gangway was lowered for him and he came up like a V.I.P. This was in contrast to our return to Greenock. When the Medical Officer there came on board, a rope ladder only was thrown over the side and he came up hand-over-hand like a pilot. The Greenock doctor was very obliging. He gave me a copy of the *Glasgow Herald* and a copy for the Captain, and asked me if I had anything to report. I replied that I had three cases of scarlet fever. He said, 'OK, I will telephone and get an ambulance to meet you at Princes Dock,' and went down the ladder again.

After we arrived at Montreal, it was about four hours before I had finished my duties and could go ashore. As I passed through the customs shed I saw a woman who had been very sick during the voyage sitting on top of her trunk in the customs shed. Her two small children were lying asleep on top of the trunk. I asked her what was the cause of the delay, and she said that the customs people had not come near her to pass her trunk. I was concerned as it was getting late, and I went ahead to see my friend, the Chief Steward, to ask what I could do about it.

'Go along to the customs office,' he said, 'and give someone half a crown and tell them to pass her luggage.'

I did so and found half a dozen customs men having a cup of tea. I gave one of them the half-crown and he came out and chalked her trunk. I then got a cab for her and saw her off to the station where she was going. So far I was not very impressed with Canada, but I have no doubt I was a pretty innocent youth at that time.

I saw my sister married at Montreal, and when we got back to Glasgow I received my pay for the three weeks' voyage in the shape of 15 golden sovereigns. I was rather proud because it was the first money I had earned. This was one of those periods, which come round occasionally, when there was a great scarcity of doctors and the pay had recently been raised from £2 a week to £5 a week.

After I had received my pay I was told that the manager would like to see me in his office. He showed me a full page article in the *Daily Mail*, the popular newspaper at that time, describing the conditions of our voyage out in the *Corsican*. It was very critical in many respects about the way the emigrants were accommodated, and the only people who received any compliments at all were the crew and myself. Apparently the reporter had fallen down one of the stairs and scraped his leg.

I remembered the man quite well and the fact that he had talked a great deal and tried to get information out of me. Fortunately I had been loyal to the ship and had not groused to him about the inadequate hospital provision or the deficiencies in my equipment. I told the manager, however, what I thought, and said that there should be some hospital accommodation in the centre of the ship. He said that he would see what could be done about it. It was many years afterwards, however, before proper medical accommodation in ships became general.

Despite this, the manager persuaded me to sign on for another trip as surgeon. He said that it was almost impossible to get anyone, and his ship could not sail without a surgeon. This second trip was uneventful, except that on the way home the *Empress of Ireland*, which was preceding us down the St Lawrence, was in collision with a collier in a fog and sank in about one hour. The passengers had not been long aboard and did not know their way about when the ship was suddenly plunged into darkness. Many of them were injured when the ship heeled over, and about 300 people were lost.

We arrived on the scene about six hours afterwards, and as we had spare accommodation about 200 passengers were transferred from shore to our ship. Many of these people had minor injuries and were in a bad way, so I had a busy time again on the way home.

——

After returning from this second voyage I did several locums to gain experience of general practice. I spent the month of June 1914 at Taynuilt near Oban, relieving the late Dr McNicol for the month. I particularly enjoyed that experience. The practice covered a large area, from the south side of Loch Awe nearly as far north as Ballachulish on Loch Linnhe. There was no Highland medical scheme at that time, and medical practice in the Highlands was a very poorly remunerated job. The doctor had one of the early motor cars, but it had broken down and was away for repairs, so I made do with a bicycle or a train to Connel Ferry and then on to Ballachulish, and sometimes hired a motor boat. If one had come any distance one was nearly always offered a refreshment of whisky, and I had many long journeys which I thoroughly enjoyed as the weather was very good.

However, to give some idea of what practice there might be like in the winter time in Argyllshire, I will record one night's work. Practically all messages were delivered by telegram, and I received an urgent call one night to go to the other side of Loch Awe. I set off about 8 p.m. from Taynuilt up Glen Nant. This was a narrow, winding, hilly road and it was about nine miles to Taycreggan on Loch Awe. I got the ferryman out and crossed to Portsonachan and cycled a few miles down Loch Aweside; then left my bicycle and climbed up to a croft on the hillside. There I found my patient, a man about 78 years of age, in great distress with an over-distended bladder and an enlarged prostate. I had a metal catheter with me, but I knew at once it was not very suitable for this case and when I attempted to pass it I only caused bleeding and did not persevere. What I required was a soft rubber catheter and I had not one with me. My telegram had given me no warning as to the type of emergency I had to meet.

There was nothing for it but to start back immediately for Taynuilt to get the necessary equipment and prepare also for an emergency operation. By the time I had crossed Loch Awe again by ferry it was quite dark. Glen Nant is a narrow road for most of the way among trees, and it was so dark that I had to walk my cycle as I could not see the ditch at the side of the road. I was unable to find a rubber catheter in the doctor's surgery, but took more suitably shaped metal ones and anaesthetics etc. for an operation.

I crossed by the ferry again about 2 a.m. Having failed again with the catheter I made an incision into the lower part of the abdomen and put a tube directly into the bladder, giving my patient immediate relief.

I crossed by the ferry again about 6 a.m., and later that day we moved the patient into the District Nurse's house at Taynuilt, where we could look after him more easily. He refused to go to hospital at Oban, but he did well and was still doing well when I left the practice a few weeks later.

At the beginning of August 1914 I went with my family for a holiday to Stonehaven on the east coast of Scotland. When we were in church on the Sunday morning a few days later, the minister announced at the end of the service that the Germans had invaded Belgium and that we were at war with Germany. We sang the National Anthem, and when we went outside the church the square was full of Seaforth Highlanders. They were part of the 51st Scottish Territorial Division.

Later that day I wrote to the O.C. Glasgow University O.T.C. and asked him to put forward my application for a commission in the R.A.M.C. My father interrupted his holiday and we all went home a few days later. It had been a wonderful summer, and as we went home by train we saw that they had already started the harvest in some places. Everything looked prosperous and peaceful.

I received my commission at the end of August and was told to report to Tidworth Military Hospital near Salisbury Plain. I travelled south in the train with Roy Young, who was an assistant surgeon in Macartney's Unit in the Western Infirmary. He had received orders to report to Tidworth Hospital at the same time as myself.

When we arrived at Tidworth we were interviewed by a Colonel of the R.A.M.C. who asked us which branch of medicine we were chiefly interested in. We both said surgery. The result was that Roy Young, who at that time was an experienced surgeon, was put in charge of medical wards. I was put in charge of surgical wards.

The hospital was very busy. New recruits were arriving all the time at Tidworth and in the surrounding camps. When it came to a case which required an operation, I gave the anaesthetic and Roy Young did the operation. I remember that we did quite a number of emergency operations.

A large part of our time was taken up with examining recruits who had been found unfit and unsuitable for the army. One method of recruiting at that time was to take the recruiting papers into a pub and ask for volunteers. Many men were signed up in this way without any medical examination. We actually got one man at Tidworth who had been accepted into the army with tubercular bone disease and wearing an iron to support his spine. We had an army form called B 204 which a single medical officer could sign, and the man was discharged home without any more formalities.

After three weeks or so we were called into the Colonel's office again, and Roy Young was told that he had been appointed M.O. to a cavalry brigade in France. I was posted to Salisbury Plain to help to train the new Kitchener Army. I had four years in the O.T.C. and an A certificate. Roy Young had no previous army training. I was very disappointed at the posting and thought that the Colonel had made a mistake.

When I arrived at the camp in Salisbury Plain I found two officers, a sergeant major and about a thousand men in tents. The men were in civilian clothes. They came from all walks of life. Some looked like down-and-outs; some were respectably dressed and had pot hats. Several were wearing 'plus fours'. These were knicker-bocker trousers which are not worn now. Our senior officer was Captain Bramhall, a regular R.A.M.C. officer who turned out to be a first-class officer. The other officer was Edmund T. Burke, a contemporary of mine from Glasgow who had been in the O.T.C. with me. He was very keen on military affairs and had gone the length of taking his 'B' certificate in infantry training. This had meant training for some time with the regular army and taking further examinations.

On the day I arrived, Bramhall and Burke were busy in the office and Bramhall casually said to me, 'Take these men for a walk, will you Glen.' My heart sank at the thought. There were about a thousand of them. They could hardly even 'form fours', although they had had a little instruction from the sergeant major.

I got them into double ranks and the line stretched so far I was afraid that they would not hear me. I shouted as loud as I could, 'From the right, number!' and then, 'Form fours. Right. By the left, quick march!' We got off in some sort of order, and I marched at the head of the column. I had no idea where I was going. The Great War had started for me.

The following day was a Sunday. Sergeant Major Cotter called the parade and I was the only officer present. Cotter, who was a typical sergeant major of the old school and had a fine voice, shouted, 'Church of England fall in on the right. Wesleyans, Baptists and all other fancy religions fall in on the left. Atheists fall in behind.' He then saluted me and announced, 'Lieutenant Glen, Sir, you will take the English Church parade,' and I marched off with between 400 and 500 men to the local English church. He took the fancy religions parade himself and the atheists were set to work to clean up the camp.

The first few weeks were occupied with ordinary infantry drill. In the afternoon Burke and I took the men for route marches. Soon, more medical officers began to arrive. Reveille was early and we had a morning run before breakfast. When we were washing ourselves in cold water outside our tents in the morning, Major Bramhall would shout along to me, 'Glen, detail for form fours', or some such command, and I had to shout the detail back to him. This was his idea for helping me with my slight stammer, which by this time was improving very much. I always got on better when I had to shout out loud, and I got on quite well lecturing to the men when I was more intent on thinking what I had to say than how I was saying it.

The thousand recruits in the camp were divided into five units of about 200 men, each of which was to form a field ambulance[7] for a brigade of the new army. Later each ambulance was divided into three sections, A, B and C, and we began to train the men in stretcher-drill and first-aid work. I was given charge of C Section of the 40th Field Ambulance and was almost wholly responsible for their training.

Most of the men were still in civilian clothes, although after a few months a temporary blue serge uniform arrived, which we gave to the men whose clothes were most disreputable. The officers were in uniform. I was lucky in that I got mine in Glasgow before I came away: it was in fine pre-war cloth and the leather in my Sam Browne belt and leggings was also pre-war. Our uniform included spurs. Field Ambulance Officers were at that time supposed to be mounted.

———

The section which I had charge of was rather a mixed lot. A number of them were office workers who had enlisted very early in Birmingham. Most of the others were men who had volunteered for ambulance work from the Brigade which was nearby. Most of these were miners and proved to be invaluable men in many ways. Some who came from the Brigade, however, were not so good. Any C.O. knows that if he is asked to transfer any of his men it is a good opportunity to get rid of some of his problems and I got a few of these. Two or three men were constantly in trouble for such things as overstaying leave, getting drunk in town and landing in jail. Two of them were obviously deserters from the regular army. You could tell them by the way they stood on parade. One said he had been in the U.S. Navy,

7. A mobile medical unit that treats soldiers in or near the combat zone.

but I expect he had been in a lot more places. Personally I rather liked them, and they made fine soldiers when we got on active service. Later on, C section won the competition for stretcher-drill and first-aid work out of 15 sections. It was the miners in the unit who were largely responsible for that success.

———

The autumn of 1914, to make up for the good summer, was particularly wet, and the camp at Tidworth Park soon became a quagmire inches deep in mud. Major Bramhall did everything he could to get us moved into billets, without success. Finally he went down to Devonshire and arranged billeting in Paignton, Teignmouth, Dawlish and Budleigh Salterton. He then informed the War Office that he had done this and they told him to 'carry on'.

Our ambulance, the 40th, was billeted in Paignton from early December 1914 until April 1915. It was a wonderful place for billets and we got 10 to 15 men in each billet, which was very good for discipline. The landladies were extremely helpful and kind to the men. We had a fine green on the sea-front for our parades and the cricket pavilion and other halls for lecturing and wet weather. The officers were billeted in the Redcliffe Hotel on the sea-front, and the local Conservative Club made us honorary members. We trained a pipe band and got a present of musical instruments and drums. Fine route marches into the countryside were made and we were invited to some of the cider farms for a free drink of cider on our route. Dances were held in the local cafe and we made many friends among the Paignton people.

One curious incident happened to me. I was going along the sea-front one evening towards the Redcliffe Hotel about 8 or 9 p.m. when I saw a motor car standing at the side of one of the houses on the front. Suddenly it shone its headlights straight out to sea. In a moment or two it did it again. I was just beside a shelter on the esplanade, and I went inside and watched. It was against the local rules even at that time to show lights on the front and I was a little suspicious. As I watched, a maid lit up the rooms in the front of the house one by one, and pulled down the blinds.

I sat on to see if anything else would happen. The house was all in darkness again and the car headlights were out; and then as I watched the whole sequence was repeated. The motor car shone its headlights and then the maid went round and put up the lights and then pulled down the blinds.

I was convinced that something was going on and that they were probably signalling to a submarine out in Tor Bay. I took one of the other M.O.'s into my confidence, and after one or two blank nights we saw the same performance again. We decided to tell the C.O., Major Bramhall. He came out of the hotel with us after dinner. Outside the hotel there was a sea-wall, and as we stood looking at the house and talking about the occurrence, Bramhall looked over the wall and exclaimed, 'There is a man down there.' As he spoke the man started to run. Bramhall shouted, 'Catch that fellow!' The cliff in front of the hotel was too high for us to drop down, so we ran round through the hotel grounds; but by the time we got down to the beach there was no sign of the man.

I think there is no doubt that Bramhall reported the incidents to the War Office. A few weeks afterwards the people in the house were charged with showing lights, and two of us had to give evidence. We were told that all we were to say was that we saw lighted windows at the house on several occasions and that we were on no account to mention the incidents which I have described above. The local magistrate dismissed the case and gave us a telling off for slandering innocent people. I understood this was a blind so that a proper watch could be kept on them. Many months later I was told that they had been arrested.

———

By the end of March the unit was made up to full strength in officers. There were ten medical officers, including the C.O. and a quartermaster. We were given a new C.O., Lieutenant Colonel Stoney Archer. I think that Bramhall was very disappointed that he did not get command of the 40th Field Ambulance, but he was too valuable as a training officer and had to continue at that work. Our new C.O. was fat and stodgy and seemed to me to be too much of an old wife to make a good officer.

Some of my bad lads had been in trouble again and one of the first things the new C.O. did was to demote me from my command of C section. He put a temporary enlisted officer in my place. His name was Lt. Weeks. Weeks was older than myself but was a temporary enlisted man, i.e. he could go home if he liked at the end of a year.

Weeks was a very decent fellow and I believe a good surgeon, but I felt a bit sore about it and complained to Bramhall. He said that he was very sorry, but that Archer was senior to him and he could do nothing about it.

At the end of April 1915 we moved back to Salisbury Plain under canvas. Very soon our equipment began to arrive, and all the ambulance wagons, medical equipment and trained transport men were attached to the unit. We had been having riding lessons during the winter and we now got horses. During May we had field days on Salisbury Plain and about the middle of June we were suddenly supplied with tropical kit and topees.

I was given embarkation leave and left Salisbury Plain on Saturday about midday, travelling from London to Glasgow on the night train. I spent Sunday at home and travelled back to London again on Sunday night. I had something to do in London on the Monday and caught the last train back to camp on Monday night. I had to get off the train at Ludgershall Junction, but the train stopped at every small station and I found myself dropping off to sleep despite making a great effort to keep awake. It was now after midnight, and when I awoke I had gone three stations past my stop and had to walk nine miles to the camp. I got there in good time for the morning run.

A few days later we left with all our wagons and equipment for Avonmouth and went aboard the S.S. *Argyllshire*, along with a brigade of artillery.

The *Argyllshire* was an old ship with four masts and three large cargo holds. There were a few cabins which the officers occupied, but most of the men slept on deck or in the holds. We had an uneventful voyage to Alexandria but we were very short of fresh water, getting only a few pints each per day. The sanitary arrangements were very bad, because the ship was never intended and had not been equipped for such a large number of passengers.

Several incidents occurred during the voyage which may be worth recording. One day Lieutenant Colonel Stoney Archer, the senior medical officer of the ship, gave a lecture on tropical diseases to the officers on the ship including the artillery officers. The O.C. ship was a very peppery elderly artillery officer. One of the things which Stoney Archer said in his lecture was that cholera belts were no use.

Apparently the artillery officer was of a different opinion and did not like Stoney Archer much in any case, because he stalked angrily out of the saloon, went straight up to the bridge and asked the Captain to sound the alarm and call everyone to boat-stations. This put a stop to the lecture.

I later learned from personal experience that Stoney Archer was wrong and that the Artillery officer, who had spent many years in the East, was right. After having dysentery once or twice I found that, when lying in the open at night in winter, I used to get abdominal cramps. I found it beneficial even to take off my puttees and wrap them round my waist. It did not seem to matter so much if my feet got cold.

Another incident which did not improve my personal relations with Stoney Archer occurred just as we were nearing Alexandria. Archer called all the M.O.s on the ship into his office and read out, with some satisfaction, I think, a report which he had written on the voyage. He condemned the officers of the ship as being most incompetent and unhelpful. He said that the water supply was quite insufficient, the sanitary arrangements disgraceful and the food very bad.

Having read his report he looked up and asked if we had any comments. I think that he expected us all to agree immediately. Instead, I was the only one who spoke. I said that I agreed that the water supply, the sanitary arrangements and the cooking facilities were quite unequal to the demands made by the large numbers on board the ship. I said, however, that I disagreed entirely with his criticism of the crew, who had done their best under extremely difficult circumstances.

Stoney Archer looked daggers at me and said that he disagreed with me and added, unnecessarily to my mind, that he did not think much of my opinion at any rate. No-one else spoke. I think they were quite taken aback by my speaking at all, and by the reception my remarks got from the C.O.

Actually I had good reason for what I said. The *Argyllshire* was a Glasgow ship with Scots officers. I had discussed these matters with them quite a lot and heard their side of the story, and the great efforts which they had made to cope with the situation. I knew also that such a report would get them into serious trouble at the end of their voyage.

Greatly to our dismay we unloaded all our ambulance wagons, transport and horses at Alexandria. We stayed there for three days tied up against the quay. None of the men were allowed ashore, but some of the officers were allowed to disembark in small parties. I was one of these and went into Alexandria for a half day. It was very tantalising for the men to be cooped up in such uncomfortable conditions after a long voyage, and quite a number escaped ashore. About two days later, when the ship was about to sail, she started blowing her horn at intervals and men began to appear from all over the dock. Some came aboard by the gangway, but some men did not appear until the ship was actually moving away from the quay. About half a dozen men grabbed ropes which were hanging down from the ship's boats and climbed up hand over hand. This was quite a feat and caused some excitement. We reached the island of Lemnos, the base for Gallipoli, in about two days and anchored in Mudros Bay.

V

Gallipoli

After about 24 hours in Mudros Bay we transferred from the S.S. *Argyllshire* to a smaller coastal steamer, one of the Burns Line of Glasgow Irish steamers. Mudros is about 50 miles from Cape Helles, and it was dark when we approached the peninsula. It was a calm night with an offshore breeze, and we could hear rifle-fire and occasional gunfire in the distance. We also became aware of a peculiar, sweet smell which one of the crew told us was the smell of human flesh decaying in the open. We were soon to get so accustomed to that smell that we ceased to notice it.

We landed on barges alongside the S.S. *River Clyde* before dawn and marched over the hill, just as dawn was breaking, to W. Beach, where we occupied dug-outs or holes in the ground. Alongside us was an ambulance of the 52nd Scottish Division.

Shortly after we arrived, someone in an observation post rattled an old tin can. This was the sign that 'Asiatic Annie', a long-distance Turkish gun on the Asiatic side, had fired. Everyone went into his dug-out or took shelter as far as possible. After what seemed about one minute we heard a singing sound in the air and a high-explosive shell burst into what seemed a busy part of the beach. Nobody appeared to be hurt and immediately everyone resumed his duties.

This went on at intervals all forenoon, but then one of the shells plunged into a bell-tent which was just below our dug-outs. Immediately there was a much larger explosion, the bell-tent disappeared and there were cries of distress. I got several men and two stretchers and rushed down to help. Almost simultaneously a party of stretcher-bearers arrived from the field ambulance alongside us. Two of the stretcher bearers in that party, Binks Lawrence and Dan Purdie, I knew well. They had been at the same school as myself. The tent had been occupied by about a dozen men making hand-grenades from empty jam tins. The shell had landed right among them and exploded their gunpowder. Several of the men were badly wounded, some fatally.

A few days after we arrived at Cape Helles, while we were still at W. Beach, the medical officer of the 6th South Lancashire Battalion, Lieutenant Cattanach, was killed. Our field ambulance was asked to supply an M.O. to replace him. I was detailed by Colonel Stoney Archer for the job. I was rather surprised, because I had been with the unit since its foundation and taken part in all its training. Six of our NCOs had only joined the field ambulance a few weeks before we left home. They had taken no part in the training and did not know the duties or the men so well as I did.

The South Lancs were already in the front-line trenches, and one of the battalion medical orderlies was to guide me up to the battalion. On my way to report to the Colonel after I arrived, we had to cross a ridge of bare rock which they had been unable to cut when making the trench. My guide told me that Turkish snipers had their rifles trained on it constantly, and it was there that Cattanach had been killed. My guide made a sudden dive over the obstacle and as he did so a bullet whacked into the rock beside me. A few minutes later I dived over also and arrived safely.

The weather was very hot. By this time one hardly noticed the stench, but the flies were incredible. If one put a little jam on an army biscuit it was literally (I mean literally) black with flies before it reached one's mouth. Dysentery was already very prevalent among the troops and I knew that under these conditions it was bound to get much worse. In a few days I was passing frequent stools with blood and mucus myself and feeling miserable.

We only evacuated the sick, however, when they were no longer fit to carry on duty. The sanitary conditions were terrible, just slit trenches inside the other trenches covered with flies. I wasn't very popular when I advised that they all should get a good covering of earth. It meant digging new trenches. Sometimes the men fell into the trenches from weakness.

I was feeling very sick myself and to add to my misery after about ten days I developed a large ischio-rectal abscess or boil, which was very painful. One night I could not sleep for the pain, and in desperation I felt in my medical haversack for an opium tablet. In the dark I took a tablet of Calomel by mistake. In a short time my dysentery and colic were increased tenfold. I think, however, that my abscess burst, and in the morning I felt better. I gradually improved after that.

I was kept busy. There were a few casualties each day, chiefly from

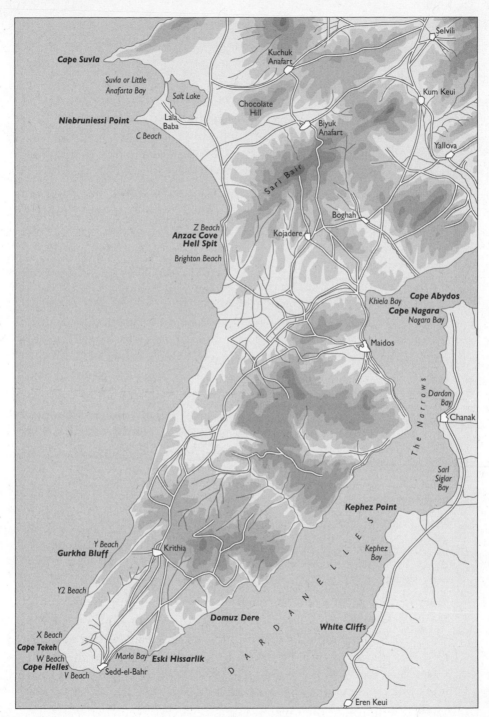

Gallipoli, 1915.

shellfire, but most of our casualties were from dysentery, and I was inclined to think that there was enteric fever also.

After about three weeks of this trench warfare our Division (the 13th) was embarked again for Mudros. We were being reserved for the major attack which was to take place later at Anzac and Suvla Bay. Our stay at Helles was only to give us a little war experience.

As I passed with my battalion along the narrow beach (about two yards wide) under the cliff we passed through several battalions of the 52nd Division. This was a territorial division mostly recruited from near Glasgow, and I knew many of the men. I learned on inquiry that one of my cousins, Andrew Glen, had been killed about a month before. I asked for Jimmy Agnew, and they pointed to someone swimming quite far out in the sea. Jimmy was a very keen swimmer. He afterwards became my brother-in-law, but I did not see him to speak to that day.

At Mudros again we lay in a dusty field for a fortnight; I treated many cases of dysentery and sent a number to hospital. I think that we must have had some reinforcements, because when we left again for the peninsula we had over a thousand men and more than our full complement of officers. Two days before we left I was having a sick parade of about thirty men daily, but on the evening before we sailed again only two men reported sick. I told the Colonel and he was quite pleased. He said that it showed that the morale of the battalion was good. I wasn't so happy myself because I knew that many of the men were far from fit.

We landed this time at Anzac. The front line appeared to be right above us. We could see this from searchlights occasionally playing on it. The rifle-fire sounded extremely loud. It was obvious in fact that they saw us also, because bullets began to hit the ship and a man on deck was hit. It was difficult to get us all below deck, since the ship was very crowded.

When we got ashore we marched along the crowded narrow beach, littered with stores, to a small valley or ravine where we settled into dug-outs which had been made by the Australians to receive us. The following day a lone enemy plane flew over quite low. It was a quite small, primitive plane but the occupant could not have failed to see the thousands of men (a full division) crowded into the small valley.

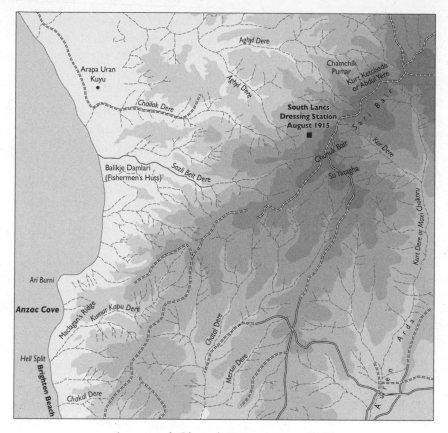

Anzac and Chunuk Bair, August 1915.

That evening, as I was having supper with the Colonel of the battalion, he read out General Hamilton's order to the troops. None of us were very impressed; we thought it was a bit too melodramatic. The following late afternoon all hell suddenly broke out. It started with a terrific bombardment from the sea and from our own land artillery. The Turks responded, and seemed to me to throw most of their shells into our small valley. This was the beginning of our all-out attack which was to last for several weeks. The Australians just above us had started their advance.

The result of the shelling of our small ravine was pretty terrible. There were calls for stretcher-bearers from every side, and soon my aid-post, which was an extra-large deep dug-out, was full of wounded men. In the middle of the trouble one H.E. shell exploded right in the centre of the aid-post. I was kneeling down at the time in one corner

43

of the dug-out attending to one of the wounded and I was unhurt, but was covered with dirt. When I recovered from the shock of the concussion and looked around, what surprised me was that so many had survived. One man who was lying on a stretcher and whom I had attended a few moments before had lost half his head, and several others were in a very bad way. One man was moving his lips but making no sound. He continued like this for the next ten minutes or so and I sent him down the line with the walking wounded labelled 'shell-shock'. This was the first case of shell-shock I had seen.

I was still engaged in clearing up the mess and getting those who could be moved down to the beach when the adjutant of the battalion arrived to tell me to leave everything and pack up my medical equipment. He was somewhat shocked at the state of my aid-post, but said that the Australians were taking over.

This was the 6th of August 1915, and as darkness came on we moved slowly away in a long snaking column down to the beach and along under the cliffs to the north. Our progress was very slow. Sometimes we stopped for half an hour or so and the men fell asleep leaning against the parapets of communication trenches.

The Major who was second-in-command came at the end of the battalion with myself and my stretcher-bearers. The Major, whose name I am sorry I cannot remember, had become quite a friend of mine. In the six weeks or so that I had been with the battalion we had been a good deal together as he looked after the men's general welfare.

We went along the beach past a valley called Sazli Dere, where the New Zealanders had broken out at the north end of the Anzac line a few hours before. The next valley was Chailak Dere; we turned and slowly trailed up it, taking long stops. We heard fighting in the distance at Anzac but only occasional rifle shots in front of us and saw no Turks, though we passed a deserted Turkish bakery with the fires still hot.

I talked a lot with the Major during these halts and I remember him telling me that if he survived the war he was hoping to tour England with his wife in a car which he had bought just before the war. Cars were quite rare in these days.

Towards dawn we climbed up the steep sides of Chailak Dere on to a high plateau further north. There was a great jumble of high precipitous hills in front of us, which I now know was Chunuk Bair and the Sari Bair range of hills. As dawn was just breaking and the battalion was crossing this plateau, a sharp rifle fire opened on us from the high range of hills, or mountains as they appeared to be, in front of us. The Colonel immediately led the way down into the next valley, the Aghyl Dere, further north and east.

As we were now getting a few casualties I sent them back at first the way we had come by Chailak Dere. When we got down into the Aghyl Dere we came up with a battalion of Gurkhas. They must have been under very heavy fire, because the bottom of the Aghyl Dere, which was like a large open dry ditch, was littered with dead Gurkhas. I could see the Gurkhas in open formation going up the slopes of the Sari Bair range. It was very steep and I remember wondering if it was possible at all to climb it.

The South Lancs, my battalion, went past the Gurkhas right to the top of the valley and began climbing up the hill there. I passed the M.O. of the Gurkhas and he said he was sending his wounded down the Aghyl Dere. The Aghyl Dere ran parallel to and below the Sari Bair range for quite a distance, and troops moving up and down were completely exposed to fire from the top of Sari Bair which was held by the Turks throughout almost the whole battle. Any attempt to go over the hill opposite was even more exposed. The fact that the valley was so exposed was I think the chief reason why our reinforcements and supplies did not reach us. Meantime I followed the battalion and established my aid post in a small ravine at the head of the Aghyl Dere, and as I learned afterwards, just under Chunuk Bair, one of the highest peaks in the range.

The battalion was spread out along the sides of this very steep mountain. The fire was very heavy and there began to be a number of casualties. I collected the stretcher-cases in the ravine and sent the walking cases down the Aghyl Dere. I was expecting the ambulance stretcher-bearers to come up and take my stretcher-cases. This was the drill we had been taught. They did not come, however, and no field ambulance personnel reached me throughout the whole battle, which lasted about five days. I later sent my corporal down the Aghyl Dere with a stretcher-party to try to make contact but they did not come back. I suspect that they were casualties themselves.

That forenoon, the 7th August, I saw the Gurkhas and New Zealanders attacking up the slopes of Sari Bair to our left. They appeared to get well up the slopes. The range of hills got very steep, almost perpendicular at the top. My own battalion, the 6th S. Lancs, was right up above the ravine where I had my dressing station. They were on the slopes of Chunuk Bair, the highest part of the range.

All that day I had many casualties, but I managed to get most of them away. Many of them must have been casualties again on their way down the valley, and I seemed to have very few stretcher-bearers left. That night I think we got some water brought up by Indian pack mules in small tanks. Above me the tanks had to be manhandled up the hill to the battalion.

Next morning, the 8th August, another attack took place and I saw some of the Gurkhas go right up to the top of the hill. For the rest of the day the fire in the upper part of the valley slackened considerably and we could move about more easily. I dug a hole in a sandy part of the dry gully and a little muddy water trickled in very slowly. This supply proved of great value to the wounded men whom I could not move.

About 3 a.m. on the morning of the 9th August, a brigade captain of the 39th Brigade whom I had met before and whose name, I think, was Wood, came up to my dressing station and asked who I was. I said M.O. 6th S. Lancs. He said, 'Thank God, I have been looking for your battalion most of the night. Could you take me to your headquarters?'

I replied that I could as I had just come back from there. I told him that it was a very stiff climb. Actually it was so steep that we had literally to pull ourselves up by our hands on roots of shrubs and grass.

We found the C.O., his second-in-command, the Major who was planning to tour England after the war and the Adjutant all together. They told Wood that the battalion was a little bit higher up, dug in as well as they could, just under the crest of the hill. Wood told them that they were to attack again at dawn, that was in about an hour's time. This was the last time I saw any of these officers.

About 4.30 a.m. there was a terrific naval bombardment for a short while. After that, firing into the Aghyl Dere ceased and I was able to move about freely and attend to the wounded in exposed places. But still no help reached me from the field ambulance. The S. Lancs and Gurkhas were actually on top of Chunuk Bair that morning.

The following morning, the 10th August, there was another battle. It was soon obvious that our men had been displaced, because the firing from the top of the hill became very severe, worse in fact than it had ever been. For shelter we had to crouch very low and I got a bullet through the top of my topee. I thought at first I had been hit.

Men drifted in single numbers down the ravine all day, most of them wounded. They said it was 'murder' at the top and no one was left alive. No officers came down all day whom I could ask for news about the battle. By the afternoon I was all alone among the wounded. All my stretcher-bearers were gone. My medical supplies were finished. I had no morphia left. There was practically no shelter now in the gully; unless I lay prone I realised I probably would not survive long, so I started to walk down the Aghyl Dere.

The small ditch in the middle of the valley was in patches almost full of dead men. As I did not care to walk on them I walked along the top, which did not appear to be much more dangerous.

When I had gone down quite a bit I came on a staff officer on top of a small eminence directing a line of troops which were spread out in a thin line advancing up the Sari Bair slopes. I have already described what these hillsides were like; I knew that their task was hopeless and their losses would be terrible. I went up to the staff officer, whom I recognised as belonging to my own 13th Division. I did not know his name then but I know now that it was Brigadier General Baldwin. He asked me who I was and where I was going. When I told him, he said, 'Carry on'. He was in full view of the Turks firing from the top of Sari Bair, and he and most of his staff did not survive that day.

I carried on down the valley, and near the foot of it I came across my own old unit, the 40th Field Ambulance. I asked them to give me some medical supplies and they gave me some food and drink. They told me afterwards that I had fallen asleep and it was several hours later and getting dark when I awoke. I set off immediately to try and contact my battalion or what remained of it.

It was now quite dark, but some distance up the Aghyl Dere I found some of the battalion collected together in a reserve position. There were two officers and about 120 men. We had started the battle with 30 officers and 1,000 men. I could not help thinking about the score or so of badly wounded men who were lying in the small ravine where my dressing station had been, and I asked the officer now in charge of the battalion if I could have some volunteers from the men to go up and bring some of them down. I got over a dozen volunteers immediately and we managed to pick up four stretchers.

It was quite a distance up the valley to our old position, but we got there without great difficulty. I told the men to take the stretcher-cases down to a position of comparative safety and leave them there and come back for others. The men worked splendidly and we got all of the survivors away. Meantime I had found a wounded officer not far away, and I asked one more stretcher-party to come back and get him. I was waiting anxiously for them to come up the hill again when the dawn began to break quite suddenly. Just then I saw my two men coming up the hill with their stretcher. We got the officer on the stretcher and were moving quickly down the steep hill. I was supporting the side of the stretcher. Suddenly there was a loud crack of machine-gun fire and we all fell in a heap together. The two stretcher-bearers appeared to have been killed instantly. The same bullet or bullets must have struck both of them as they were in line at either end of the stretcher.

The officer was apparently not hit because he cried out and groaned. Shortly afterwards more bullets cracked round about us and I think he must have been hit again, because he became silent and I saw that he was dead also. I lay perfectly still myself, as I knew it was my only chance. Actually at that moment I did not want to do anything else but be still. I was quite exhausted. I was terribly annoyed with myself for being so careless as to get caught by the dawn. I felt myself responsible for the loss of those two fine lads who had helped so willingly during the night.

After a bit the sun came up. The firing seemed to grow less. The chirping of the innumerable grasshoppers seemed to grow louder. I don't remember feeling afraid but I think I sobbed a little, and then I remember nothing more. I must have fallen asleep very quickly.

The familiar sound of heavy rifle and machine gun fire woke me up. The sun was setting again, and the usual heavy firing which occurs at that time had started. I had slept throughout the whole day. I waited till it was quite dark and then I got up and walked unsteadily down the hill and along the Aghyl Dere.

There was no sign of any living British soldiers. I must have gone about half a mile down the valley before I was challenged by an unmistakably Irish voice: 'Halt, who goes there!' I answered feebly, 'Friend, Medical Officer.' I was helped over a well-built sandbagged parapet by a sergeant major of an Irish battalion. It was a great surprise to me, as I did not even know that there were any Irish troops on the

Peninsula and there had been no line of trenches when I passed that way last.

The sergeant major said, 'Good God, Sir, where have you been? You could be doing with a cup of tea.' I replied, 'Thank you, I could do with it.'

I sat down on the parapet step. After a little I felt much better and continued my way down the valley to look for my battalion. There was only one officer left now, Lieutenant Ward. The other officer had gone down the line. He had had a slight flesh wound for several days and had been persuaded to report as a casualty. I had been reported missing myself to the Divisional Headquarters. I will have more to tell of Lieutenant Ward later.

A few days afterwards I got word to report back to my old unit, the 40th Field Ambulance. I was told that I was to take command. They were now considerably north of Anzac on a shingly beach called C. beach. The remains of the Division were in reserve not far away. The Division had lost about 6,000 men out of 10,500 during the battle. Ten commanding officers out of thirteen had disappeared. Several of the battalions, like my own, had lost practically all their officers.

C. Beach, where I found the Field Ambulance, apart from occa-sional stray bullets, was a delightful place. There were some sandhills among which we were stationed and then a gravelly beach leading steeply down to crystal-clear water.

I found that all the medical officers (nine of them) had gone either with wounds or sickness, except the commanding officer Lieutenant Colonel Stoney Archer and Lieutenant Quartermaster Rees (non-medical). The men were lying carelessly about and Colonel Archer was lying on a stretcher. He said that he had developed a sore knee and could not move it. I found it somewhat stiff and grating a bit on movement. I had great pleasure in attaching a label to a button on his tunic that read 'Chronic arthritis of the knee', and sending him to the clearing-station as a sick casualty.[8]

8. Perhaps Alec's assessment of Lieutenant Colonel Stoney Archer did not take account of the stresses imposed on a regular army surgeon in Gallipoli. An obitu-ary of his daughter Kathleen (Gemmill) includes reference to her father as never having recovered from the experience of having to do so many amputations and tend so many maimed men.

Lieutenant Rees, the Quartermaster, was very helpful. He was an old Regular RAMC soldier and had actually been at the battle of Omdurman in the Sudan war. We got the camp tidied up and divided the men into their sections and made them construct dug-outs among the sand hills. I constructed an incinerator and arranged all the medical stores, which were very limited, in some order.

I was very glad I had done this, because a few days later we had a visit from General Stanley Maude with his staff. He had just taken over command of the shattered division. I was to get to know him very well later, but our first meeting was not too happy. As we walked round the lines he pointed out some food debris covered with flies which a man had apparently vomited. The General turned to me and said, 'Do you allow this sort of thing to lie about in a medical unit, Glen?' I replied, 'No Sir.' He waited a minute and then asked: 'Are you not going to do anything about it?'

Much to my own surprise, and that I think of my men, I suddenly got angry and addressed the sergeant major who was with me in as loud a voice as I could, 'Sergeant Major, get a man to clear away that bloody mess, immediately!' The rest of the inspection went quietly, but I could see that the General was anything but happy with our appearance.

A few days later we were moved further north to a small eminence near the entrance to the Salt Lake, to take over from a field ambulance of the 53rd Welsh Division. The Welshmen were miners and had made a good start with dug-outs. Unfortunately the hill was made of shaly rock, but if dug by an expert came away in layers and made excellent shelters. We had one section, C. section, my own original section, which was composed mostly of miners. I borrowed as many picks and shovels as I could get, and soon had the men busy building rows of excellent shelters which were to stand us in good stead as it happened, for the next few months.

For the next fortnight there was very little doing as our Division was in reserve. I got several junior medical officer reinforcements and also a padre. Towards the end of August the Division went into action again on Chocolate Hill, which was directly on our front above the Salt Lake. This was a very fierce battle, but again it was unsuccessful and we had many casualties from other divisions as well as our own.

The 29th Division had been brought from Helles and was fighting alongside our own division. As I knew one of my cousins, John Glen, was in it, I went over one day to see if I could find him. I found his battalion all right but he had been killed a few days previously. His C.O. said he had been one of their best officers. I was very disappointed, because he was about my own age and a particular friend of mine.

———

Our Field Ambulance was in full view of the Turks, but we had a Red Cross flag flying on our flag-pole and we were very seldom shelled by the Turks except when transport came too near us. Stray bullets, however, continued to come all the time. We had put up bell-tents for the casualties and we built shelters round these with the rocks we took out of the dug-outs. There is no doubt that the Turks respected us as a hospital.

The weather turned colder at night in September, but the men were getting fitter and I personally started to put on some weight. Flocks of geese began to fly over going south, and when they passed above us it was like a battle, the whole front line were trying to shoot one down.

On 27th November the great storm struck us. It was a rule that an officer had to go at night to the supply dump at Lala Baba with the A.T. carts.⁹ The Turkish gunners had the range of the dumps and always shelled it at night. It was a dangerous place and discipline had to be very strict. Although I was in command of the unit I took my turn of this duty, and on the night of 27th November I went with the carts.

There was the usual occasional shell falling at the depot, but we got away safely. It was a very dark night. Suddenly, when we were about half-way home a violent thunderstorm started. I have never seen anything like it, except once afterwards in Mesopotamia. The lightning was practically continuous and the thunder very violent. We were caught in an exposed place. The mules panicked and we all had to hold on to them. Then the rains came, first hail and then terrific rain. It continued for about 24 hours.

After an hour of this we made our way slowly to our camp. We found it in a terrible state. About three-quarters of our dug-outs were nearly full of water.

Fortunately, since we had had showers in the previous weeks, I had arranged every covering we could get. We had some wagon covers

9. Animal Transport carts, hauled by mules or horses.

which covered a few dug-outs. In the others, the men's waterproof sheets had been carefully strung together to make a roof, but the rain made short work of these. Luckily we had the tents and we let the men occupy a few of them that night. The others crowded into the dry dug-outs. I had a wagon-covering over mine and all the officers got into it.

After 24 hours the rains changed to snow and very cold wind. Everything wet froze solid. This lasted for another three days. Both lines of trenches were flooded and the men sat on the top of them, numbed with cold and frostbite.

There was an old house behind our front called White Farm, which we used as a dressing-station. On the first day of the blizzard I went up there and found it full of casualties, so closely packed that it was difficult to pull them out. They refused to move. Some could not, they were dead. We helped some to walk, but it was impossible to carry them all.

I decided to take an ambulance wagon across the Salt Lake. By the second day of the blizzard it was frozen hard and I took the wagon right across the lake up to the White Farm. I continued doing this for the next two days, and got very many men out. On the third day it began to thaw, and on the return journey the wheels went through the crust. The Turks started to shell us. The mules got hit and stampeded and we let them go. One M.O. who was with me got a shell wound in the chest. We helped those who could walk and later sent stretchers for the remainder.

The ambulance remained stuck in the lake visible to the Turks, the British, the Navy and all. In fact it became a landmark.

I have read in the War Records that during those few days 200 British soldiers were drowned, 5,000 cases of frostbite occurred and there were 5,000 other casualties. The worst casualties were on our front, the Salt Lake front at Suvla.

Shortly after the storm, E.T. Burke arrived back at the unit. Burke had been one of the original officers of the unit and had always been recognised as second-in-command. He had been evacuated with dysentery while I was with the S. Lancs. Without thinking about it for a minute, I handed over the command of the unit to him. I had never been keen on administration in any case.

A few days later the ADMS (Assistant Director Medical Services), Col H.M. Morton, visited the unit and said he wished to speak to me. He took me aside and said that I had no right to hand over the command of the unit without permission. He said that my name had gone forward with a recommendation to be appointed acting Lieutenant Colonel to the Ambulance. I explained to him that Burke had been the first special reserve officer to arrive at the ambulance training camp in England in 1914, and that I had followed a week or two later. He had always done the office work and was a good administrator. If I stayed as Lieutenant Colonel I felt that Burke would require to go to another unit and I did not wish to be responsible for that, as he had been with the unit from the start. He agreed to talk it over at Divisional Headquarters, and Burke remained in command thereafter.

In early December it became obvious that preparations were being made for the evacuation of Suvla. We received orders to move the ambulance wagon, which was stuck in the middle of Salt Lake. I inspected it and found that it was quite a job. It was sunk beyond the axles and I had no tools to do the job. However, the following night with the help of a section of pioneers we dug it out and put it back in the field ambulance lines. Our ambulance wagon was the most conspicuous object on the horizon and I think this was a very good piece of deception on General Maude's part.

I left with half the unit for Mudros a few days before the final evacuation, which was on the 19th December, and Burke brought up the remainder of our medical unit on the final night. How cleverly the Turks were deceived in this evacuation is a matter of history, and for me at least it was quite uneventful.

We had only been a few days on Mudros when we were told that our Division, the 13th, was to go back to Cape Helles to relieve one of the Divisions there. Our Brigade, the 39th, had already gone and we were waiting on the jetty to embark on Hogmanay 1915 when the order to embark the ambulance was suddenly cancelled and we marched back to camp. The decision to evacuate Cape Helles also had been taken and it apparently was decided that the medical units already on Cape Helles would be sufficient. We had seen the last of Gallipoli.

VI

Egypt and Mesopotamia, 1916

We left Mudros for Port Said about the end of January 1916. I do not remember the name of the ship in which we sailed, but I remember arriving at the quay at Port Said. Major Brownrigg and one or two staff officers had gone ashore as soon as the ship tied up. Just at that moment the ship began to blow off steam. The hissing noise sounded exactly like a shell falling, and Major Brownrigg and the other officers who had been so long accustomed to that sound fell flat on their faces on the quay, greatly to the amusement of the troops on board.

The Turks were at that time threatening the Suez Canal, and the 13th Division took up defence positions at the north end of the Canal. Our field ambulance was encamped in an empty space near the centre of Port Said.

Life was very pleasant, and a great change from our recent experiences. We got chickens and eggs and all the good food which Egypt can supply. It was not very long, however, before there were rumours that we were to be on the move again. Kut had been surrounded by the Turks, and Townsend and the forces in Mesopotamia who had made a stand there were being very hard-pressed. A relieving force was making very slow progress and required reinforcement. The 13th Division was chosen for the job.

On February 3rd we were inspected on the beach at Port Said by Lt. General Sir A. Murray. We had received quite a number of reinforcements and the Division at that time was about 10,000 strong. Our transport and equipment was made up from reserves in Egypt as quickly as possible, and by the middle of February we were sailing down the Red Sea on our way to Mesopotamia. It was beautiful calm weather on the Indian Ocean and I saw flying fish for the first time.

We anchored off the bar at the mouth of the Shatt el Arab, the great river which pours the waters of the Tigris and Euphrates into the

54

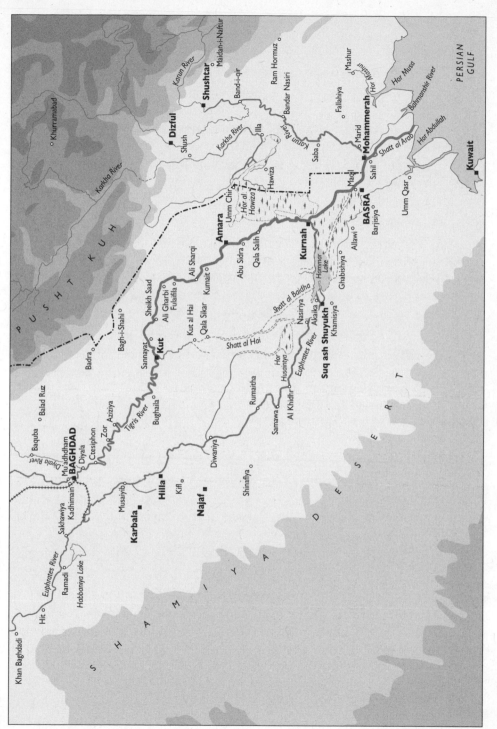

Mesopotamia, 1916.

head of the Persian Gulf. Not far off we could see the mud walls of the little town of Kuwait shimmering in the heat. At that time it was a very insignificant, primitive place.

When we started upriver the ship slid over the bar turning up thick muddy water. After about 24 hours sailing we tied up to palm trees alongside the bank of the river and disembarked. The river here was very deep and slow-flowing, and our ocean-going ship seemed to have no difficulty in getting alongside the bank.

The Division was being landed very rapidly from many ships, and at first there was a lot of confusion ashore. Lieutenant Colonel Morton, ADMS of the Division, told us one day that General Maude, who normally was a very quiet-spoken man had actually been heard to swear about it. For transport animals we had been supplied with a great many partially broken-in Australian horses and many huge Argentine mules which were very difficult to manage at first. Colonel Morton told us that General Maude had said that day to a meeting of the Divisional Staff: 'I was coming along the *bund* [the river bank] today and I saw two men leading four horses which were behaving very badly. I overheard one man say to the other: "Let the bloody things go." So far as I can see they have let the bloody things go, and the bloody things are all over the bloody place.'

Once more, however, it was our fate to leave all our transport and heavy equipment, and we embarked shortly afterwards on a river steamer without any transport and with only medical equipment and a few bell-tents. These river steamers were paddle steamers which had come mostly from the Irrawaddy and Indian rivers. They had a large barge attached on either side. The barges were full of stores and equipment, and every inch of space on the barges and on the ship itself was occupied by troops.

After we left the broader Shatt el Arab, progress up the winding river was very slow. The load was heavy and the current was strong. Sometimes the ship was carried against the river bank, and the barges were useful to prevent the ship from grounding and getting stuck on the mud banks which were constantly shifting. Sometimes at night, after plugging up the river all day, we would only be a mile or two away from the point where we started in the morning owing to the great bends in the river. On one occasion some of the officers went ashore and walked across one of the river bends, meeting the ship again in the evening. We tied up to the bank each night. It took us about 14 days to do the 200 miles or so to Sheikh Saad, our base, about 10 miles behind the front line at that time.

We camped alongside the river, and for a week or two carried out training exercises with the Division in the desert away from the river. At this time of the year the river was rising rapidly, and a good deal of our time and that of the Division was employed in building up the *bund*, or bank, of the river to prevent it from flooding the camp. Actually the river was several feet above the level of our camp, and was only held back by the raised *bund*.

It was here also that I first had experience of marauding Arabs. I was lying half-asleep one night in a tent with a fellow M.O., when I awoke in alarm and felt someone bending over me. I put out my hand and touched an object. The object gave a grunt, and for a moment blocked the light of the sky as he went out of the tent opening. My tent was at the back of the camp next to the desert, and a sentry was standing a few feet away. I asked if he had seen an Arab and he said he had seen nothing.

Almost at the same moment we heard shouting from the hospital part of the camp, where there were a few sick men. In a field ambulance a sick man lies with his rifle alongside him. The Arab had made four slits in a bell tent and stolen four rifles. One would think that they knew exactly where the men left them. The Arab leaning over me had been looking for any weapon I might have. I had only a revolver which he did not find. Rifles, however, were what they chiefly wanted, and were considered of great value.

We had brought about a dozen of our transport personnel with us. They were armed with rifles and were detailed to us to act as guards for our camp. Our ambulances and dressing stations were often in isolated places and our position was sometimes quite precarious because the Arabs did not hesitate to attack and kill those in isolated posts if they could get away with it.

Our Brigade, the 39th, marched from Sheikh Saad to Hanna during the night of April 1st. The idea was, I suppose, that the Turks would not notice our arrival. It was a terrible night. We had a march of about 10 miles. Torrential rain with almost continuous thunder and lightning went on all night. It was pitch-dark and we only got glimpses of one another occasionally in the lightning flashes. We were soon soaked to the skin and tumbled into old trenches and mud holes.

When dawn eventually came I had only about a quarter of my unit of stretcher bearers with me. During the day we sorted ourselves out and had some cold bully beef and biscuits.

On the following day the Division took over the trenches at Hanna from the 7th Indian Division, which had previously attacked the position unsuccessfully. I went into the second line of trenches with my stretcher-bearers. I was now separated by at least 10 miles from my unit. The only transport I had to carry rations and equipment was in fact my stretchers. I was told I would probably get some A.T. carts later to help if necessary. These A.T. carts had Indian drivers. They were very strong and simply built. Since they had no springs they were very unsuitable for carrying wounded, but were extraordinarily useful and economical for their real purpose of transport of supplies. Their harness was such that they could be transferred into pack transport in a few minutes.

In the description of the unsuccessful fighting for the relief of Kut which follows, I am not concerned with the history of the campaign which may be read in the history books. I can only describe what happened to myself and my stretcher-bearers, and perhaps give some account of the medical arrangements at that time which seemed to me, from the very beginning, to be terribly inadequate. It may help the reader, however, to understand the position better if I explain that the Turks' main position for the defence of Kut was a narrow strip of land of between 1,000 yards and 1½ miles in width between the left bank of the Tigris (when facing downstream) and a great marsh, the Suwaikieh Marsh, which extended many miles inland and was completely impassable, so that our only road forward was a direct attack on the narrow front. Hanna was the Turkish position at the south end of the corridor, and there were twenty miles of the corridor behind Hanna which the Turks could make into defensive positions.

At this time of the year the river rose rapidly and could only be prevented from flooding over this narrow strip of ground by the preservation of the *bund*, which was about six feet high along the river bank. One of the games by both armies was to break the *bund* opposite the enemies' trenches. Fortunately at this time we controlled the opposite (right) bank of the river for a considerable distance north of the Hanna position. Nevertheless, the trenches were half-full of

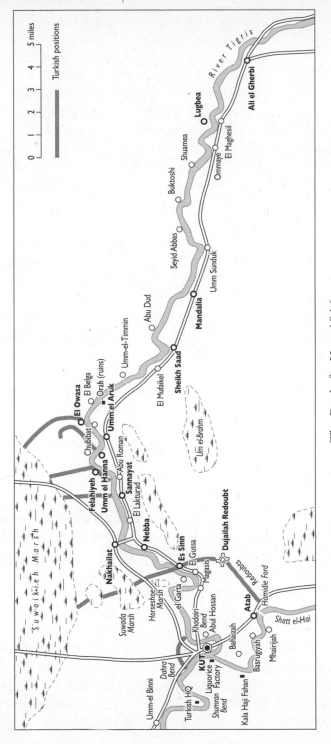

The Battle for Kut, 1916.

Within the map:

0 1 2 3 4 5 miles

Turkish positions

River Tigris

Ali el Gherbi

Lugbea

El Maghesil

Onmaye

Shuamea

Buktoshi

Seyid Abbas

Umm Sunduk

Mandalia

Umm el-Timmin

Abu Dud

El Mutaikel

Sheikh Saad

Um el-Brahm

Orah (ruins)

El Belga

El Owasa

Chubibat

Umm el Aruk

Abu Roman

Felahiyeh

Umm el Hanna

Sannayat

El Lakturd

Nebba

Nakhailat

Es Sinn

El Gussa

Magasis

Dujailah Redoubt

Redoubts

Hamidie Ford

Atab

Shatt el-Hai

Mhairijah

Basrugiyah

Bahaizah

Abul Hossan

Khadairi Bend

el Garta

Horseshoe Marsh

Suwada Marsh

Suwaikieh Marsh

Umm-el Binni

Dahra Bend

Turkish HQ

Liquorice Factory

Shumran Bend

Kala Haji Fahan

KUT

water and mud from the recent heavy rains when we took them over.

The attack on Hanna took place in the morning of 5th April 1916. My men were in the second line of trenches and my orders were to follow the second wave of attack with my stretcher-bearers. Maude was always very meticulous with his orders and this looked as if he intended to go right through the Turkish position. This is what actually happened. There was a heavy bombardment. We found only a few wounded Turks in the trenches and very few of our own wounded. I left a few stretchers to look after the wounded and pushed on after the Brigade.

After a few miles we came up with General Maude himself with his staff. He asked me about the casualties. A few miles further on we ran into heavy fire at a very narrow part of the corridor, Felahiyeh, where the Turks had another defensive position. The country in Mesopotamia is absolutely flat, and for a mile or two behind the front there was always the whine of stray bullets, which one after a while ceased to notice, but an odd casualty was always occurring. The troops of the Division dug themselves in sufficiently to give themselves head-cover.

After a short bombardment, the Division attacked just after dusk. A night attack is always a difficult operation and requires very good discipline on the part of the troops, but the attack was entirely successful and they captured the whole position. The 7th Indian Division came through shortly afterwards and advanced further along the corridor towards the next Turkish position at Sannayat, which they attacked unsuccessfully at dawn on the 6th.

During the night we did what we could among the men round about us, but when dawn came it presented a terrible sight. The ground in front of Felahiyeh was littered with dead men in all sorts of contorted positions, just as they had died. I had put up my Red Cross flag and we gathered as many of the badly wounded together as we could and gave them first aid. All that day we were collecting stretcher-cases. We managed to carry a few to the riverside where they were put in barges.

We were on the right of the line near the marshes, which meant we had a long carry to the river. My sergeant told me late that day that he had been unable to get any rations. Under normal conditions we would have been in touch with the headquarters of our ambulance unit and we would have got our rations from them by means of our ambulance transport, but our unit was at least 15 miles away, acting like a general hospital, and we were a small detachment who belonged to nobody.

When darkness came that night, the 6th of April, I had a large number of wounded men around me. My own men had received no rations since the evening of 4th April, the day before the attack on Hanna, and neither had any of the wounded. We appeared to be quite isolated and were out of touch with the troops in front of and behind us.

Very reluctantly, because I knew that it was against orders, I instructed my own men to use the tea and biscuits from their iron rations. These iron rations consisted of a tin of bully beef, a tin of tea and a quantity of small hard biscuits. We gathered some brush-wood which was fairly plentiful near the marsh and brewed tea for the wounded and my own men. The biscuits were all reduced to a dry powder from friction with the tin of bully beef, as the rations were carried in a small bag attached to each man's belt. We gathered the biscuit powder and made a sort of porridge with it. I refused to let the men touch the bully beef.

Next morning the ADMS of the Division got in touch with us and sent us three or four A.T. carts, with the help of which we cleared our wounded by midday. The casualties in the Division in that night attack on Felahiyeh were about 1,800 killed and wounded. That night I rejoined the Division who were in reserve about the Felahiyeh line.

The 13th Division took over from the 7th Division in front of the Sannayat position after dark on the 8th April and attacked that position at dawn. The Turks were alert and put up flares when the leading troops were about 100 yards from the trenches, and opened up a ter-rific rifle and machine-gun fire. In that dead-level ground there was no shelter for anyone anywhere. The second line was just as badly hit as the first line, and although some of the first-line troops got into the Turkish trenches they were not supported by the second line and were thrown out again. The attack was a failure, and the whole Division was spread out on the level ground in front of the Turkish position, digging in for any shelter they could get. We knew that there must be a great many badly wounded men, but the fire was so intense and the shelter so little that it was impossible to approach them.

About noon I got word to go and see Colonel Morton, the ADMS of the Division. O'Brien, who was in charge of the stretcher-bearers of the 41st Field Ambulance, was there also. Colonel Morton said that General Maude had suggested that a party of stretcher-bearers should go forward with a Red Cross flag. Morton tossed a coin to see whether O'Brien or I should go. I guessed correctly and it was decided that the 40th Field Ambulance stretcher-bearers would go forward with the Red Cross flag.

We hoped that the Turks, who had always recognised the Red Cross, would cease fire and let us collect our wounded. I was a bit doubtful myself, because this was a desperate position for the Turks as well as for us. It was really the Turks' last strong position before Kut. If the Turks ceased fire our men would have a chance to get into some kind of formation and dig themselves in preparatory to another attack.

We went forward as arranged. I put three men to each stretcher. I think we could only man about a dozen stretchers. The enemy fire slackened somewhat at first, but later it got more intense. A number of my men got hit, but mostly in their legs, and were able to limp back. We lifted a number of helpless men on to our stretchers. Some of those we wished to take refused to come, and several officers shouted to us and told us to go back.

As most of our stretchers which were still in action were now full, I told the two men who were carrying the flag to retreat, and we returned to the old front line trenches. I found when we got back that we had brought in about two dozen casualties, about half of whom had walked. Eight of my own men had been hit, but all of them were hit in the legs and were not too serious. The fact that most of them were hit in the legs was an indication that the fire-control of the Turks was very good and they were aiming at men on the ground. I made a report to Division Headquarters and reported the fact that a number of my men had leg-wounds. I was told not to repeat the experiment.

I think it was the following day that Colonel Morton came to me and asked me if I would ride back to El Hanna where the headquarters of the 40th Field Ambulance now was, and get some more A.T. carts which had become available for carrying wounded. The headquarters of the Division had several riding horses, one of which I was to get. I of course had no horse at that time, most of our transport haveing been left at Basra. Hanna was now about 8 to 10 miles at least behind us. The road through Felahiyeh by which we had come was not now in regular use, as all our supplies came by river.

After a few miles I found myself completely alone. Here and there were bits of abandoned equipment and relics of battle. Shortly afterwards I saw a number of Arabs on horseback riding parallel to my route, about 150 or 200 yards away. Then a rifle-bullet whistled uncomfortably near me. I spurred on my horse and fired my revolver at them to show that I was armed. I had a very good horse, and at full gallop I saw that I was leaving them behind. Several other shots were fired at me but I was out-pacing them and they soon gave up the chase. No doubt they thought I was not worth wasting ammunition on, and there was plenty of loot to be had much more easily.

I got back to the Ambulance Headquarters about midday and had a fairly good meal, starting back in the afternoon with twelve A.T. carts manned by Indian drivers. These drivers, although very good at their own jobs, were quite unarmed and were no good at all in a scrap. I was anxious about the Arabs on the return journey, but I thought that our numbers would deter them and that they might think we were all armed. Actually we had to face a somewhat different hazard on our way back.

After we had gone some miles, we ran into water, and all I could see for miles ahead and apparently on all sides was water. It is difficult to explain what a Mesopotamian landscape is like. It is absolutely flat and there is not a tree or landmark of any sort. I had a rough idea of the direction and I was following the tracks of the army as it had advanced. Now these quickly became covered up and I had nothing to guide me except my compass, and I was not at all sure of my bearings. To the east of me was the great Suwaikieh Marsh which extended for miles, and no doubt the water through which we were now wading almost up to the axles of the carts was flooding over into the marsh.

I calculated that we had probably gone more than half the distance and I thought it was best to carry on. Here and there were small nullahs or ditches, some of them partly made by the water and probably some of them the remains of Turkish works. Suddenly the leading A.T. cart went into one of these, and all I could see was the heads of the mules and the upper part of the driver sitting on the cart. I got off my horse and waded around, found that it was an isolated hole and guided the other carts round it. Meantime the cart which was in the hole remained stuck there, and in spite of frantic efforts by the driver it would not move.

It was now late in the afternoon and I was afraid of darkness coming on. Looking around I might have been in the middle of an ocean. I could see nothing but water. There was no landmark anywhere. I decided therefore to try moving on as if I was going to abandon the cart. My intention of course was to go back and get the driver and his mules if he could not move the cart. Fortunately my stratagem worked. When they saw the rest of the column moving off, the driver and mules made a terrific effort, and out came the cart. They were wonderful little mules, these Indian mules.

We carried on for several miles, with frequent interruptions from getting into holes. I was not afraid of walking into the river, because I knew that it was protected by a *bund* several feet high and that I was sure to see that, but I was afraid I might wander into the marsh.

Then the darkness came down quite suddenly, as it always does there. We stumbled on, but the water seemed to be getting shallower gradually and then I saw a few flickering lights. Shortly afterwards we came on some 13th Division troops looking for dry ground. Soon after that I found my own men and we moved nearer the front, where the ground was still dry.

Next morning the ADMS found us and was greatly relieved to hear that I had arrived. He said that he had been in serious trouble with General Maude for allowing me to ride back alone. A number of small parties had disappeared and only large columns were allowed to use the road.

We were now relieved by the 7th Division again, who took over the trenches in front of Sannayat. Not long afterwards the 13th Division crossed the Tigris by a bridge of boats which had been put up a few miles behind the lines.

We went into reserve for a few days behind the 3rd Indian Division on the right bank of the river, and I took the opportunity of indenting for the iron rations which I had used when we were on the other side. There was an immediate reaction and I received orders to report to General Maude at his Divisional Headquarters, which consisted of several small single fly tents. He took me out of his tent and away from his staff. He explained to me that I had committed a very serious offence. Only a senior officer in the position of command of an isolated force was permitted to order the consumption of iron rations. He wanted to know why I had done this. We walked slowly along together during this interview.

I answered that I was not aware that the regulations were so strict and that my position at the time was exceptional. I should normally have been in close touch perhaps a mile or two from the headquarters of my unit. Instead it was at least 20 miles away at Sheikh Saad, acting more or less as a general hospital. I had no transport facilities except my stretchers. We had to carry out patients a mile or so from my part of the front to the river bank. We drew rations also from a barge on the river bank and carried them back. I had only a sergeant in charge of the rations and he had not the same authority as the officer quartermaster of the field ambulance would have. I was only given rations for my own men and none for the patients whom we might have with us. The field ambulance could do this but I had no authority to do this. Normally the field ambulance would have supplied us by returning ambulance wagon, but there was not such a thing as an ambulance wagon on the front. On this occasion we had about 100 stretcher cases in my aid post for about 24 hours, and we had been unable to draw any rations for ourselves on the previous day. With the equipment which I had I could do very little for the casualties, and they were crying out for a cup of tea. I ended by saying that I would do the same again in similar circumstances.

The General was silent for about half a minute and then he said, 'Glen, I think we will go and have a cup of tea ourselves.' We went into the Headquarters mess tent. There was a bare board table, and in the middle was a battered enamel plate with three large army biscuits on it. Several officers came in and had a mug of tea, but I noticed that none of them touched the biscuits.

I know now that at this time supplies to the Army at the front were extremely short. We were living from day to day on the supplies that were able to come upriver. A few days later, when I was in the reserve trenches with my stretcher-bearers behind the 34th Brigade in front of the Abu Roman position on the right bank of the river, for four or five days our rations consisted of one large army biscuit per day (this was like a dog biscuit and extremely hard) and tea without sugar.

It might be a slight relief to this grim account if I tell a story about two tins of condensed milk. When I went forward on the right bank of the river with my stretcher-bearers when the division moved out of reserve I was accompanied by a Padre. Lieutenant Rees, the ambulance quartermaster, slipped a small tin of condensed milk into each of our haversacks. These were medical supplies and we had no right to get them, but neither of us objected. The following week, when our rations consisted of one biscuit and tea, I opened my tin and the Padre, myself and our batmen, who messed together, had a few drops out of the tin in our cups of tea. After a few days the Padre moved on, I think to another battalion. My batman came to me in great indignation and said, 'That damn Padre has moved away as soon as our tin of milk was finished. I bet he is not sharing his tin with anyone!' I explained to him that I was quite sure the Padre had moved on only from a sense of duty.

About this time I saw a copy of the Divisional Orders which were issued from time to time. After complimenting the Division on its fine record of fighting at Hanna, Felahiyeh and Sannayat on the other side of the river, there was a paragraph towards the end which said: 'An officer in a junior position has recently ordered the consumption of iron rations by the men under his command. This must never happen again.' The officer commanding the battalion alongside us showed me the order, and I told him that I was the junior officer concerned.

General Maude was a great commander, and it was extraordinary how officers and men trusted him completely, but he was a very strict disciplinarian. Men were court-martialled and shot for dereliction of duty. Not long after this incident a young soldier was court-martialled and sentenced to death for falling asleep on sentry duty. A medical officer had to be present at the execution. Naturally the man's own M.O. was excused and our field ambulance was told to supply a medical officer. We drew lots and I was lucky to escape the task. I do not know how often such executions happened, but I can testify one did take place on this occasion.

———

Some very hard fighting was now taking place on the right bank of the river where we now were, along with the 3rd Indian Division. I believe General Maude always considered that this was the side where our chief effort should have been made. It was possible on this side to outflank the Turks; the line became stretched and was very thinly held in parts.

One night before an attack the 41st Field Ambulance and our own ambulance were told to establish dressing-stations with stretcher-bearers behind the line. It was an extremely dark night. There was no moon, and as I have often said the land was as flat as a pancake, with no features to guide one. J.A. Burton, a Glasgow doctor, was in charge of the 41st Ambulance stretcher-bearers. I used my compass and I expect Burton did the same. In this part of the front there was no continuous line, and it was held by strong posts with wide spaces between them. There was no rifle-firing and I began to be anxious after a while that I had missed the line and we might be going right into the enemy lines.

I ordered a halt and told the men to try and dig in a bit if possible and we settled down to get what sleep we could before the morning, when we would see where we were. Suddenly there was a heavy outbreak of firing on our left and a Very light[10] went up. It turned out that Burton had done just what I had been afraid I would do myself; he had missed our line and walked right into a Turkish post. The Turks thought it was a night attack and the whole line woke up. The firing did not stop all night and in fact lasted well into the next day.

I think the incident upset the arrangements of the command considerably. We were very uncomfortable with bullets falling all around us, but we had no casualties. Burton did have quite a few casualties, but he got back safely himself.

Burton was quite a character and had many very good qualities as a soldier, but he did not approve much of Army ways and he had his own idea of discipline. On the day following my return with the A.T. carts through the floods on the other side of the river, the ADMS came to me and told me that Burton and his stretcher-bearers were missing. He asked me if I had any idea where he might be. Knowing Burton and his stubborn determination, I replied, 'He will still be where he was before the floods happened if you have not told him to move.'

The ADMS asked me if I would go with him to see if we could find Burton. He borrowed a horse from Division Headquarters for me and we rode off together into the floods, guided by compass. After going a mile or two through the floods, we saw small black specks in the distance, which turned out to be Burton and his party. He was at the edge of the river near the *bund*, and he and his men were sitting on top of the A.T. carts trying to keep dry. He said that he was 'waiting for orders'. Burton later became Muirhead Professor of Surgery in Glasgow University, and was affectionately known as 'Pop' by students and nurses.

10. A flare fired from a pistol as a signal or to illuminate the battlefield.

It was now nearly the end of April, and although we had made some progress on the right bank it was not sufficient. The Turks had counter-attacked in strength and regained some ground, although they lost very heavily in doing so.

The river was now very high and flowing along some of the nullahs and old, long since disused, irrigation channels. I was called out to a battalion where several men had taken very acutely ill with enteritis. One of them was dead when I got there and several others looked like they were dying. I immediately suspected cholera. There was an irrigation channel just behind the lines which actually flowed through the Turkish lines nearer the river. Owing to the water flowing slowly the mud had largely settled, and the water looked very enticing in the heat of the day.

I asked the Brigade Major if the men had been drinking the water. He said that there were strict orders against that, but that the men had been bathing and washing in it. The Brigade Major seemed to be very nervous while talking to me, when I told him to stop all washing in the channel and that only the chlorinated water brought up by pack mules must be drunk. I had barely got back to the field ambulance with the men when I received a message to return. When I got back an hour later the Brigade Major himself was dying, and died before we got him to the ambulance hospital. The epidemic stopped soon afterwards and there was no doubt where it had come from.

On the 22nd April the 7th Division attacked again at Sannayat. They were supported by machine-gun fire from our Division across the river. The attack, however, again proved unsuccessful. On the 24th April the *Jumna*, a small tug-boat, tried to run the gauntlet of the Turkish defences to Kut. I saw it pass upriver in the late evening. It was well protected by sandbags. It was run ashore, however, by a cable which the Turks had stretched diagonally across the river.

On the 28th April, Kut surrendered. In this unsuccessful fighting for the relief of Kut, our division lost about 4,500 men in casualties alone. The losses in officers were particularly heavy. We had arrived in Mesopotamia between 8,000 and 9,000 strong. In Gallipoli also the Division lost about 6,000 men out of 10,000 in about a fortnight. Very few armies in history have suffered losses like that and remained a fighting force.

The weather was now becoming very hot. The men were very depressed; they had been very badly nourished and sickness increased rapidly. In June the Division was moved back to Sheikh Saad to be nearer supplies. We got several large single fly marquees which we joined together to form large wards. The officers lay on stretchers and most of the men lay on paliasses on the ground. The normal capacity of a field ambulance is about 180 to 200 patients, and it is only supposed to look after them for a few hours or a day or so at most. We were now acting as a general hospital, and had 800 to 1000 patients.

Most of them were suffering from P.U.O. (pyrexia, or fever, of unknown origin). Much of this was probably sandfly fever, a fever rather like influenza; but some of it was probably typhoid and paratyphoid. However, we had no laboratory or means of making an exact diagnosis. There was also much dysentery as the flies were very bad. Later the flies seemed to die off as it became too hot, or perhaps our sanitation inproved, but dust-storms were of very frequent occurrence.

We had many cases of what we called heat-stroke. These cases occurred usually in men who were already suffering from a rise of temperature from some other cause. Owing to the intense heat of the sun, the heat-controlling mechanism of the body broke down and the body temperature rose to 108° or more. The men became unconscious, foamed at the mouth and went into convulsions. We had a tent down at the riverside where we kept splashing them with river water to cool them. Nearly all of the patients died, but a few recovered. Many of the men in the hospital tents became delirious and lost their reason, and we had to put a guard by the river to prevent them jumping in. The Tigris is a very steep-banked, swift-flowing river and we were seldom able to save anyone who fell in.

These days in the Field Ambulance in the summer of 1916 were to me, I think, the most distressing time I experienced in the army. It is bad enough to see men die of wounds received in battle, but to a physician like myself it was terrible to see men die by the score of sickness from which proper care and nursing might have saved most of them. Our nursing orderlies were magnificent, but were only partly trained. The conditions were appalling. The dust blew constantly and even the soldiers' limbs and faces were covered with it as they lay. We had no proper washing or sanitary facilities.

At one time I took what was diagnosed as sandfly fever myself. The sergeant nursing orderly told me afterwards that I was the worst patient they had had. They found me examining the sick officers, but when they brought me back to my stretcher I refused to stay in it, instead wandering about among the tents talking nonsense most of the time. Fortunately I recovered quickly and was back on duty in a little over a week. Sandfly fever is very liable to be associated with delirium.

We did get some reinforcements during this hot season, but we would have been better not to get them. Most of them went sick before they reached us. We got several new medical officers to help, but all of them went sick and only five of us who were there at the beginning of the hot season survived. Of ninety M.O. reinforcements who arrived in Mesopotamia in April 1916, ten died and forty-five were invalided.

In Mesopotamia there were no military cemeteries; after a battle, parties from the battalions buried their comrades and smoothed down the ground so that the Arab thieves, the Buddoos as we called them, could not find the graves to rob them. I believe some attempt was made to record the places where large numbers were buried, but it would have been extremely difficult to locate them afterwards.

One thing I noticed in Mesopotamia really did not surprise me, although it must have been very different on the Western Front; after a week or two in hospital, most of the men wanted back to their battalions. Home was very far away, and they knew there was no chance of getting back there. They wanted to be beside their comrades; they were happier there.

General Maude visited the hospital every Sunday without fail, and went round to speak to all the men who were able to speak to him. When he was there he always had a glass of water. The Tigris water was very muddy, but we collected it in canvas tanks and chlorinated it. This seemed to make it quite safe to drink, but it was really horrible stuff. We used palm-tree wood for our fires for cooking and the ashes made very good charcoal. I used this charcoal to make a crude filter with petrol tins, and we got crystal-clear water which came through very slowly. We used this as a special treat for patients, and General Maude always asked us for a glass of it when he visited us on Sundays.

On one of the visits to the Ambulance that summer, General Maude handed an envelope to an officer who had been recommended to be invalided home. It was to be handed personally to General Robertson, who was then at the War Office. Some of us thought that this envelope contained a report that may have had something to do with General Maude's rapid promotion. He was made Corps Commander about the middle of July and given command of the whole army in Mesopotamia shortly afterwards.

I think it was about the end of August 1916 after General Maude took over that the 13th Division was moved downriver about 100 miles, to Amara. There were probably several reasons for this. It got us nearer to supplies and saved transport. The divisional transport which had come from Basra all the way by road had now arrived at Sheikh Saad. A stationary hospital had arrived to take over our ambulance hospital duties. It was good for the troops to get on the move again and get accustomed to our transport. We had had many new troops arriving to fill up the battalions during the summer. More than 50% of these had been sent back down the river again sick in the following months.

We moved downstream in columns about full battalion strength. I was M.O. to one column with a section of the Field Ambulance. We had our full quota of ambulance wagons now, with enormous South American mules. I had a small Arab stallion as a riding horse. At first he was difficult to control, but latterly I got very fond of him and he was very comfortable to ride.

As it was very hot we just did about ten miles a day and it took us ten days to reach Amara. We struck camp usually about 2 a.m. and marched till about 6 a.m., when it began to get too hot. I remember that the sunrises were a wonderful pale-green colour.

The Buddoos were particularly active during this march. We used to collect all our wagons and supplies in the centre of the camp and the troops slept on the ground on the perimeter. Outside the sleeping troops, guards were posted at intervals. The men would dig a hole in the ground, put their rifle in the hole and sleep on top of it. Even then sometimes the rifles disappeared. The Arabs would tickle the men as they slept until they turned over, and then take the rifles which were the equivalent of a small fortune to them.

One night on the journey I was sleeping among the men at the perimeter of the camp. I was wakeful for some reason, and I thought I saw a shadow move against the starry sky a short distance from me. Suspecting it was an Arab, I put my hand round to my side to get my revolver, which I always carried. The Arab must have seen my movement, because he rose up immediately and his shape flitted across the starry sky right in front of a sentry.

I got up and asked the sentry if he had seen the Arab, but he had seen nothing. At Amara shortly afterwards I saw a post-mortem on a

British sentry who had been found dead at his post. He had a small puncture wound over his heart not more than ¼ to ½ inch in breadth, but his heart and main blood vessel (the aorta) had been cut across and he must have died almost immediately.

At Amara we had a comparatively pleasant time. We were encamped in large, double-fly E.P.I.P.[11] tents on the outskirts of the town, and we carried out daily training with our transport. The officers of the Field Ambulance were asked by the nursing staff of the general hospital there to come along one afternoon for tea. Burke, Poole, Littleworth, Macneil, Rees, our old quartermaster, and myself, I think, formed the party. We were a little shy at first, but with the help of a cup of tea and some nice cakes we gradually thawed out a bit and spent a pleasant afternoon.

About the middle of October the Division, which was now under the command of General Marshall, was inspected by the Army Commander General Maude and Sir Charles Munro. In Divisional Orders published on the day of the inspection, four officers and men were awarded the V.C. and I was among a number who were awarded the M.C. for our services during the campaign for the relief of Kut.

11. English Privates Indian Pattern tent, a large tent with a double fly-sheet accommodating between 20 and 26 men.

VII
Mesopotamia, 1917

We started marching north again about the beginning of December. With all our transport and new reinforcements filling up the depleted battalions, we were now a formidable force. We were all fit and well, and many of us were now hardened veterans. About two or three times the number of ships seemed to be plying up and down the river. There were now much larger paddle-boats. They had searchlights and went night and day. We marched directly north, through Sheikh Saad and into the battle of the Hai River which commenced the day we arrived at the front, the 13th December 1916.

The Turks still held the lines at Sannayat on the left bank, but had withdrawn their front on the right bank and made a fortified position on the right bank opposite Kut. The Hai River runs right across Mesopotamia from Kut to Nasiriya on the Euphrates. At flood times it is navigable all the way, but at the end of the summer, when the river falls, it practically dries up. It was dry when the troops of our Brigade, the 39th, crossed it with little opposition shortly after the start of the offensive.

The Turks withdrew to their positions near the river and the troops of our division followed them up as closely as they could. There was a fair number of casualties in the Brigade. We could not get our ambulances across the bed of the Hai River, even though it was dry. It was quite deep and broad and unfortunately the banks were very steep.

After studying it for a while, I selected a place where I thought we might manage to get a wagon across. The Argentine mules were very big and strong, and I got the transport men to harness an extra pair in front. We had got the wagon down into the bottom of the river bed and were getting ready for a run at the other bank, when suddenly the river bank behind me became lined with a troop of cavalry carrying lances with a small flag at the end; I recognised the Army Commander of the Mesopotamian Forces surrounded by his staff.

They beckoned to me to come up and speak to them. I went up quickly and General Maude addressed me: 'That is a dangerous way to use an ambulance wagon, Glen, what are you trying to do?'

I answered, 'I am trying to take it across, Sir. We have about two miles of a carry on the other side now, which is much too far. I thought that if we had one wagon across we could use it back and forward to the river and carry the casualties across by stretcher. I think we could manage it, Sir. Do you mind if we have a try?' We had been just about ready to have a go at it when we were interrupted.

I collected all the men I could get to push and pull. We then made a rush at it, and by a terrific effort on the part of the mules we got up on top. The General's party gave us a wave before they left.

I was very pleased, and also surprised that General Maude had remembered my name. In about an hour's time a party of pioneers arrived and in no time there was a road across the river and guns and other wagons were crossing.

The next day, whether it was because the Tigris had risen as it was expected to do at this time of the year, or the Turks had broken a *bund*, there was a swirling torrent where we had crossed dry-footed. In a few hours, however, there was a pontoon bridge at the same spot.

The slow advance against the Turks in the Kut position that had now begun was to continue for two months, with hard slogging work on dead level ground where there was no shelter. The only way to attack was to work up towards the Turkish positions and then capture the trenches bit by bit. The Turks were extraordinarily good fighters, especially in defensive positions.

A week after the attack started it began to rain, and it rained torrents for several days. The Mesopotamian desert is just dried mud, and when the rains came it was almost impossible to move. Cart-wheels sunk about a foot deep and could barely be moved, except with very light loads.

I was again with the stretcher-bearers, but this time I had a recently qualified Edinburgh graduate with me. He arrived just as the rains commenced and was attached to me as my assistant. We struggled through the mud all day and lay down at night in the mud and rain to get what sleep we could. I was watching Paterson Brown carefully to see how he was standing up to the conditions, but he never once grumbled. The nearest he got to a complaint was when he said to me, 'Is it always like this in Mesopotamia?' I replied, 'No, it is often much worse!' We soon became very good friends and he proved to be a fine officer. After the war he became a senior surgeon in Edinburgh Royal Infirmary.

The slogging work continued and the casualties were heavy, but not nearly so heavy as they had been the previous winter during our attempt to relieve Kut. This time the medical arrangements were much better. The Field Ambulances moved right up to the front, and we were in touch with our unit practically all the time. We drew rations from our own unit, and unless there was a fight on, frequently got back to our unit at night.

I think I mentioned when I was writing about the attack on Chanuk Bair, in Gallipoli, that at the end of that battle there was only one officer, Lieutenant Ward, myself and the quartermaster left after the battle. Lieutenant Ward had survived the heavy fighting in Mesopotamia the previous winter, and during the summer he often visited me and frequently dined with us in our mess. I was very fond of him and he seemed to be particularly attached to me. Although he never told me so, I learned somehow that he was the son of Mrs Humphry Ward, the novelist.

About this time he came into our mess at the Ambulance one night, as he often did, to have a refreshment with us. This night he said to me, 'The South Lancs are making an attack on our front tomorrow, and as second-in-command I am leading it. I don't think it is at all likely I will survive without being hit at least. I have told my men to send for you, Glen, at once if I am hit, and I know you will come.'

I got the message the next day, but when I reached him he was dead. He had been shot through the head at the beginning of the battle, and only survived a short time.

By the middle of February the Turks had been cleared from the whole of the right bank after very hard fighting and a magnificent defence by the Turks. Then General Maude started deceiving the Turks as to what he would do next. He had a pontoon bridge on wheels, and he kept moving this up and down the right bank in full view of the Turks. One day we marched about ten miles up the river and did not meet any opposition from the Turks except for some cavalry, and made an attempt to cross the river there.

The fire from across the river was too heavy and we had a good many casualties. I do not think this was meant as a serious attempt at crossing. There was an alarm that the Turkish cavalry were going to make an attack, and at this the main body of the troops and unfortunately our ambulance wagons retreated. We were left to come along with the rear-guard, carrying about eight or ten men on stretchers. We carried them for at least five miles, and were exhausted when we at last made up with the main body who had halted in a defensive position. I am afraid I was not very polite to Colonel Burke about this incident on my return. He should not have retired with his ambulance wagons until he knew how many wounded we had.

The River Tigris was about a quarter to half a mile broad, and flowed at about five knots an hour. However, you can read in the history books that it was crossed. It was crossed at a bend, the Shumran bend above Kut, by men from the 3rd Indian Division, Norfolks and Herts on 23rd February. They went over first in boats in the dark and gained a footing. Reinforcements then went over in boats and pushed up the bend further to protect the building of the bridge. Meantime the Turks had been marching about from one place to another where they expected a crossing to be made. Only a few were at the exact spot when the actual crossing took place. Those who were on the spot, however, fought well and the crossing had to be paid for.

By 4.30 in the afternoon the bridge was in place and our Division started crossing the following morning. The Turks were soon in full flight, and we were moving as fast as possible up the road to Baghdad. We came across abandoned Turkish ambulance wagons with severely wounded men in them. We transferred them to our own wagons and moved on.

The Turks had occupied a position in a nullah (gully) about eight miles from the Shumran bend. Our cavalry, which had gone on ahead, were unable to take the position, and two battalions of the 13th Division attacked late in the afternoon of the 25th. There was a sharp fight and losses were heavy on both sides, but the Turkish trenches were finally occupied by the evening and the Division moved on.

Our Field Ambulance was left with several casualties. Shortly after the battle everything became very quiet as the Division moved on after the Turks. The Army now had a fleet of Ford motor ambulances which should have evacuated our Ambulance so that we could move on after our Brigade, but the fleet was still busy with casualties from the 14th Division which had taken about 1,000 casualties the previous day in clearing the Shumran bend, so that we could not move that night.

Lieutenant Colonel Burke, who now had a Ford Motor Tourer, went out to see if he could make contact anywhere, but he was fired on heavily by a party of mounted Arabs. He had two bullet holes in his car and one through his windscreen, so he hurried back to the unit. We had a number of armed drivers, and we formed a defensive position with men and wagons on the outside and patients inside. The night passed quietly, except for one or two shots fired to warn off the Arabs. Next morning we were cleared by the Motor Ambulance Column and moved on after the Division. We made up with them before dark. There had been no more fighting.

We went on during the next few days to Aziziya, which was fifty-five miles from Kut and halfway to Baghdad. Meantime the river fleet had moved up and captured most of the Turkish river fleet, boats in which there were large quantities of guns and stores and large numbers of wounded Turks and wounded British prisoners captured in the recent fighting. It was a Turkish rout, although the Turks as always kept fighting and kept their discipline. We stopped at Aziziya till March 4th, when enough supplies had been accumulated, and then the Division pushed on after the Turks.

The cavalry had a brisk battle two days later at a place called Lagg, but they cleared it with a gallant action. The Turks had apparently intended to make a stand there.

We marched on past Ctesiphon, the great ruined palace built by the Parthian Kings. The ruins of the Greek city of Seleucia are on the other side of the river. Ctesiphon was captured by the Roman Emperor Julian in A.D. 363 and he was killed in the battle. His troops crossed the river in the dark, as our army did at Shumran. Although he captured the city, this was the end of the Roman advance to the East. Townsend captured Ctesiphon in 1915, but again, although it was a victory for him, he also had to retire for want of reinforcements. Ctesiphon when we saw it was a bleak dusty place, with many deep nullahs and old irrigation channels where the Turks had again prepared a strong position, but owing to our rapid advance they had evacuated it before we arrived there.

In these advances, although I now had a horse, I usually left it with the transport and marched with the men behind the Brigade troops. As we passed Ctesiphon, one of the men marching near me asked, 'What's this 'ere Cestisyphon anyway, Sir?' I answered that it was a very old palace built before Christ was born, that is to say, a long time ago. It is marvellous that the great arch still stands. I don't know what height it really is, and have been unable to find the figure.

There were some irrigated parts about here, and one day we camped in a field of growing barley in the bottom of a wide nullah, like a wide valley, which was called Nebuchadnezzar's Canal. It was made by the Babylonian king who lived about 600–550 B.C. It was as great a work as some of the Egyptian constructions. I thought it was rather a sin to camp on a field growing crops like this, but the animals certainly enjoyed it and required fresh food badly.

We had unfortunately only been encamped an hour or so when we saw a black cloud on the horizon. It came quickly nearer, and in no time we were in the midst of a great swarm of locusts. They hopped all over, jumping in our food, and they had a filthy smell. Within an hour, before our horses had a chance to eat any barley, the crop was gone and only the stalks remained.

The Turks eventually made a stand at the Diyala River. This is a large tributary of the Tigris on the left bank about ten miles south of Baghdad. A bridge was thrown across the Tigris River and the cavalry and 7th Division crossed over to the other bank. Our 38th Brigade, which was leading on the left bank, was ordered to attempt a crossing. The Diyala there is about 120 yards wide, and is deep and swift-flowing. There was no surprise and no shelter. The first night the Kings Own Lancs attempted to cross, but their pontoons were all sunk and very few survived this initial assault. The following night, the 8th to the 9th, the Royal North Lancs attempted the crossing following a bombardment, and some men managed to get across hidden by the great dust raised by the shelling. About 60 men got across and held on for two days against repeated Turkish attack. On the third night 9–10th the river was crossed further up by the Wiltshires and the position turned. This crossing of the Diyala River was a terrific battle and our losses were again heavy. The courage of the men of our Division in making this crossing of the Diyala River has never, I am sure, been surpassed, but very few of our countrymen have ever heard of it.

On the 10th March our Brigade, the 39th, crossed the river and took over the van. We ran into a Turkish position in the palm and orange groves by the routes to the city which the Brigade cleared and then carried on outside the city. Our transport was full of wounded, and we were told to go straight into Baghdad and leave them at the

British Embassy Hospital. When we got there it was largely filled with Turkish wounded, but we left our wounded there too, and our nursing orderlies. Colonel Burke stayed at the Embassy, but I was told to go right through the city streets with my men to join the Brigade at the north of the city. The previous night there had been a dust-storm and our faces were covered with dust; we looked like millers. The streets were already lined on both sides with crowds of cheering Baghdadis; I think some cavalry had gone through before us.[12]

Actually the Black Watch in the 7th Division had been the first troops into Baghdad, but they were on the other side of the river, which is not the centre of the city. Our Brigade, the 39th, was lead-ing that morning and they, along with the 40th Brigade, were told to march around the outside of the city. I think that our men were all very disappointed not to enter it after their hard fighting in the desert. In our Brigade certainly many of them never saw Baghdad again. Apart from some hard fighting which was still ahead of us in Mesopotamia, the Brigade carried on through Persia and the Caucasus, and eventually went home by the Black Sea and Constantinople. The only troops of the 13th Division to march through Baghdad apart from our Field Ambulance was the battalion of the Kings Own Lancs, who had made such a gallant crossing of the Diyala River a few days previously.

Our Division carried on up the left bank of the Tigris, and troops of the 37th Indian Division advanced up the Diyala River towards the Persian border and the Jabel Hamrin mountains, where they met the 13th Turkish Army Corps which was now retreating out of Persia fol-lowed by the Russians. This Turkish army corps was commanded by a very able general, Ihsan Bey. His troops were regular army Turkish soldiers. Some of the prisoners who were later captured said that they had been on continuous active service for ten years. Many of them had only sacks on their feet instead of boots, and they had been living on the country in Persia. It was no wonder that we found the Persians starving when we eventually got there.

12. Although not included in this account, Alec told his sons that while he was marching through the streets of Baghdad with the Field Ambulance, a Turkish officer rushed forward towards him, sword in hand. Alec was on horseback. He bent down and grabbed the sword, not knowing if it was an aggressive act or a surrender. This Turkish officer's sword, with its crescent and star marking, remains in the family's possession.

In the hard fought battles on the Diyala at the foot of the Jabel Hamrin hills, the 3rd Division were forced to retire and lost about a third of the men engaged. Ihsan Bey then attempted to cross our front and join up with the Turks on the left bank in front of our position. The Turkish troops from our front, who at that time were holding a position on the Shatt el Adhaim, a tributary of the Tigris, north of us, attempted to cross our front. Two of our Brigades, the 39th and 40th, advanced to meet them.

Our Brigade, the 39th, did a night march of ten miles. We ran into the Turks at dawn on the 29th March on a dead level plain. The battle was called the Battle of the Marl Plain, because here the ground was covered with small, white, flat stones about 1 to 1½ inches in diameter. It was a most unusual thing to find stones like these in Mesopotamia, and my own opinion was that there once had been a city here and that these were small pieces of weather-worn pottery.

That may or may not be so, but this was a most unusual battle, for modern times at any rate – an encounter battle in the open at close-quarters. There was no shelter for anyone. Bullets and shells whistled all round and there were many casualties. One of our M.O.s was shot through the abdomen. We had a lot of wounded and tried to set up an operating tent quickly, but our M.O. died very soon. I cannot remember his name. He was rather older than most of us. I wrote to his parents myself and told them the circumstances.

The battle lasted till about midday and then the Turks retreated. The 3rd Division troops dealt with Ihsan Bey and he retired into the Persian Hills again, but further north, leaving the road into Persia clear. It was then that some Russians joined us. There were only a few of them and they did not stay long, but retired again into Persia. The Russian Revolution had happened by this time.

On the 10th of April, Ihsan Bey again came out from the Jabel Hamrin Hills to try to join the Turks on the Tigris. He was met first by the 40th Brigade. Our Brigade, the 39th, which made a rapid march to help, only came in at the end. This was the battle of Shialah. It was again an encounter-battle in the open. Our artillery caused great havoc among the advancing Turks and they left 385 dead on the field before they retired.

If we were to consolidate our position in Baghdad before the summer, it was necessary to take the Turkish positions on the Shatt al Adhaim. The troops on the left bank could not advance to Samarrah, which was the Turkish railhead, until we had advanced on the left bank.

The 38th and 40th Brigades of the 13th Division and the 35th Indian Brigade attacked the position on 29th April. This was called the Battle of the Boot, and was one of the bloodiest battles of the campaign. I was not there and cannot say much about it. Ihsan Bey came down the Shatt el Adhaim from the Persian Hills and joined in the fight. Our battalions, in spite of drafts, were far below strength after the continuous fighting since February 1917. The Cheshires lost 126 men out of 330 in the battle, and the South Wales Borderers 203 out of 340. The Turks were finally dispersed. Ihsan Bey fled with a few survivors to the Persian Hills. A few days later, after another very hard fight, the 7th Division took Samarrah on the right bank and captured much railway booty. Shortly afterwards trains were running from Baghdad to Samarrah. The whole front was now safe. It was the end of April. The sun was now up. Fighting was over for the season.

—

Since 13th December 1916, when we marched right into the battle for the Hai River, our division had been fighting continuously. Our two previous campaigns in Gallipoli and the attempted relief of Kut had ended in defeat. This one had ended in victory because we had completely broken up the Turkish armies, and now occupied a strong, easily-defended position. The British forces in Mesopotamia had destroyed the German dreams of advancing to the East and we had opened the road to Persia. The news of our victory spread rapidly throughout the East and was a great help to the Allies. Although on a small front, it was our first real victory over the Germans and their allies, and helped to cheer up the people at home and on the Western front, where there was still stalemate.

From the medical standpoint this part-campaign was very different from our previous campaigns. The field ambulances were just behind the front-line troops, doing their proper duty. Within an hour or so after their occurrence, casualties were under medical care. The Ford motor ambulance columns were an enormous advance over the old animal transport wagons. At the Battle of the Marl Plain, for example, they came racing over the flat desert and the casualties were away to a proper hospital ship on the river in an hour or two. It is hard to believe today that it was only towards the end of this campaign that we saw a few army motor transport wagons. Many of the men with slight wounds were back in their units a fortnight after they were wounded, and only a few were evacuated so far as India. There was no leave to Blighty. Occasionally the men returned to duty with their bandages still on.

There is no doubt that the British Army learnt lessons in these Eastern campaigns in the First War that we put to very good use in the Second World War. In the North African campaign we had mobile surgical units with skilled surgeons right up at the front. Our sulpha-nilamide drugs for the treatment of dysentery were much superior to the German drugs. The German anti-typhoid vaccine was very much inferior to ours. We gave blood transfusions in these surgical units and latterly we had penicillin, which saved many lives. Some medical men believe that our medical superiority played a large part in winning the campaigns against the Germans and Italians in North Africa and there seems to be little doubt that the reason why the Japanese lost the Burma Campaign was because they had practically no medical service at all.

A great many of these improvements in the medical services in Mesopotamia were due to the influence of General Maude himself. I have told you that when he was divisional commander he visited the field ambulances every week without fail, and discussed all our difficulties. More important still, he proved to be a very great commander in the field.

The morale of General Maude's troops was always good. They very quickly realised that he had the interests of the individual soldier very much at heart. No doubt all the improvements which seemed to occur almost immediately after he took over command of the whole force were not due to him, but there is no doubt that he was responsible for the continuing improvement. Field-bakeries arrived, and we began to get baked bread instead of biscuits all the time. Whenever transport conditions were possible, beer became available in the canteens. As an example of the sort of thing that happened, Colonel E.T. Burke, C.O. of our Field Ambulance, started a canteen at the Field Ambulance where he supplied a mug of tea and a bread and bully beef sandwich to anyone who asked for it. This was a great boon to the motor ambulance men and transport men, who often went many hours without food or drink. This became known throughout the Division. We were always on the lines of communication and very few, even officers, passed us without giving us a call. Sometimes the officers got a tot of whisky also. That put our mess bills up a bit, but we did not mind that. The authorities approved and we got extra rations of bread and bully beef and tea for the purpose; Rees, our grand old quartermaster, who was still with us, looked after the supplies of whisky.

For his campaign in 1916–17 General Maude got no new formations. He had reinforcements for the Divisions which he had, but owing to continuous losses he never got them up to anything like full strength. This may have deceived the Turks and Germans, who probably thought that they could hold us quite easily. This time, however, the British and Indian troops were well fed and well looked after, and were led by a great commander in whom they had complete confidence.

VIII
Home Leave

The Turks had retired on the right bank as far as 100 miles from Baghdad. On the left bank, on the 13th Division front, the 13th Turkish Army Corps or what was left of it had retired north into the Persian Hills. Our Division held a line from Sindiyah about 50 miles north of Baghdad to the Jabel Hamrin foothills on the Persian border. We called it the Sindiyah Windiya line. The Turks were far away and scarcely troubled us. It was a much more pleasant country than the country round about Sheikh Saad where we had spent the previous summer. Part of it was irrigated and green and there were occasional groves of palm trees. It was now about two years since our Division had left home and we had been two years on very active service.

It was announced at the beginning of May 1917 that leave to India was to be granted. The first to go in our Division were those who had been with the Division since we left home two years before. It was a small party. There were very few in the infantry battalions. We were better off in the Field Ambulance, where we had about a score of NCOs and men and three officers out of our original RAMC strength of 180.

I applied for special leave to go home to Britain from India. My family had run into serious trouble in the past year. My eldest sister, with whom I went to Canada in 1914, had died at the birth of her first child. Her husband had been severely wounded in France with the Canadian Forces and she had sailed home to join him. She was about eight months pregnant at the time, and she was very seasick throughout the voyage. Her child was born shortly after she arrived home. She went into a comatose condition after the birth and died after a few days. The cause of the death was not properly understood at the time, but it was probably due to acute atrophy of the liver. The child, a boy, survived.

My father had taken ill about the same time with symptoms of lung tumour, called at that time mediastinal tumour. I got word that he

84

was dying. I was granted home leave for one month along with forty other officers from the whole Mesopotamian force, on the understanding that we went home by passenger steamer and paid the cost of our own passage.

One of the Indian officers from a neighbouring unit asked me if I would take his Indian servant back to Bombay as he wanted to return to India. He told me that he would be helpful to me on the way, and as he was a private servant he could only travel home in the company of an officer. Our leave party went down to Baghdad by river in a large barge towed by a small tug. I got word to board a steamer at Baghdad at 9 p.m. some days later. I had collected a box of rations for myself and my servant for the journey downriver. There was only sitting room on the deck in these steamers, and we had to feed ourselves, although we occasionally got hot tea. My servant helped me on board with my baggage, and then went back for the box of provisions. He did not appear immediately, but I thought that he must surely be aboard and that he would soon find me. However, the boat left in the darkness, and after a good search the next day I realised that he was not on board. I had lost my servant, but not the least of my troubles was that as a result I had no rations. However, a kindly Scottish Indian Medical Service officer offered to share his rations with me and we did quite well, because we made up a party and shared together. This officer's father was a Church of Scotland minister near my home.

When I got to Basra a week or so later, I reported the loss of my servant. They said that they would keep a lookout for him and send him on to India if he told the right story. I had little hope of seeing him again. However, a week later I was lying on my camp-bed in the great heat of a Basra afternoon when I heard a most pathetic voice crying, 'Sahib, Sahib!' It was my Indian servant. He had apparently suffered great tribulations. He had lost his way to the ship in the dark. Afterwards nobody would take any notice of him without his officer. However, he had smuggled himself aboard a ship going downriver and had eventually found me in the rest camp. The box of provisions was untouched and intact.

We travelled comfortably to Bombay on a B.I. (British India) boat, and I put up at the Taj Mahal Hotel in Bombay. This was a very good hotel, but unfortunately I suffered a bad relapse of my old dysentery. It was quite acute and I felt very ill. I had booked on a P.&O. ship to sail in a week's time, and I dared not go sick in case I was put into hospital and lost my leave home. I sailed as a second-class passenger about the middle of June.

It was the monsoon season and the Indian Ocean was very rough. My cabin was in the stern of the ship, one of the worst parts of a ship to be in during a storm. The lavatories in fact were actually over the propeller. I was very sick and ill and did not come out of my bunk until we reached Aden and the Red Sea.

When I got home I found my father very ill but he was still surviving by the time my month's leave was up when I had to report to my ship for the return journey. This time we were notified very generously by the War Office that our passage back would be free.

I decided to ask for an extension of my leave. I reported to the War Office in London where I told them my reasons. The response was that many other officers had applied for extensions, but the orders were that none were to be granted. I said that I would like to see Sir Laming Worthington Evans, who was the Minister in Charge of the medical service. I was told I had no chance of seeing him. However, I was an old soldier by then and I sat down in the office and said I intended to wait till I saw him. I sat there from 9.30 a.m. till 12 noon. Latterly I saw one or two of the staff whispering to one another, and then a Major came forward and said that Sir Laming Evans would see me. I was very kindly received and I was given a letter to Scottish Command in Edinburgh.

I arrived early in Edinburgh next morning and was waiting at the door of the office when it opened. It was a Saturday morning. They told me I was lucky, because Colonel Cullen the DDMS (Deputy Director of Medical Services) Scotland was only coming in for half an hour that morning as he was taking the weekend off. The office staff advised me to give him a good salute. When he came I was taken into his office and I gave him as good a salute as I could.

He said at once, 'You have been in the East. You have had malaria.' I agreed that I had had a number of tropical diseases and did not dispute his diagnosis, although at that time I had not had malaria. He read my note from the War Office and asked, 'Where do you wish to go?'

'Glasgow,' I replied.

He gave me a letter to report to Maryhill Barracks in Glasgow and I went home the same day, greatly to my mother's surprise. I stayed at home except on the days I was on orderly duty when I slept at the barracks.

After a week or two at Maryhill I was sent down to the Flying School at Turnberry. There I was assistant M.O. to William Gardiner, who was a Glasgow practitioner and on the staff of the Samaritan Hospital. We had a small hospital in the house on the front. Parachutes were not used at this time and accidents were fairly frequent. We also had a small epidemic of cerebrospinal fever among the air-force personnel and mechanics, who were living in huts in too crowded conditions. Willie Fernie, the golf professional, was convalescent at the time from the Western Front, and he and I played frequently. We had an arrangement that an ambulance would come for me on the course when required. Fernie gave me a stroke a hole, so my golf can't have been too bad.

One day, after I had been at Turnberry a few weeks, I was visiting my father in Glasgow. For several weeks he had been unable to lie down and had sat in a chair night and day. I was sitting with him when he suddenly expired. He had been advising me to get rid of his share in his business if possible, because he was sure that it would not do well. The son of the original proprietor, who was co-director with my father, was not very able or very reliable. His prophecy proved only too true, and unfortunately my mother never got anything out of that business again and a considerable part of my father's capital was lost.

As soon as my father's affairs were settled, I applied to the ADMS (Assistant Director of Medical Services) for Ayrshire, Lieutenant Colonel Forrest, to get back to my unit in Mesopotamia. He was a territorial officer and a practitioner on the south side of Glasgow. Forrest was rather annoyed. He said that his staff were always being changed and he refused to forward my application.

Next time I was in Glasgow I went to the DDMS West of Scotland and told him that I wished to return to active service and if possible return to Mesopotamia. I told him that the ADMS Ayrshire had refused to send in my application and I think that helped. I don't think the ADMS and DDMS were on very good terms.

When I called Lieutenant Colonel Forrest to tell him what I had done, his language over the telephone was somewhat strong to say the least of it. After the war was over he forgave me and I actually became his medical attendant when he had a long illness from which he died.

In a few days, much sooner than I expected, I got word to proceed to London *en route* for Mesopotamia. Apparently a batch of MOs was just about to leave as reinforcements for Mesopotamia, and I got instructions to join them. We crossed from Southampton to Le Havre at night in an old Clyde paddle steamer about the beginning of December 1917. It was a wild night. The boat was very crowded. The saloons had been stripped of all their upholstery, and the men sat about on the decks.

Almost all of them were seasick. I was not feeling too well myself and I went along to the stewards office to see if there was any medical comfort (whisky) available. There I met a tall Scottish RAMC Captain about the same vintage as myself. He had the unmistakable slightly superior attitude of the Edinburgh graduate. His name was Bryce McCall Smith. He was originally from Morayshire and we were to become great friends.

We boarded a train at Le Havre for Marseilles. The men travelled more or less comfortably in covered goods-wagons. At least they could lie down in them. McCall Smith and I and four other newly qualified MOs were put in an ordinary local passenger train compartment. It was very old and dilapidated and had only three complete windows out of six, including the doors of the compartment. We were told to put all our kit into another wagon.

McCall Smith and I, being old soldiers, insisted on opening our valises and taking out three blankets each. We found when we started that the other MOs had not done so and only had their greatcoats. We were two and a half days on the journey to Marseilles. It happened to be a very cold spell and was freezing hard all the way to Marseilles. We of course shared our blankets but it required two of them to help to keep out the draught from the broken windows, so that we had only four blankets between six of us and we could not lie down.

We had two meals on the journey, which was very slow. We were frequently rushed into sidings while express passenger trains passed. On the first day we had a tin of McConnachie (stew) which was heated in boilers at a siding. The second day we marched a short way to a hall where we were given another stew. This time it was dark and purplish in colour, unmistakably horse-flesh. It was certainly not a very comfortable journey.

At Marseilles we were kept confined in a rest camp most of the time. One night we were all marched down to the docks and then marched back again. The submarine attack in the Mediterranean was at its worst. There were a great many of them and they were based in Austrian and Turkish ports. One night we were suddenly put aboard a ship called the S.S. *Nile*, an old P.&O. ship, which went right out to sea as soon as we were aboard. There was no attempt to detail us to quarters; we were simply dumped aboard and at once put to sea on a dark moonless night.

It was very stormy in the Gulf of Lyons, and many of the men were again seasick. They lay about on the decks and corridors. I spent the night in one of the public lounges. Next morning we were detailed to cabins and quarters. I think it is unlikely that we would have been torpedoed during the night, but I hate to think what would have happened if we had been torpedoed in the early morning.

We went straight to Malta and anchored in a bay on the south side of the island. While in this bay we had practice at abandoning ship. We were all told to jump into the water with our lifebelts on. Some of the officers, to show a good example, dived or jumped from the deck of the ship into the water. I chose to jump. I think I must have kept my legs straight too long because I went very deep, and thought that my lungs would burst before I surfaced.

We left Malta in convoy with the S.S. *Aragon*. This was a large ship which had been the headquarters of the staff in Gallipoli and had lain in Mudros Bay all through the campaign. The troops said that they had difficulty when they came to move her after the campaign, because she was stuck on a shoal of bottles.

We had one British and two Japanese torpedo boats in charge of the convoy. The *Aragon* had a large party of nursing sisters aboard as well as troops, and we steamed close to one another most of the way surrounded by the torpedo boats. During the night before we approached Port Said, the two ships separated. In the morning when I went on deck I found we were escorted by the two Japanese torpedo boats and the *Aragon* and the British torpedo boat had disappeared.

As I was looking over the ship's side I saw a streak of white foam coming towards us. Just as I noticed it one of the Japanese torpedo boats sounded the alarm. The torpedo, for that was what the white streak was, passed just behind our stern. The *Nile* was an old boat and actually had a clipper bow, but it had quite a turn of speed, which was probably what deceived the German submarine into missing the target.

Immediately our ship's signal for boat stations sounded, and the ship made a right-angle turn and made off in a different direction, while the torpedo boats went looking for the submarine.

The chief steward was in my boat, and he and I were standing behind the troops just at the door of the saloon bar. He said to me, 'It's a pity to waste all that good drink, Doc. This is the third time I have been down. They always get you at the second or third try. I'll bet we are surrounded by submarines and we'll be torpedoed in a minute or two.'

I declined the offer of a drink, however, and said I would prefer to be sober if I had to swim for it; so he went into the bar on his own.

We escaped unscathed, however, and returned to our course. When we got into Port Said the next day, we learned the sad news that the *Aragon* had been torpedoed just about the same time as we were attacked. She was sinking fast and the single torpedo boat had gone alongside to take off the troops who were having difficulty getting the lifeboats out. The torpedo boat was itself torpedoed alongside the *Aragon* and 800 lives were lost. The nurses escaped on the boats. This was one of the most serious submarine losses of the war.

When we got into Port Said the officers were having a bit of a celebration in the saloon and some of the officers insisted on sending for the captain to toast him. He appeared in a nightgown down to his ankles. We drank his health and he went off to bed again. I expect he was badly needing sleep.

—

When we got to Basra we were put into a rest camp, and I went right away to the headquarters of the RAMC to see about getting back to my unit. When they heard how long I had been with it, they told me that they could send me back to my old Division, and said they expected I would then be able to arrange a return to my old unit. McCall Smith had asked me to get permission for him to accompany me if possible, but they would not grant that. However, I promised McCall Smith I would try to arrange an exchange when I got to my Division.

Next day I set off again up the river. The last time I was there the trip used to take about a fortnight, but there were now new steamers which had reduced the time. When we got about eight or ten miles south of Baghdad the steamer stopped and tied up against the *bund* in a deserted spot and we were all dumped ashore. We were told that smallpox had broken out in the rest camp and we were to camp where we were meantime. We had no tents or cooking facilities. The CO of the ship had taken charge and was sitting in front of some ration boxes in lieu of a table. There was a wind blowing with a lot of dust and I began to think I could do better than this. After all I was an MO. We had had an epidemic of smallpox the previous summer, and our Ambulance had formed an isolation unit for a month or two. We had all been vaccinated, and I wasn't the least afraid of taking smallpox. I thought I might even be of some use and get back quicker to my own unit.

I therefore approached the Major in charge warily. He was shouting orders all over the place and I could see his temper was not exactly good. I saluted and said to him, 'Excuse me, Sir, I am a medical officer on my way back after leave. I might be useful in Baghdad and I think I could find my way there myself.' He answered angrily, 'Get to hell out of this!' I went back and sat on my kit for a while rather disconsolately, then suddenly I remembered that he had said, 'Get to hell out of this.'

A number of Buddoos had arrived at the edge of the camp, and were attempting to sell the men 'oranges and eggs'. I approached one of them who seemed to have a reasonably good donkey, pointed in the direction of Baghdad and muttered, 'Baghdad hai.' He understood and replied, 'Acha, Sahib.'

I got one of the soldiers to help me with my kit and we loaded the donkey. No one seemed to notice us, and I set off behind the donkey for Baghdad. It was about 4 p.m., and after a while I began to doubt the wisdom of my move. I had my pistol, however, and I let the Arab see I had it. He walked in front with the donkey and I walked behind.

By the time we got into the suburbs of Baghdad it was quite dark. We crossed one of the bridges of boats and I asked the Arab to go to the Hotel Maude. He appeared to know the way all right and we arrived at about 8 p.m.

The hotel-keeper told me all his beds were occupied, but he would give me some dinner and I could sleep in the courtyard. The courtyard was quite luxurious for an Arab courtyard. There was a pond in the middle with some water-lilies, and a verandah all round under which I put up my camp-bed. I was brought an excellent meal with actually a bottle of German hock, which must have been a relic of the German occupation. I thought that the Germans must have left a great deal of it for it to last so long. I had an excellent sleep and in the morning went out to find out about transport to my Division, which I had been told at Basra was where I had left it about six months previously, at Sindiyeh, about 50 miles north of Baghdad.

To my great joy, a few minutes after I left the hotel I spotted one of our own motor ambulance wagons. I knew it was ours because I recognised the drivers. They seemed almost as pleased to see me as I was to see them, and they promised to call back for me in an hour or two after they had collected their stores.

On the journey to Sindiyeh they told me that they had got several new officers. One of them was a Scotsman from Glasgow called Mavor. They said he was a great sport, that he had organised concerts and at present was producing a play which he had written himself. A stage had been erected and they were going to put on a show for the Brigade very soon.

I replied, 'I think I know this fellow Mavor,' and wondered what extraordinary chance had brought him to our unit.

The men told me that there had been no fighting since I left. There had been an expedition into the Persian Hills to chase the elusive remains of the 13th Turkish Army Corps which were still holding a position there. The 40th Brigade had quite a stiff fight but our Brigade, the 39th, had only come in at the tail-end of it. They had had a long journey and had to march nearly 100 miles north-east of Sindiyeh into the hills.

After a journey of about 50 miles over very rough roads, we arrived at Tuwair camp, the same place as I had left them six months before, shortly after 7 p.m. It scarcely seemed to me six months. I had left in June 1917 and it was now January 1918. I seemed to have been travelling ever since I left. I was a week or two in Bombay and took six weeks to go home. I spent part of July and August on leave, then there followed six weeks at Maryhill and six at Turnberry before I left again in December for Mesopotamia.

The officers had already gone into the mess for their evening meal when I arrived, and I went in unannounced, much to their surprise. There were very few changes in the personnel and I knew most of them.

Shortly afterwards there seemed to be a great deal of noise outside the mess. The Colonel asked the waiter what it was all about, and he answered, 'The whole field ambulance is outside, Sir, asking to see Captain Glen.'

The Colonel turned to me and said, 'You had better go outside, Glen, and tell them to stop that bloody row.'

When I got outside and the 'bloody row' had quietened down a bit, I said, 'I think your discipline must be getting a bit slack. This is a most unusual way to behave in the Army. However, I thank you very much for your welcome. This seems to be a haven of peace now and a great change from former days. The war seems to be pretty bloody yet on the Western Front and I think you are very lucky to be here. Some of you, I know, have been a very long time away from home, but I have no doubt now that we are going to win the war and that it won't be so very long before we all get home again.'

The officers' mess was a most luxurious place. The Indian personnel who were now attached to the Ambulance had built a mud hut which was much cooler than a tent. The inside walls had been whitewashed, and Mavor had painted a dado round the top depicting strings of camels. Apparently there was a once-weekly routine. Mavor would draw a cartoon of an officer, which was hung up on the wall of the mess and was ceremoniously unveiled with speeches and toasts. A week or two later my own cartoon was unveiled and I still have it.

The officers had recently been supplied with small bivouac tents, double-fly, Indian pattern. That night and for several months until we eventually moved camp, I shared Mavor's bivouac tent. My batman, an Aberdonian named McDonald, had adopted Mavor in my absence and now he took charge of both of us. The tents were very small and there was just room for one person to lie on either side. A trench was dug in the middle so that one could stand up. I noticed a photograph of a lady at the end of the tent. It was a photograph of Mavor's mother.

The next three months, February, March and April, were very pleasant. After the winter rains the Mesopotamian desert is transformed. A thick green grass grows up and there are masses of flowers, particularly orchids and flowering bulbs. Some of the grass is like miniature wheat and provides food for great numbers of birds. There were flocks of very fine game birds called Sand Grouse and also many Partridges.

Quartermaster Rees had picked up a couple of very old shotguns in Baghdad, and when we could get ammunition, which was very scarce, we occasionally supplemented our rations by hunting these birds. There were also wild boars in the swamps which some of the cavalry officers hunted. The ground was much more fertile than further down the river and areas were cultivated near the banks. There were also groves of date palms. At night immense numbers of starlings came and roosted in the palm trees. They flew about in great flocks and went through extraordinary gyrations, and sometimes, when a hawk or predatory bird dived into the middle of them, forming great saucer-shapes.

As the river fell after the floods, the local Arabs came out and staked their claims on the sandbanks as they appeared. They seemed to be able to produce water melons in a few weeks.

We occupied ourselves with various pastimes. Mavor produced his play, a melodrama such as would appeal to the Tommies. I can't remember the title he gave it. We had boxing matches in the Division which were very popular, football matches and we even held a sports and race meeting.

There was one great change in the Mesopotamian force which I deeply regretted. That was the loss of General Maude, who died of cholera in Baghdad on 18th November 1917. I heard the news just before I left home and had a feeling of personal loss. I knew that the British Army had lost one of its greatest generals, but I felt, as I know that many of those who knew him well also felt, that I had lost an old friend and comrade. General Marshall, who had previously been in command of our Army Corps on the left bank of the Tigris, was now Army Commander.

IX

Persia with Dunsterforce, 1918

The Germans had been penetrating into Mesopotamia for years before the outbreak of the First World War, hoping to increase their influence in the East. After their defeat by General Maude and the break-up of the Russian army following the Revolution, the Turks and Germans changed their line of advance and began to move into North Persia and the Caucasus. The 13th Turkish Army Corps, to which our Division had been opposed on the right bank of the Tigris for some time, retreated further north and joined the Turkish forces which were advancing into North Persia and the Caucasus with no opposition from the Russians. They lived to a large extent on the country they occupied, and ravaged the Armenian country in North Persia round about Lake Urmia. The Armenians began to flee from them in thousands, pouring into central Persia and down the Baghdad road into Mesopotamia behind our lines.

Early in the year 1918 we began to hear talk of a new force which was gathering at Ruz,[13] a place on the Diyala River on the road to Hamadan. We called this force the Hush Hush Force. We understood that it was going places. Two hundred officers and 400 NCOs had been collected in France and elsewhere as volunteers to take part in a dangerous and difficult enterprise under the command of General Dunsterville. Actually their purpose was to go into North Persia and the Caucasus and to organise and train the Armenians to oppose the Turks.

It was about this time that the Germans and Turks began to quarrel. The Turks had always had a great ambition to form a trans-Caucasian Islamic state between themselves and Persia. Part of this area had originally belonged to Turkey. The Caucasus contains a variety of different races: Armenians and Georgians in the west and centre who are Christians, and the Tartars in the east around Baku who are Muslims. This eastern part of the Caucasus is called Azerbaijan.

13. Now known as Balad Ruz.

The Germans had now occupied the Ukraine in Russia and began to advance down the railway to Baku which is a great oil-producing region. At one time there were six German battalions in Georgia. Their aim was to form a Georgian State there under German influence. The Turks, however, beat them to it, and six Turkish divisions were advancing on Baku by the time General Dunsterville with his Hush Hush Force, now known as Dunsterforce, arrived in North Persia.

To complicate matters when he got to Enzeli,[14] the port in the Caspian Sea, he found the Bolsheviks in control. I don't think that we had previously given them much thought, but General Dunsterville found them very difficult customers to deal with. They refused at first to let him have ships to take him to Baku. It was probably about this time that the decision was made to send our Brigade, the 39th Brigade of the 13th Division, to his aid.

The movement of large bodies of troops through Central Persia at that time was almost a physical impossibility. In most places there was only a track suitable for pack animals going over high mountain passes. It was impossible to supply an army by road transport, and the troops which went into Central Persia had to live largely on the country. Meantime the surrounding area had been despoiled by the Turkish army and by the Russians, especially since the Revolution.

However Alexander the Great had crossed Persia in 800 BC and no doubt the British thought they could do it too. Our Brigade left Ruz for the 1,000-mile march through Persia early in May 1918. I was unfortunate on this occasion, as I was detailed to stay behind and clear up the camp and bring on some reinforcements to our RAMC personnel which were expected to arrive at any time. It was understood that we were to follow on quickly using modern motorised vehicles, and that we would soon make up with the main body, who were marching with animal transport.

I did not relish the prospect; from experience I did not like being separated from my unit. It was pointed out to me that I had always been in the van and that this time it was my turn for the rearguard. The ADMS told me that it might be a difficult job, that there might be several hundred reinforcements also for the battalions and he

14. Now known as Bandar-e Anzali.

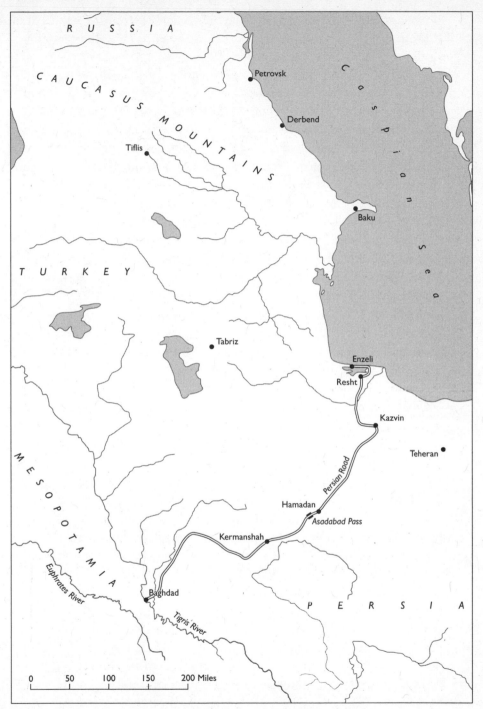

Persia and Russia, 1918–19.

wanted an experienced officer to be left to deal with it. He was right. It turned out to be a very difficult job and we had to walk practically all the way under difficult conditions.

Perhaps I should detail the officers who were attached to the 40th Field Ambulance when we started our journey into Persia. We were to have many adventures together. Our O.C. was Lieutenant Colonel E.T. Burke, a Scottish medic and contemporary of Mavor and myself at Glasgow. He had been a keen politician as a student and was something of an orator. He had made exciting speeches as an Irish Nationalist in student political debates. Osborne Mavor, who had been appointed a Major just before I returned to the unit, was Second in Command. I also was appointed a Major shortly after my return to this unit. In addition we had Tomory, who was an Edinburgh graduate and a crack rugby footballer at school and university. He stayed on in the Army after the war and reached the second highest position in the Medical Services.

Bryce McCall Smith, whom I met on my journey out to Mesopotamia, joined us. After I arrived back at the Ambulance I was able to arrange a transfer for him with an older MO who preferred to return to the base to do hospital work. McCall Smith arrived in time to join the Ambulance just as it left for Persia. He was a tall athletic man, and Mavor with his genius for characterisation called him 'Muckle'. The name stuck to him.

Salisbury Craig was another Glasgow graduate who later became a consultant physician in Glasgow. Then there were Paterson Brown, an Edinburgh graduate who later became one of the senior surgeons in Edinburgh Royal Infirmary and J.M.Watt, also an Edinburgh student, who went to South Africa after the war and became Professor of Pharmacology and Dean of the Faculty of Medicine in Johannesburg. Drummond Campbell, another Scot, was in charge of the horse and mule transport. He qualified as a dentist after the war.

Lieutenant Rees, our quartermaster, when told of our new campaign, said that he was afraid he could not go. He had never gone sick at any time, but we all knew latterly that he was an ill man; he was very stout and short of breath on slight exertion. He was invalided home as no longer fit for active service. He had done an extraordinarily good job, but he did not survive very long after the end of the war.

'Deacon' Boyes, who was in charge of motor transport, was an Edinburgh lawyer. The ADMS of the Division, Colonel H.M.

Morton, brought him along one day to us after we got the motor transport. Mavor asked him if he would have a drink. In front of the ADMS, Boyes answered, 'I never touch it laddie, I am a Deacon of the Church.' Mavor of course christened him 'the Deacon', a name which also stuck to him. When the ADMS left we soon found that he was anything but a teetotaller; he was full of fun and a great addition to the Mess.

We were a very happy unit. Mavor very soon became well known throughout the Brigade and the Division, and very few officers or even generals passed our camp without making an excuse to have a talk with him and see what he was up to next.

Just before the camp broke up an incident occurred which is worth recording. Salisbury Craig came in one morning in a very collapsed state with acute enteritis. He had been doing a round of sick parades with isolated units One look at him convinced me that he had cholera; I had seen quite a number of cases in 1916 in the fighting near Kut. The only recommended treatment at that time was to wash out the stomach with Condy's Fluid[15] and give saline transfusions to make up for the loss of fluid from the patient through vomiting and diarrhoea. The books said that this treatment should be continued until improvement began to show. We moved him into an isolated tent and started the treatment with Condy immediately. We poured it into him by the gallon through a stomach tube. Later we managed to give him some sterile intracellular saline. By the evening his symptoms began to improve and he made a rapid recovery. I have no doubt that it must have been a fairly mild infection or it is unlikely that he would have recovered, but I am sure also that our treatment was helpful to a considerable extent. He was able to move on with the unit to Persia in about ten days.

I was left with an NCO and about a dozen RAMC personnel. We moved on to Ruz, the base headquarters of Dunsterforce, after a few days. There we camped with about 200 reinforcements including two officers for the 39th Brigade. We waited impatiently for four to five weeks, but the story was always the same – 'no transport'. This was not surprising, as I learned afterwards that it took a convoy of 750 Ford wagons to keep about a battalion strength in Hamadan in rations, and Hamadan is only about halfway to the Caspian. Further on it was a case of living on the country and there was famine in the

15. A disinfectant based on potassium permanganate.

land. At the time we were there, about 50,000 Armenian refugees were flooding down the road, and we had to feed the Armenians as well as ourselves. We carried sacks of silver Indian Rupees and paid with silver for all we took. It was surprising how much came out of hiding when the money appeared.

Finally, after about five weeks' waiting we were told that the 39th Brigade reinforcement and my party were to join a company of Gurkhas and march to the Caspian. We had a few pack mules for transport.

It was now early July 1918 and getting very hot. The first part of the road to the foothills was very dusty, and we marched at night for coolness. There were about 500 men in the column including the Gurkhas. I was the only MO and marched, as an MO usually does, at the end of the column. The dust was so thick that I could hardly tell when we passed into the narrow defile at the foot of the Jabel Hamrin range. It is at the entrance to this defile that the Memorial to the 13th Division was placed after the war, and here it was that the Division finally split up. The 39th Brigade went into Persia and the 38th and 40th Brigades continued up the Tigris to Samarrah and Mosul. Our Brigade did not come back this way but finally went home over the Caucasus mountains and the Black Sea.

We marched on day after day, or rather night after night, for 10 to 15 miles or more between camps. Most of the reinforcements were unused to the heat and difficult conditions, and we had to go slowly to get them acclimatised. Very often I was carrying at least two rifles before we had gone far on the road, to relieve men who were finding it difficult. If they fell out we gave them a lift on a mule.

We passed through the villages in the foothills at the border of Mesopotamia, such as Kizil Robat and Khanikin. It was near Khanikin that I saw an area with oil seeping out of the ground. I believe there are now oil wells there. We passed through Kasri Shirind and then started to climb the Paitak Pass. The Persian mountains appeared like an impenetrable mass of naked rocks. We spent most of the day trudging up the narrow road, built originally, we were told, by Alexander the Great (320 BC) on his way to India. On some parts of the road paving stones said to be laid by Alexander the Great's soldiers are still to be seen. On this particular day we went up 5,000 feet or more, and in the evening we found it distinctly cooler and pleasanter. In fact we never again felt the heat of the Mesopotamian plains, and were never to see Mesopotamia again.

One day, after we had been marching for about two weeks, two Ford wagons arrived with supplementary rations – tea and bacon and biscuits. We had a flock of sheep for meat rations and bought others on the way when we could. The men who brought the rations told me that there was an epidemic in Baghdad called 'Bombay Fever'. Everybody was taking it, the hospitals were all full and there were many deaths. This sounded a funny tale to me because I had never heard of Bombay Fever. I congratulated myself that we were well out of it.

As it happened, however, we were not out of it. Thirty-six hours exactly after these men had made contact with us and we had done a day's march in the interval, it struck us. We had just made the stop after the first half hour's marching of the day to adjust loads etc., and had fallen in again to march off when a man collapsed beside me with a crash. Suddenly men began to faint all along the line. The O.C. column, who had the only horse, rode back to me and asked what was wrong. I said that I really did not know, unless it was food poisoning.

After an hour or so, we got the very sick men on to mules and carried on. I suddenly got a severe headache and began to sneeze violently. Fortunately we struck a good camping spot very shortly afterwards with a remarkably clear running stream alongside. The C.O. decided to camp, and we stayed there for about ten days. All of us were very soon affected. My headache cleared by the evening and I felt reasonably well the following day. I realised by then that this was Bombay Fever, and I guessed that it was probably a virus belonging to the influenza group.

This record of a column in the open on the march being affected is interesting from the medical point of view. It is amazing that the men who no doubt carried the disease affected so many of us at once, and the disease developed in many of us almost at the same minute, 36 hours after the first contact. Some of the men were quite ill during the next week and a few developed symptoms of pneumonia. We were lying in the open all the time, but we had no deaths and were able to move on in ten days. In Kazvin,[16] 400 miles ahead, where many of the Brigade happened to be at the time in billets, our Ambulance Headquarters had 500 in hospital and 60 deaths.

About this time we began to pass many thousands of Armenians who were refugees. Sometimes we would pass several thousand

16. Now spelled Qazvin.

in a day. It was an amazing and tragic sight. There were old men and women and children, some riding on donkeys and some riding on cows. The younger ones walked and pushed barrows with their belongings. Now and then we passed at the roadside a dying person, or one already dead and half-eaten by dogs and jackals. We could do nothing for them, but we lifted some of the younger ones who looked as if they might recover on to the mules and carried them forward to the next village. The Dunsterforce had arranged posts in most of the villages where rations were handed out to the refugees and some primitive arrangements were made for looking after the sick. Salisbury Craig told me later that he attended an old refugee in the road who, before he died, gave him a leather belt full of sovereigns, which he asked him to spend to help the refugees.

It is almost 250 miles from Baghdad to Kermanshah. The road was terrible, full of holes and boulders and sometimes with very stiff gradients. There were four passes over 5,000 feet high in this part of the road, and at one of them we had as much as 40 miles between watering places. One can imagine the plight of the refugees on roads like this.

On one long trek we did 20 miles in the evening, stopped for about two or three hours at midnight, and then marched on again till about noon. As we were approaching the village where we were to make our halt, we came to a muddy ditch of shallow water. The Gurkhas broke ranks and wallowed in the dirty water, sucking it into their mouths. The officers were furious and hit them with sticks, to no avail. Not one British soldier broke ranks; they just looked on rather amused, although their tongues were as dry as sticks and they had long finished their single water bottles.

We always moved to the top of a village and there I put up a canvas tank and chlorinated the water before we were allowed to drink it. That evening, and every evening for the next fortnight, the Gurkhas were paraded and did drill for an hour as a punishment.

The Gurkha C.O. was the third generation of a family who had all been officers. I am sorry that I cannot remember his name. He was a fine soldier and I became very fond of him. We had long talks together about many things. One night I watched with him a special Gurkha dance and religious ceremony which he said very few people except Gurkha officers had ever seen.

X
Persia and Russia, 1918–19

Then we came to the town of Kermanshah. It is mentioned frequently in ancient history, and the poet Omar Khayyam speaks of it. It is a picturesque walled town surrounded by strangely shaped mountains. The people seemed more civilised than usual and one could believe, looking at them and their town, that one was living in the Middle Ages.

A few nights after Kermanshah we camped at Bisotun, on the grassy sward beneath the great cliff, 1,700 feet high, upon which King Darius of the Persians (521–480 BC) inscribed the record of the achievements of his reign. Among other places, he captured Babylon, Egypt and Macedonia. The record was inscribed with pictorial carvings and written in three languages. After Colonel Rawlinson copied it, it played an important part in the deciphering of cuneiform writing.

Near Kangavar we passed a great many more refugees in this part of the road and at one point they continued passing for a whole day. They seemed to be rather better organised than the ones we had passed earlier. Before we reached Hamadan we crossed the highest pass so far, the Asadabad Pass, about 8,000 feet high.

At Hamadan it was raining, and my memory of it is mud, mud, cold and misery. We camped outside the town beneath the old walls. It was a bare desolate spot, very dirty with lots of rubbish lying about. I am sure it had been used by the Turks and Russians many times as a camp, and they had not been particular how they left it. For the first time I was not feeling too well myself, and I lay on the muddy ground all day. I did not go into Hamadan myself but gave one of my NCOs a note to the hospital to see if he could get any quinine. I had only one tube of tablets in my medical pannier, and I began to suspect that there was some malaria about as several of the men had been showing slight temperatures. The NCO came back without any quinine, saying that they were very short themselves at the hospital and had none available.

We handed in our mules and were given camels instead – wild camels! Shortly after we left on our first march from Hamadan to Kazvin, they stampeded and scattered our baggage on the country-side for miles. We spent the whole of the rest of the day trying to salvage it. We got most of the kit, but some of it was missing and we suspected the camel-drivers. A small brown case of mine which I had carried since I left home had disappeared, though I thought it had been secured to my valise. It contained all my valuables: shaving kit, hairbrush, toothbrush, books (*New Testament* and *Poems* of Burns), photographs, a small vest-pocket Kodak etc. We had camped temporarily and I went out myself for a mile or so and actually found it lying intact, with only the handle broken.

It was still 145 miles to Kazvin where, I learned at Hamadan, our Ambulance had formed a large stationary hospital. The road was better here, and we were now marching during the day as it was cooler. We were buying almost all our food on the road. Mostly we got chapattis, which seemed to be a mixture of sand and flour. We got sheep occasionally. These were poor and tough, but the Gurkhas would not eat the offal and we did well with liver etc. Sometimes we got large jars of curdled milk. There were almost as many flies and wasps as curds mixed with it, but I ate it and enjoyed the sour taste. We did not see any more refugees but saw many starving Persians and children and often gave them what food we could spare.

After some days I began to suffer from severe headaches each day. I started off all right in the morning, but after marching for an hour or two I began to get a very stiff neck and severe headache. When I got into camp I could do nothing but lie down and rest. Later in the day I would feel better and take some food. One night I took my temperature and realised I must have malaria. By now, however, I had used up all the quinine and could not treat myself.

The country round about was not marshy so I had not suspected malaria, and in fact had not been warned about it. One or two of the other men I found had raised temperatures, but none of them were very bad. We had none of the typical rigors. That, however, is characteristic of the quotidian (daily) type of malaria which is endemic in North Persia. It can also be a very malignant type if not treated. We had now only 50 miles or so to go to Kazvin, and I began to wonder whether I could make it without getting on a camel, which I thought would be worse than walking.

The following day, after we had gone a few miles, two large American trucks which had been taking guns up to the Caspian met us as they returned towards Hamadan. They stopped and asked if the men of the 40th Field Ambulance were in the column. They were to take us on to Kazvin, where the headquarters of the Ambulance was very badly needing reinforcements and they had been sent to pick us up. In a few minutes we were in the trucks and I took all the sick men along with us.

A few hours later we were in Kazvin. It appeared that the Ambulance had 500 sick and wounded. They were short of two sections and MOs, who were out on special duty with the Brigade. We were taken to the Russian Officers' Club, where the headquarters of the Ambulance was. Mavor met us at the entrance and said to me, 'You are looking a bit seedy. We haven't much to offer you, but you had better have something to drink.'

I went inside and sat down, but I remember nothing after that. I collapsed and went unconscious and remained so for two days. Mavor told me that I gave them a bit of a fright. He used to say afterwards that he saved my life.

The Ambulance had been getting quite a lot of malaria of the malignant quotidian type, and they had had several cases of cerebral malaria like my case. They had used up all the quinine they had brought with them but they had been able to buy it at exorbitant prices in the local bazaar. Our pharmacist had prepared it in sterile solutions, and they kept plugging it into me in very large doses intra-muscularly rather than intravenously.

After two days I suddenly came round, to find a woman in a kind of nurse's uniform arranging my pillow. She was one of a number of nursing sisters who had been abandoned by the Russian army and were adopted by Colonel Burke, who was badly needing any help he could get. Burke at this time was in charge of the whole medical arrangements of North Persia and had only one Field Ambulance, much below strength, to carry out the job. Actually they were not very good nurses according to our standards. One did not find out what their real duties were in the Russian army, but they were certainly better at arranging pillows than at skilled nursing procedures.

This is not a history of the War, only the story of what happened to me and those round about me, but I ought to describe what had been happening to the Brigade in the meantime. While I was still struggling up the road to Kazvin at the beginning of August, three battalions of the Brigade, the Worcesters, Warwicks and North Staffords, left Enzeli, the port on the Caspian Sea in North Persia, for Baku. The battalions were much reduced in numbers and there were only about 800 all told.

They arrived at Baku before the Turks by only a week or ten days. They had scarcely got into position outside the town before they were attacked by the advancing Turks. The local levies of Armenians and Baku townspeople proved to be very little use as soldiers, in spite of the fact that they were scattered throughout companies of the British battalions. The town was full of Germans and Austrians who had been prisoners of the Armenians and had escaped. General Dunsterville thought they must have a telephone line to the Turks; at any rate there were plenty of spies.

The first full-scale attack was made on August 26th and was repulsed, but the Turks attacked continuously after that. They received further reinforcements and it was reckoned that they had about six divisions in the area. Another full-scale attack was made on the 14th September, and again beaten off, although important positions were lost owing to defections of the local troops. That night Dunsterville withdrew all the British troops onto ships which he had commandeered, and sailed off under fire of the batteries at the entrance to the harbour. It was a very fine piece of work by the Brigade and the whole story is an epic.

None of the Field Ambulance personnel got to Baku on that occasion. The only MOs which they had were the battalion MOs. These were greatly helped by the surgical staff of the Baku Hospital, especially one surgeon who was an exceptionally able man. All the time that Dunsterville was in Baku in the attempt to defend it against the Turks, there was a serious threat to our left flank by the Turks from Tabriz. A section of the Ambulance was at Zanjan on the road to Tabriz from Kazvin with part of the Brigade. At that time there were about 500 patients, suffering from influenza, malaria and battle wounds, in the emergency hospital which the Ambulance had opened in Kasvin.

Although Dunsterville was unable to hold Baku, his attempt to do so was of great value. It drew off troops from Palestine, where Allenby at the same time was inflicting a crushing defeat on the Turks. Meantime the Turks and Germans were quarrelling badly, especially in the Caucasus. At the end of October the Turks gave in and asked for an armistice, and the First Great World War came to an end in France if not in our part of the world. At first it made little difference to us. In Kazvin none of the local population believed the story which we had got by wireless, and so we held a celebration to try to convince them. The Turks at first refused to leave Baku, and were actually still fighting the Royalist Russians at Petrovsk, north of Baku, a month after the Armistice.

Eventually, however, the Turks did leave Baku, and on 17th November General Thomson and the 39th Brigade returned there. A Tartar (Azerbaijan) state had been formed, and as they were the strongest party in Baku, General Thomson, who was now in command, allowed them to continue.

—

Shortly after the Armistice our hospital at Kazvin was taken over by a Casualty Clearing Station, and the Ambulance continued its journey by road to the Caspian. This road, which was made by the Russians and is quite good, crosses the Elbruz Mountains, a high mountain range in the north of Persia. On the south side the hills are dry and bare, but as soon as one crosses the top of the ridge the country becomes green and lush with oaks and ashes, deciduous trees that one was familiar with at home. The road was lined with bracken and tongue ferns.

As we descended, however, the country became more barren and towards the Caspian Sea it became marshy and very malarial. It is said that when Alexander the Great wanted to get rid of any of his generals he sent them to this part of the country called Mazanderan. He knew that they would not survive there long. We examined some of the children there and found that they all had large spleens, a sure sign of malaria. There was obviously great poverty among the population. We now had ample supplies of quinine and our men took a daily dose as a preventive.

After about ten days we came to sand-dunes and heard the waves of the Caspian Sea breaking on the other side. We had about a day's march along the sandy shore to Enzeli, and from there we took ship to Baku. A detachment of the Brigade went to Krasnovodsk on the east side of the Caspian and McCall Smith with a small section of the Field Ambulance went with them. They eventually moved along the railway to Merv and Samarkand, and fought a battle against the Bolsheviks as late as March 1919. They joined up with an Indian Brigade which had marched there from Quetta, a distance of between

1200 and 1300 miles. This was the last battle in which our Brigade took part.

I was on a small ship with a lot of our transport which sailed to Baku. The trip should have taken about 18 hours. Instead we took about two days, as we ran into a storm and the engines broke down. We rolled about in heavy seas and were all very seasick. In fact it was so bad I began to wonder if we were going to be shipwrecked in the Caspian Sea after all our travels. However, after about eight hours the Russians, who were quite good seamen, got the engines going again and we clanked into Baku a day late.

We took over a large college as a hospital and we all went into billets. Our officers' billet was in a flat which had belonged to a rich Persian. It had a large L-shaped room, one arm of which had a table for a dining room and one of which contained a large handmade Persian carpet and actually a grand piano. We had a telephone too and Mavor was in his element. He immediately started to learn Persian, even making friends with the telephone operator and carrying on conversations with her. He played the piano and sang songs to us, explored the town and made friends with everyone.

The town, however, was in a bad way. Supplies of food were very low and what food there was very dear. Before long, however, when the locals found that they would be paid for supplies, they began to flow into the shops and things began to improve.

We were soon busy in hospital. Many of the men were still suffering from malaria, and to add to our difficulties a serious epidemic of typhus fever was raging in the town. Funeral coaches in white (not black) were always moving about the streets. It was wintertime and very cold. The Medical Officer of Health of the town told us that our troops would all die of the disease and that typhus fever always decimated armies.

We had marched lightweight from Mesopotamia and our men had no change of clothes. Most of them had only one shirt besides their uniform and greatcoat. Typhus is of course spread by lice, so we rigged up Serbian Barrels[17] to delouse their clothes. We sterilised the men's shirts and greatcoats first, and then they themselves were hosed down and scrubbed. Next they went about for a day in their shirt-tails and greatcoats until their uniforms were sterilised. They ran about to

17. Barrels placed over boiling water in which clothes were hung, so that the steam would disinfest them by killing the vermin.

Colonel Andrew Munro of the Royal Artillery, Alec's maternal great-uncle, who drilled Alec and his brother in the garden at Dumbreck.

Alec's elder sister Cissie and his mother Sarah Margaret (Munro), top; younger sister Mollie, father Alexander and his younger brother Gus, bottom. Alec, middle right.

Alec in training with the 40th Field Ambulance in Devonshire during 1914. A good horse was to prove a life-saver later in his story.

(Left to right) Lieutenants Neilson, Glen, Moore and Burke in Devonshire during 1914. Edmund T. Burke, a contemporary of Alec in Glasgow, was with 40th Field Ambulance from Gallipoli to Persia, one of the few surviving officers.

The 41st Field Ambulance leaving SS Argyllshire *at Mudros Bay.*

Camp at W Beach, Cape Helles, Gallipoli.

Reserves gathered on Anzac Beach, Gallipoli.

Tending the wounded at a dressing station near Kut.

Caricature of Alec by Osborne Mavor, drawn in camp at Sindiyah, Mesopotamia (courtesy of James Mavor).

Starving children in Persia (Iran) in 1918.

Officers of 40th Field Ambulance, Baku, 1919. The war is over and they are still alive. Mavor is in front, Alec just behind him.

Some young Govanites around 1910
(courtesy of the Mitchell Collection, Glasgow City Archive).

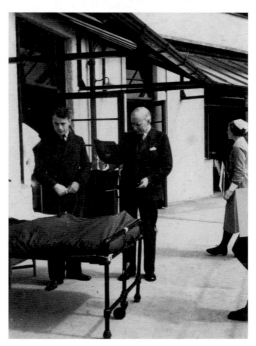

Attending patients in open-air beds for tuberculosis at Mearnskirk Hospital,
Glasgow, in the 1940s.

Alec's lifelong friend, Osborne Mavor (James Bridie) at the latter's retiral dinner from hospital work in the Art Club, Glasgow, 1937.

Alec and Bessie Glen with their oldest son, Iain, Brora, 1937.

Alec Glen about the time of his retiral from the NHS aged 65
(courtesy of Lafayette).

keep warm, and I am afraid that the Russian women were scandalised and thought we were all mad. However, we had very little typhus. Practically the only cases which occurred among the British troops were in men who were on guard at the stations and on other duties where they mixed with the population.

We opened a small isolation hospital in a school and I was given charge of it. We had only about 100 to 120 cases altogether and very few deaths. I kept careful notes of the outbreak and when I came home wrote a thesis on it for an M.D. degree. Typhus is a terrible disease. The patients run a high temperature for about fourteen days and then a sudden crisis occurs when the temperature falls. We had no specific treatment at that time and had to rely only on careful nursing and stimulants to the heart like camphor. Many of the men were in poor physical condition and suffering from malaria, which complicated the disease. Those who died succumbed from pure exhaustion about the twelfth to fourteenth day.

In the evening we sometimes got off duty and explored the town. Mavor discovered the Casino. This was not primarily a place for gambling but a large restaurant with a stage for a cabaret show at one end. It was a large hall with dining tables and boxes all round the sides. The boxes also had tables where people could have a meal and view the cabaret show at the same time. Much of the cabaret consisted of Caucasian dancing and singing. Those who saw the party of Caucasian dancers who visited this country a few years ago will realise what it was like. The dancing is carried out with enormous energy and is accompanied by shouts as in Highland dancing. There is one famous dance called the Lesginka in which they alternately sit on their heels and then spread their legs out in front in turn. Tomory, one of our MOs, who was very athletic but on the stout side, used to go up on to the stage and dance the Lesginka with them. This always brought down the house. The audience was very mixed: there were Tartars, Persians Bolsheviks, Armenian Persians and a few British officers. Their way of showing appreciation was to fire revolvers through the roof and the ceiling was peppered with holes.

One night I was in the lavatory and was washing my hands in front of a large mirror. There was a Russian officer standing alongside me looking at himself in the mirror, rather silently, it seemed to me. I think he was one of Bicharakoff's[18] men, the Royalist Russians who

18. General Bicharakoff, a Royalist Russian General.

were extremely disgruntled at that time. Suddenly there was a terrific bang. He had shot his reflection in the mirror in front of him. It was a beautiful plate glass mirror, and I felt very annoyed both at the fright he had given me and at the wanton destruction. 'Stoltoquoy! [Why!]' I exclaimed. He looked at himself disgustedly in what remained of the mirror and said something in Russian which I interpreted in English soldiers' language as 'No bloody good.' I think he must have been disappointed in love or something like that. 'Next time you shoot yourself you might give a fellow some warning,' I said.

Osborne Mavor revelled in this place and came as often as he possibly could. He and I shared a room in our billet and I felt it was my duty to accompany him as often as possible to see that he did not come to any harm. He studied the Russian language quite seriously and very soon could make himself understood. Before long everyone seemed to know him and for some reason or other they called him Dr Jim. He must have told them his name was Jim. I became known as Dr Alick.

All the food and drink was very expensive, but we had plenty of money. The official exchange rate for Baku roubles at that time was about 80 to the pound sterling. At least that was all we got if we drew our pay through the Army. We soon found that we could get about 300 roubles to the pound for a cheque written on the RAMC bankers in London, Holt and Co. All the MOs had their cheque books with them if they had not lost them – I had mine and so had Mavor. I don't know how the locals cashed the cheques, but it is true to say that they were very anxious to get them, and when I eventually got home I found that all the ones I had given had been cashed. I suppose that there would be international financiers, even in Baku.

We usually had a box at the Casino and ordered a supper of sturgeon steaks, which were somewhat expensive and very good. We often preceded this with a small glass of vodka with caviare which was very cheap. Mavor asked all sorts of people to this box. We frequently had the cabaret dancers, who usually seemed pretty hungry, and looked forward to a supper of sturgeon steaks if they could get it. All we wanted was to be amused and to try to learn Russian from them. They seemed to like us too because they never required to be asked twice. I don't think that they had ever seen anything quite like us before. We were very happy to meet them too after four years of war and dirt and death and misery.

110

Mavor was always a great host and asked them all if he could give them English names. One of them, whose name sounded like Jennifer, we called 'Jenny'. She seemed to take a fancy to me, and always came and sat beside me if she could. One night she came to me rather distressed and said that her *malinky* (baby) was very ill and would Dr Alick come and see him. I replied, 'Good gracious, Jenny, I never imagined that you had a baby.' She was in her early twenties and I looked on her as just a girl. It was after four years of war and I was 28 at that time. I went and told Mavor, who was surrounded by Russians as usual in the centre of the hall. He volunteered to come with me, but I said there was no need and that I would go straight back to the billet afterwards. He said, 'Take care of yourself, then.'

I set off shortly afterwards in a gharry, the local means of transport, with Jenny and her companion, whom we called Jackie. A gharry was a small open carriage, usually drawn by two small white horses. We went a long way into the town and eventually stopped and went up a kind of close or alleyway, and entered a wooden building up some wooden stairs. I made the mistake of not telling the gharry to wait for me.

The room was very clean and tidy and the baby was spotlessly clean, although breathing somewhat rapidly. An elderly woman left just as we came in. I examined the baby and found it to be suffering from a broncho-pneumonia, probably associated with the recent influenza epidemic. It was a well-nourished child and Jenny was actually breast-feeding it herself, which was in the baby's favour. I said I thought that it would do all right, but would take a week or two to recover.

I asked Jenny who its father was. She said that he was a Russian officer, but that she had not heard from him for over a year and believed that he had been killed. I asked her where her parents were, and she answered that she did not know, but thought that they might be dead also. With my poor command of the language it was very difficult to get this information, and it was obvious that she was unwilling to tell me much. She was darker in appearance than the other Russian dancers and I had thought previously that she might be an Armenian. She was a Christian. She probably did not wish to admit what she was because the town was now being governed by the Tartars, who were Muslims. I felt sure that she had a history and that it might be an interesting and possibly sad one. Her family might

111

have been among the refugees that we had passed on the road through Persia.

Jenny laid a table and I had a 'chasse qui chai' (a cup of tea). Actually, rather than a cup, it was always a glass of weak tea with sugar and no milk which the Russians served.

When I got outside I found it was a very dark night. I had only a very vague idea of my way home to our billet and the street lighting was poor. I knew roughly that our billet was in the south-west part of the city, so I took a bearing by the stars and found my way home after a long walk.

Night and day while we were in Baku there were always occasional shots being fired. I think most of the firing was for fun. Those who had rifles, and many of the locals had them, kept firing them off. General Thomson had ordered all the British soldiers to go about unarmed, however, and I personally never heard of any soldier being attacked or molested.

We had a great deal of fun at Baku, and those who wish to read about it should get James Bridie's first book *Some Talk of Alexander*, which is all about Persia and Russia. There is one incident, however, which Bridie does not mention in that book and which I think I can now safely tell. I had accompanied Mavor to the Casino one night. We got separated after a while, because Mavor had gone off on his own as he frequently did. Later, about midnight, he came up to me and said, 'I have met an awfully decent Russian chap and would like to introduce him to you. He speaks English and used to address meetings at Hyde Park Corner. He wishes us to go and have supper with him at his club.' He took me over and introduced me to a great bearded Russian about as ugly a looking chap as I had seen for a while. Mavor was in great form and had quite decided that he was going with his new friend. I concluded, as I often did, that there was nothing I could do but go along myself.

In a few minutes we were galloping along in the usual Baku horse carriage. Osborne, in great form, was singing opera in Russian and our friend was sitting facing him. We seemed to be going a very long way into one of the least salubrious parts of the town. Eventually we stopped, and the Russian led the way down some dark steps into what appeared to be a cellar. When he opened the door a blast of alcoholic fumes, smoke and noise came out, and we were ushered into a room with about a score or more of bearded Russians. The walls were decorated with black cloth, on which skulls and crossbones were painted in white.

We got seated at a table and our Russian friend got up and made quite a long speech in Russian, which was loudly cheered by his friends. Then we all stood up and drank a toast in vodka. On these occasions in Russia the vodka, which is very powerful spirit, must be swallowed in one gulp. I had no idea what the toast was about, but I drank the vodka with the others. Then several other Russians got up and made speeches followed by toasts and vodka drunk in this manner. Finally Mavor got up to applause. He spoke in his own Russian and was received with great cheers. The Russians got up and stood on the tables and shouted and danced and drank our health over and over again in vodka in the typical Caucasian manner.

After all the vodka we had had we were beginning to feel a bit like the Russians ourselves and I managed to indicate to Osborne that it was time we went home. Our Russian friend (to my surprise, for I feared anything might happen to us) led us to the door. Immediately a carriage appeared from nowhere and we set off, Mavor still singing his Russian opera and in wonderful spirits.

As we reached more familiar streets and came near our billet he stopped singing, and I asked him where on earth we had been. 'Don't tell anyone, for goodness sake,' he replied, 'or the General might get to know of it. We have been guests of the Baku Anarchist Society. They believe you and I are members of the secret British Anarchist Society. We were just paying a courtesy call.' Needless to say I did not tell anyone of this escapade at the time or for many years afterwards.

Mavor did not tell me what he said in his speech: I think he did not wish to get me involved any more than he could help in case we got into trouble. I am sure in my own mind, however, that anything he said was quite harmless and that General Shuttleworth, who was then in command, would have enjoyed the story. After all, these common Russian people had been living under conditions of tyranny and subjection for centuries. I have no doubt that they called themselves anarchists and I have no doubt also that they were Bolsheviks, whom we were actually fighting at that time in Turkestan on the other side of the Caspian. I think Mavor probably told them that the days of tyranny were over and that better days were coming for them. The man whom Mavor met in the Casino and who had been in London must have learned something about democracy there. Unfortunately for these people, we now know that they were only changing one form of tyranny for another.

Some months later, also in the Casino, Mavor and I got a glimpse of the other side of the picture. We dined one night with two of the Russian general staff who had just returned from London. They told us that General Denikin[19] expected to be in Moscow in about two months. I asked, rather innocently, 'What are you going to do when you get there?'

One of the Russians answered, 'The first thing that we will do will be to kill all the Jews. They are responsible for the revolution and all the trouble. Besides, they killed Jesus Christ.'

Mavor exclaimed, 'What a Christ-like thing to do!'

After that the conversation languished and Mavor soon found someone more interesting to talk to.

It is not my purpose to write a history of the events in Baku at this time but, to summarise the situation, there were several different forces there, all of whom had patched up a temporary peace under our influence. There were the Azerbaijanis or Tartars, who were in the majority, and had formed a government. They had an army which paraded about the streets. Then there were the Royalist Russians under General Bicharakoff. There was our own force, which was much the smallest group, and finally there were the Bolsheviks.

In February a number of strikes of workers began to take place. During one of these the electricity generating station staff went on strike and the city was plunged into darkness for several days. A party of engineers with special knowledge of electricity generation was organised and I went along with them to the generating station as MO. It was amazing how one could always find someone in the Army at that time who was a specialist in any job that turned up. There happened to be a sergeant in the engineers who knew all about the job. The dynamos had been sabotaged by throwing hammers and chisels among the machinery and he crawled about picking them out and inspecting everything. Finally, after about twelve hours work, he declared everything satisfactory and said that he was ready to switch the lever

19. Anton Denikin was Lieutenant General of the Imperial Russian Army. Following the Revolution and the overthrow of the Tsar, he became chief of the General Staff.

over and turn on the electricity. He warned us that anything at all might happen and there might even be an explosion. We gathered in the control room and he switched on the lever. The lights went on all over the city and that finished the strike for the time being.

There were still about half a dozen Russian gun-boats anchored in the Bay, which had been taken over by the Bolsheviks at the time of the revolution and were now manned by the Bolsheviks. I think they ran them by some sort of committee. They were a source of great anxiety to the British and to the town, because they were powerfully armed and could play havoc in the city if they bombarded it. It was thought that they were just waiting till the ice broke at Astrakhan after the winter so that they could go up and join the rest of the Bolshevik fleet which was frozen in there.

In February 1919 the trans-Caucasian railway was opened. In the first batch of reinforcements which came through were several high-speed motor boats which could do about 30 to 40 knots and dashed about the bay in clouds of spray. They were each armed with a torpedo and a machine gun. The Russian gun-boats were now told to surrender and given the deadline of March 1st at twelve noon to haul down their Bolshevik flags. There was quite a bit of excitement about this ultimatum. Our artillery, which consisted only of field-guns, was posted round the harbour. Some of the guns were placed in front of my Typhus Hospital which was on a prominence above the bay. The gun-boats had four-inch guns which could have caused enormous damage to the city, and it was doubtful if our field guns could even reach them in retaliation. A few minutes before twelve noon the motor speedboats moved at high speed into the bay. One of them fired a torpedo which missed, probably on purpose. The officer in charge of the speedboats approached the ship where the commander was presumed to be. It is said that he fired his pistol at the bridge and told the Bolsheviks to surrender. The Russian commander hauled down his flag and all the other ships followed suit. The British Navy men shortly after took over the ships and added them to the British Caspian fleet.

The 27th Division from Salonika had now occupied Batoum on the Black Sea and Tiflis in the Caucasus, and one battalion, the Royal Scots I think it was, came to Baku to reinforce our Brigade. Many of our men had not seen their families for four years or more, and they were sent home. Many of the officers also were sent home, and Lieutenant Colonel Burke, our CO, was among these. We had an RAMC officer, Colonel Hill, in charge for a short period and eventually Mavor took over command. Mavor and McCall Smith and I, who had been home only 18 months before, had not much chance of demobilisation.

Mavor asked a party of the Royal Scots to dinner in our mess one night, and I remember Jock Wemyss, the Scottish international rugby player was among them. After dinner we had a scrum in our beautiful Persian mess room. So far as I can remember the Royal Scots won.

Some time in March 1919, General Milne and his staff from Constantinople arrived in Baku to take stock of the position. The DDMS visited our hospital and went round my Typhus Hospital. We made not a bad show. We had got beds and linen in Baku. My orderlies were volunteers and they were extremely loyal and efficient. I had warned them well that if they got bitten by a louse from a typhus patient they had had it. When new patients came in their clothes were immediately taken and sterilised, and the patients themselves were scrubbed all over and deloused as far as possible. We had quite good bathing facilities in the hospital and in fact the search for lice was never-ending. None of the nursing orderlies took typhus. Their nursing of the seriously ill patients was also very faithful and conscientious for men with so little training. By this time very few new patients were coming in. I think it may have been because of this inspection that I later got orders to go to Salonika to take charge of the medical side of a general hospital. I was very sorry about this, because I had no desire to make a career in the Army, and did not wish to leave the unit I had been with all the war.

One day I went down with Mavor to the docks to see a ship which had arrived from the other side of the Caspian Sea with sick and wounded. They had been in action somewhere near Samarkand against the Bolsheviks. Among the sick were several convalescent typhus cases. One of these was O'Hara May, who was then MO of the Gloucesters. O'Hara May was a great character. He had been a colonial MO somewhere in West Africa. He never missed an opportunity to have fun and did not take very good care of himself. In spite of this he had survived a severe attack of typhus. He was extremely emaciated but his word to Mavor was, 'Anything doing in this old town, Mavor?'

'Plenty, old chap,' Mavor replied, 'you had better hurry up and get better.'

Shortly after this, all the British troops returned from the east of the Caspian, McCall Smith and his small section of the Field Ambulance with them. We left the Bolsheviks in Turkestan to their own devices.

During all this time the other MOs were doing fine work in the large general hospital which we had opened in a college in Baku. Paterson Brown and Dunlop were doing major surgical work and Tomory and Watt were in charge of the medical side. R.E. Reynolds had arrived some time before to act as bacteriologist and pathologist.

Conditions in Baku were steadily improving and an opera season started. The opera house was a very large and beautiful building with fine architecture. There was a large area inside the building outside the auditorium where everyone paraded for about half an hour between each act. All the Baku society went there and we went as often as possible.

One day I was waiting in a queue to purchase some tickets for the opera when a Royalist Russian officer walked right up to the head of the queue and pushed himself in to get his tickets. A British sergeant came out of his place and walked up behind him, caught him by the back of his jacket at his neck and the next moment the officer was lying on his back in the street. Everyone in the queue cheered. They had never seen anything like this before, I think.

About the end of March, part of a Royal Flying Corps squadron arrived by train across the Caucasus. They were going north from Baku to help General Denikin. Only half the Squadron with half of their supplies was in this train, and their MO was coming on with the second half later. As they had no MO and one was required, I volunteered to go with them to Petrovsk where they were to be stationed about 200 miles north of Baku.

The train moved very slowly, sometimes going over bridges which had been destroyed and where the rails were only supported by piles of railway sleepers stacked above one another, and which creaked ominously.

When we got to a place called Derbent, about halfway to Petrovsk, the officers were all invited to the Town Hall for a banquet. The CO of the squadron was a Highland Light Infantry officer aged 26 years. I was older than he was by three years, being aged 29, and the

117

father of the party. Later they all called me 'uncle'. The flight officers were all just boys in their late teens. It appeared that this was a training squadron, and very few of them had seen any service. I expect that the more experienced men had all wanted to be demobilised.

At the Town Hall each British boy was placed between two great bearded Russians. I wonder what they thought of us. I knew what was coming and felt rather apprehensive. They started off with speeches and toasts, to the King of England, the British Empire and so on. Our little H.L.I. captain proposed the Russian Empire and the boys drank down their glasses of vodka in one mouthful as instructed by the Russians. These Russian feasts go on for hours. They start with hors d'oeuvres, caviare, raw fish etc. and gradually go on to more substantial dishes.

When we were less than halfway through I saw that it was a bad situation and that the Russians were deliberately trying to make the boys drunk. I went up to the CO and told him, 'If we don't go now we will never get to the train. All these boys will end up unconscious and the result may be serious.'

Speaking rather thickly himself, he replied, 'I think you are right, Doc.' He then rose and indicated to all his officers to follow. The Russians shouted their disapproval, but we carried on. Several of the officers had to be practically carried to the train.

It was still very cold in Russia and the squadron had oil stoves in each carriage of the train, but they were filled with petrol, of all things. When the train started suddenly, several hours later, the stove in our compartment fell over and I could see nothing but a sheet of flames. I threw all my blankets over on top of the blaze and stamped on them and the flames went out as suddenly as they commenced. I had two young officers in the compartment with me who were still quite unconscious as a result of their vodka. They knew nothing of what had happened. On the whole we got off better from our dinner party than we might have done.

We were billeted in some old dilapidated buildings some miles north of Petrovsk on the shores of the Caspian. I had a particularly old house that was only partially roofed. I think the place had been shelled in earlier fighting between the Russians and Turks. I tried to make a small hospital in this building but it was not a very successful effort. Two companies of Gurkhas were also stationed near us, the same Gurkhas that I had marched up with from Baghdad.

One day there was a very remarkable occurrence: the whole shore was covered with ducks, paddling a few feet from the shore. There must have been many thousands of them. They must have flown a very long distance and were so tired that one could almost lift them out of the water without any resistance. A great many of the Russian people were on the shore knocking them out with sticks and gathering them by the half dozen. Our men, you may be sure, got their share and we dined well on duck for several days. The ground at the time was covered with snow from a late snowstorm and I think that the ducks must have been affected by this storm on their way north to their summer grounds in northern Russia and Siberia.

After three to four weeks the second half of the squadron arrived with their MO, and it was arranged that I would go back to Baku, taking about thirty sick Gurkhas. The Gurkhas had been in Petrovsk most of the winter. Some of them looked quite sick, and I think were mostly suffering from malaria or convalescing from typhus and malarial fever.

We were about twelve miles north of Petrovsk and I had to join some of Denikin's troops at a barracks in Petrovsk and pick up my batch of sick Gurkhas the following morning at the station. It was rather late in the evening when I reported to the Russians and I thought I was received rather coldly. I was offered no food but was asked into a great empty barrack hall. The beds consisted of wire-netting stretched over four low posts and the floor was mud. It was quite dark by the time I arrived and I could hear rats scurrying about.

I ate some of my rations which, as an old soldier, I always carried if possible, opened my valise and lay down on the wire-netting. By the light of a flickering lamp which the Russians had given to me I could see large rats inspecting me at a distance. Shortly afterwards my lamp went out. I kept one of the straps of my valise handy, and laid about me now and then when I heard the rats getting close. I put any food I had inside my valise beside me. It was pitch dark and I don't think I slept a wink that night and was very glad to see the dawn.

I told the Russians in the morning, in as many Russian words as I could command, that I did not think much of their hospitality. I don't know whether they were Bolsheviks and had some other grudge against the British, but I am sure that their treatment of me was deliberate. They gave me no breakfast and I had to walk to the station, a mile or so through slushy snow. There I was put in charge

119

of a carriage full of Gurkha patients by the Gurkha MO, an Indian doctor. I had very little Russian and had no interpreter. Fortunately a Gurkha NCO could speak a little English and we formed a guard of several convalescent soldiers.

The train to which we were attached was crowded with people. When I say crowded, there were about as many people sitting on the roofs of the carriages and on the buffers as there were inside. There were also people on top of our own carriage. The place seemed to be in pandemonium with nobody in charge. After several hours we moved off at a speed of about 6 to 7 m.p.h. We stopped at short intervals, often for long periods, and all the passengers, men, women and children, got off and performed their toilets at the side of the railway. The distance to Baku was about 180 miles. I don't think we made more than 30 miles that day and stopped at a station all night.

Next day we reached a large town called Derbent. There the railwaymen shunted off our carriage and left it in a siding for a whole day and night. This station was in even worse confusion and even more crowded. After a struggle I got hold of a person I thought was the station-master and told him to get a move on with our carriage. Sometime afterwards our carriage was attached to a train, but I noticed that the engine was at the wrong end of the train, and that it was obviously going north again towards Petrovsk. I had told the station-master repeatedly that we were going to Baku and I now realised there was deliberate obstruction.

The drivers were in the engine and the passengers were all aboard, inside and out. Our carriage was fortunately next to the engine. I explained the situation to my Gurkha N.C.O. and we put two Gurkhas with their rifles on to the engine plate. I took care to explain to the Gurkhas that they were not to kill anyone, but that the train was not to start. This instruction was necessary because the Gurkhas appear to enjoy anything in the nature of a fight. When the Gurkhas shouted and partially drew their Kukris,[20] the drivers hopped off the engine pretty quickly. Then a great uproar arose. The excitable station-master fought his way through the crowd and began shouting at me. I called him a damned rascal and pointed south in the direction of Baku.

I kept the Gurkhas on the engine plate until our carriage was uncoupled and we were again put into the siding. We spent another

20. Curved knife with a broad blade used by Gurkhas.

night in the station, but next morning we were attached to a train going in the right direction and two days later reached Baku. I was very thankful to hand over my patients to the hospital and made a report of what had happened through my CO to the General. I don't dream much, but after that I sometimes used to dream about being in a big barn surrounded by rats in the black-out.

When I saw Mavor, the first thing he told me was that Jenny's baby had been ill again with gastroenteritis. He had seen it twice and it was desperately ill. He thought we should go out and see it that evening. When we got there the baby had just died. Jenny was very upset indeed and we were very sorry for her.

We still had our transport and there were half a dozen riding horses, which in the early days of the war were necessary to take MOs about on their duties. Now we had Ford motors, but the horses and mules were still being looked after in Baku in a square near where we were billeted. Mavor, McCall Smith and I used to go out riding in the morning before breakfast, both to exercise the horses and exercise ourselves.

One morning my usual horse had gone lame and I was given a black Australian horse which had a very bad reputation. It was a very heavy horse with a neck like a Clydesdale and a mouth like iron. When it took it into its head to run away it was almost impossible to hold it. That morning it suddenly went off with me. The country behind Baku is very hilly and almost completely bare of vegetation, I think because of the nature of the soil. When the black horse ran off with me, we were going along a valley with very steep, almost precipitous sides. I could not hold him at all, but I found I was able to turn him towards the steep hills on one side. He raced at it at full gallop, and up and up the hill he went until it became almost vertical and a kind of scree with loose stones. He finally stopped, trembling all over. He was at such an angle that I actually slid over his hindquarters, but I kept hold of the reins. At first he would not move but after a lit–tle encouragement I was able to lead him down the hill and he was as quiet as a lamb. Mavor and McCall Smith were helpless with laughter, but I got on him again and we rode back to our billets.

On the way up to the country behind the town we often passed the British cemetery. This was on the bare hillside near where the

121

brigade had made a stand against the Turks in defence of Baku. Buried there were many Worcester, Warwicks and Staffords and others who had later died of disease. It is on a bare hillside and I have sometimes wondered if it is still tended by the Graves Commission and looked after by the local people.

It will be gathered from these stories that life at Baku had now become quite pleasant. In May 1919 rumours of the withdrawal of our force began to circulate, and then it was authoritatively stated that the mandate for the Caucasus had been given to Italy. We thought this was about as daft an arrangement as even the politicians could think up. It never came to anything. The Italians were wise enough to refuse the job.

In June I got orders to proceed to Salonika to take over charge of the medical side of the general hospital there. I was sorry about this, because I would much rather have waited to go home with the unit to which I had been attached all the war. Besides, I was very happy with Mavor as OC and very content with life in Baku as it was at that time.

I left in a train for Batoum. The distance is almost 500 miles, but the journey took about four days as the train went very slowly, with long stops. The scenery in the Caucasus is very beautiful and interesting, and we stopped about half a day in Tiflis. A naval officer whose name I have forgotten occupied a covered truck with me. We had camp beds and were very comfortable.

The only unusual thing about our journey was that we had an extra passenger in the truck, a large goose which apparently had been adopted as a pet by the naval officer. It seemed to me to be a very remarkable goose. Its master talked to it very frequently and it seemed to understand. When we stopped for a while, as we often did, a naval rating from a nearby truck came along and took it for a walk with a leather lead round its neck, much to the amusement of the Tommies on the train who were on their way home to be demobilised. Apart from the peculiarity about the goose the Naval Officer was a very decent chap and we got on quite well together.

When we arrived at Batoum, we were billeted in what seemed to be a large disused factory. It had been divided by temporary partitions, and as I was now a field officer (a major), I had one of these compartments to myself. Batoum is a very pleasant place. It is, I believe, quite a favourite Russian holiday resort. It has a fine frontage to the Black Sea, with a shingly shore and an esplanade well shaded by trees.

We were about a week there waiting for a ship. On the night before we sailed I was having a walk along the esplanade with an officer belonging to the 39th Brigade, who was on his way home. It was a Sunday evening and the esplanade was crowded with the local people having their evening walk. I suddenly heard a voice crying, 'Doctor Alick!' and a young woman detached herself from the crowd and came across to me and grabbed my arm. It was Jenny, the dancer from Baku. How she had got there I do not know, and I did not ask her.

My friend discreetly left me, and Jenny and I walked on together to a quieter part of the beach where the esplanade stopped and sat down on the shingle near the water. We were silent for a while and then Jenny said in Russian, 'Ya loobloo, Doctor Alick!' (I love you, Doctor Alick), and indicated by signs that she wanted to go home with me to England.

I had only picked up some simple Russian words and phrases, and it was very difficult and took a long time to make ourselves understood but the following is something like the conversation which took place. I explained with great difficulty that what she proposed was impossible. The British Army did not allow women to accompany their soldiers, and anyway I was not going home but was on my way to Salonika in Greece.

She was inconsolable at first, but after a while she said, 'Malinky Serge [little Serge] is dead. I want another baby, this time from you, Doctor Alick.'

'Oh no, Jenny,' I replied. 'I would not like you to have a baby and then desert you here and never see you again. I have a feeling that if I went with you tonight that you would be sure to have a baby.'

Jenny said, 'Come with me Doctor Alick, I have a nice room in Batoum. I do not mind if you go away if I have your baby.'

I did not know what to say. After a while I raised her hand and kissed it and said, 'I love you too much, Jenny, to treat you like that.' I do not know whether she understood this or not, but she became very passionate and wept a lot.

She got quieter after a time and then I did something which I will always regret. She was five or six years younger than me and I always looked on her as quite young. I thought I would give her a present to remember me by. I pointed to a brooch and a bangle which she had, and then I took out all the money I had with me, probably about

£20, and tried to explain to her that I wanted her to buy a present for herself and laid the money in her lap.

She said nothing for a moment or two, and then she suddenly took the notes and threw them down in the shingle; stood up and said, 'Dahsidayna, Doctor Alick [Goodbye Doctor Alick],' and turned to walk away.

I called after her but she never looked round once.

I thought at first that she had not understood my meaning, but on thinking it over afterwards I am sure that she did understand and knew that I did not mean to insult her.

I walked home to my billet a sadder, but not, I am afraid, a wiser man. I felt, and still feel, that Jenny came out of that incident much better than I did. I was very unhappy about it.

I suppose a modern young person might have a good many comments to make about this story. I do not propose to make any, except to say that the story, like the rest of this book, is exactly true.

XI

Salonika and Home

Next day we set out over the Black Sea for Constantinople. We slept on deck and the following day sailed down the beautiful Bosphorus. I was one of a very few who got off the ship at Constantinople. Most of the men and officers who were being demobilised sailed on to the Dardanelles, where there was a demobilisation camp on the Asiatic side at Chanak. I was instructed to report to a general hospital in Constantinople. I arrived just before lunch, and a padre who was the only occupant of the mess when I arrived offered me a refreshment. We got into conversation and he told me that he was a brother of Conan Doyle, the author of Sherlock Holmes.

I spent a very pleasant time there for three weeks or so. I was given no professional work, but a day or two after I arrived the matron of the hospital approached me and asked if I would be good enough to escort some of the nurses for a sail by paddle steamer in the Sea of Marmara and give them a bit of a holiday, which they needed badly. Every other day or so for the next two or three weeks, I took several nurses on a sail to the island of Prinkipo. It was like going to a sail down the Firth of Clyde, except that the weather was much better. The wooden piers at which we called were very similar and the paddle steamer on which we travelled had actually been built on the Clyde. We called at several islands. Prinkipo, the island where General Townsend had been interned, is a very beautiful island, quite hilly and in those days very primitive. The transport seemed to be all by pack animal. We always had a picnic basket and usually had a picnic on the shore in beautiful surroundings.

Constantinople at that time was a very cosmopolitan town. It was full of officers of all the Allies, for example there were Italian military police with their triangular hats which were rather comic. One day I was coming up from the docks in a tramcar with several nurses on our way home from a day's trip, when the tramcar stuck on the hill. It stuck because it was completely overloaded. We were inside the tram, but workmen had crowded on and stood packed in the doorway and hanging on outside. Several Italian police and the guard were shouting at them to get off, but nobody complied. Two British Red Caps (military police) arrived on the scene, and instead of adding to the argument by talking, they got hold of the two nearest men to the doorway by the collar and pulled them off the tramcar. In a few moments there was a rush to get off the tram and we were able to proceed on our way.

There was a lot of jealousy between the different Allies. There was a large Italian battleship anchored in the Bosphorus as well as several British and Russian battleships. A story was told about a very dirty British collier which arrived and signalled the British flagship as to where he should anchor. The answer came, 'alongside the Dago'. He anchored alongside the Italian battleship, much to its Commander's annoyance. Actually the *Dago* was another British collier which was anchored some distance away.

As well as escorting the nurses I did some sightseeing and visited the Mosque of St Sophia among other places. I was sorry at the end of about three weeks when I was ordered to go aboard the first train to do the journey between Constantinople and Salonika since the end of the war. The bridges had all been destroyed but had now been rebuilt or repaired.

I found that I had a compartment to myself, and that the train had Greek, French, Italian and American passengers also. It was not long before a French officer came into my compartment and told me what a poor crowd the Italian officers were. An Italian officer came in and told me the same about the French and Greeks. A Greek officer was more generous to his allies and I liked him best. The American officers belonged to some voluntary agency like the Red Cross and were going to Greece on relief work. They were very interested in everything and enthusiastic about their journey.

I had been on good terms with the catering department of the hospital owing to my trips with the nurses, and they had given me a large box of provisions with bottles of wine and beer. I was an old soldier by this time and I had told them I had no idea how long the journey would take. I was able to provide refreshments, and my compartment was therefore very popular.

The train went very slowly with frequent long halts. On the second day there was a violent thunderstorm, and after that we stopped for several hours. We were then told that some of the temporary bridges had been washed away and the train was going to return to Constantinople. We had gone, I think, about 200 miles from Constantinople, nearly halfway to Salonika. We were told that if we wished, we could continue the journey by road, and that we would be met after some distance by a train which was coming from Salonika. The Americans decided to go by road and got out of the train. They wanted me to go with them, but I decided that Constantinople was a good place and that I would stick to the train. I knew that a journey by road such as was proposed, without any preparation or official help, would be no picnic. The war was over. I was not particularly keen to go to Salonika and I was rather tired of dirt and discomfort. I had noticed also that the Greek officer had decided to remain on the train.

Just as the train blew its whistle preparatory to leaving on the return journey, the Americans changed their minds and bundled their kit into my compartment. They had previously been arguing with me that I was not behaving in a very British way in turning back. As it happened, by this time they had finished all their rations, and I had to supply them on the way back to Constantinople.

———

After a further week I was put on board a ship for Salonika. This ship was bound for home, and she made a very considerable detour to land me, the only passenger to get off the ship at Salonika. I got a cheer from the homeward-bound passengers as I went down the gangway to a small tender. My kit consisted mostly of Persian carpets which I had bought in Baku – I had very little clothing except that which I wore!

I found the general hospital to which I was to be attached on the eminence called Kalamaria, to the east of the town. It was one of the healthy parts of the town and there had originally been several hospitals situated there. There were a great many wooden huts, some of which were empty.

I was rather appalled when I had time to look over my charge and realised the responsibility that had fallen to me. There were nearly 1,000 patients in the medical side and only about a tenth of that number in the surgical side. I had four or five medical officers assisting me with the medical patients, most of whom were quite junior and had little experience of Middle East diseases. This was the only military

127

hospital left in Salonika at that time, July 1919. It served the sick from the British Salonika garrison, Turkish and Bulgarian prisoners and Macedonian Labour Corps etc.

The large majority of the British patients were Army Service Corps personnel who were looking after the great numbers of horses and mules left by the British Army, most of whom had gone home. I think the idea was to sell these animals if possible in the Middle East, where there was a market for them, to save the expense of taking them home where motor transport was beginning to take the place of horse transport. These animals were kept in a swampy, unhealthy area to the north of Salonika. As a result, the men were nearly all suffering from chronic malaria and were in a depressed and unhappy state. I do not think that their discipline was very good, and this prevented anti-malarial treatment from being effective. At any rate we had many daily admissions of men suffering from severe malarial infections. Some of them were in coma from cerebral malaria.

The malaria in Salonika was the malignant quotidian type, similar to that from which I had suffered in Persia. When I spoke to the O.C. of the hospital about my concern for these patients, he told me that there was a British Army order in Macedonia that if a patient suffering from cerebral malaria did not get an intravenous injection of quinine the medical officer in charge was liable to court martial. I was never able to confirm whether such an order really existed, but that was what he told me.

A few days after I arrived, I was giving an injection of quinine into the veins of an unconscious soldier when he suddenly expired. On going into the matter more fully, I found that many of these soldiers were suffering from disorders of cardiac rhythm, and I considered that injections of massive doses of quinine into the veins was liable to cause cardiac arrest and stoppage of the heart in such cases. I then gave orders that no intravenous quinine was to be given in the medical division until I had first seen the patient. Very soon afterwards we stopped giving intravenous quinine altogether, and we thought that our results were at least as good, if not better, than formerly.

Almost all the men in hospital had multiple infections of malaria, and instead of having a rise in temperature every third day they had a daily intermittent temperature. Many of these men had enlargement of the spleen, a symptom of chronic malaria, and were in poor condition. These were the men who took fatal attacks when they got a fresh infection. What was happening was that the men were being returned to their units as soon as they recovered from their latest bout of infection. It seemed the reason for this was that the transport services in particular were short of staff. Too many men had been demobilised, and the authorities had been unable to sell the animals as they had expected. To add to their troubles, 1919 was a particularly bad summer for malaria. I decided after observation of the situation for a few weeks that it was my duty to send most of these chronic malaria cases home. Most of them were anaemic and in a poor state of health, and it was endangering their lives to send them back to duty.

A weekly medical board was held at the hospital to consider cases for repatriation on account of invalidism. The board consisted of the CO of the hospital, the senior surgeon and myself. The first time I was on the board I put up about a dozen men whom I recommended to be sent home. About half were accepted and the rest returned to duty. I was in a minority of two to one and I could do nothing about it. This happened for several weeks, but after a week or two instead of sending them back to duty I returned them to hospital.

After about six weeks I realised that the time had come to take drastic action, and one morning I paraded over a hundred men before the board. They were marched up by a senior sergeant in column of fours and halted outside the boardroom. The Colonel inquired what the parade was for, and was told that they were men to be invalided from the medical division. He turned to me and said, 'What the hell do you think you are playing at, Glen?' I replied that I was quite serious and was of the opinion that all these men should be invalided home. However, with the consent of the surgeon, the other member of the board, he dismissed the whole parade.

I went back to my office in the Medical Division and wrote a letter to the D.D.M.S. Mediterranean Forces at Constantinople, telling him my story. I said that in my opinion the majority of the men who were suffering from chronic malaria were no longer fit for duty and should be invalided home. I added that my Commanding Officer and the surgeon in charge of the Surgical Division disagreed entirely with me. I was so strongly of my opinion, however, that I could no longer remain responsible for these patients and asked to be relieved of my post immediately. I knew that I was well within my rights in doing this; in the army one can in exceptional cases appeal over the head of one's immediate commander to a senior officer. I left the letter open and wrote a covering letter to the CO, asking him to read it before sending it on to Constantinople.

In a short while he came down to see me himself, and this time he was in quite a changed mood. He said, 'Let us discuss this thing calmly, Glen. You can't send that letter on to Constantinople. That would be a most unusual and very serious thing to do.'

'I do not think so,' I replied. 'After all, men's lives are at stake.'

After a while he suggested that he should write himself and ask for the medical consultant to the Forces at Constantinople to visit us and give his opinion. I replied that I could not agree to that. It might be a month or two before he came and that was not good enough. I considered the matter very urgent.

Finally we agreed that he would send a telegram himself in, so far as I can remember, the following words: 'Malaria situation Salonika very serious, request urgent visit from senior Medical Consultant.'

I agreed to destroy my letter. I had no desire to do the CO any personal harm. He was a regular army officer and I did not wish to do anything that would affect his career. I think it was just want of thought and carelessness on his part; he never visited the medical wards to see the situation for himself. He and the surgeon's chief subject of conversation at the mess was about stocks and shares, and they were constantly sending off wires to buy and sell them.

Meantime other things were happening. One evening as we were sitting at mess it became very dark and I judged that a bad thunderstorm was brewing. I thought it wise to go along to the wards and warn them about the possibility of a hurricane, as I had seen something like this in Mesopotamia. I had just got into one of the huts and was in the act of shutting a window when it struck us with terrific force. I felt as if the whole place would collapse at any moment. The hut in which I was stood up to the blast, except for several window panes which were blown in. The next hut had its roof completely blown off and the rain descended in torrents, with thunder and lightning. One can imagine the effect of this on sick patients in bed. For hours we had a terrible job on our hands. An aerodrome a short distance away had most of its hangars blown away.

Fortunately there were several empty huts nearby which had more or less escaped and we got the patients moved into them. As mentioned earlier, there had at one time been several hospitals on Kalamaria and there was plenty of spare accommodation.

On another evening the sergeants' mess went on fire and made a wonderful blaze, greatly to the amusement of some of the medical orderlies. Fortunately it was in an isolated spot and there was no danger to the other patients.

After about two or three weeks, Lieutenant Colonel Willcox, a well-known London consultant at that time, arrived in answer to our request for help. He went round the medical wards and fully agreed with my assessment of the situation. He said that between 400 and 500 of my patients should be repatriated immediately.

Afterwards he took me aside and asked if there was anything he could do for me. I said that I had been a very long time on active service, and that as soon as the present trouble was cleared up and the men sent home, I would like to get home myself. He said that he would do what he could when he got back to Constantinople. Three weeks later I got my demobilisation orders.

The concentration camp for demobilisation was at Chanak on the Dardanelles, and I arrived there by ship from Salonika in mid-October. We had to wait there for a larger ship to take us home. Chanak is very near the ruins of Troy. The camp was not a very interesting place and I went out for a walk to look around shortly after I arrived there. I was walking among some sand dunes when I saw a familiar figure also walking alone coming towards me. I could scarcely believe my eyes when I realised it was Osborne Mavor. He had demobilised our old unit, handed in all his stores, etc., and was now ready to go home. He said that with the money we had collected in the unit welfare fund over the years, he had been able to hand over a fairly substantial sum to each man.

We sailed together to Taranto in the heel of Italy, where we went into another camp. I thought Mavor was unusually quiet and subdued for him during the trip; he was usually full of fun and games. I think we both realised that one stage in our lives had passed. We were going home to start civil life, and it would be a great change from the life we had spent for five years. We had managed to stand up to war. How would we face up to peace?

We both thought that we would like to be consulting physicians. Neither of us, however, had much in the way of independent resources. In those days, in order to become a hospital physician one had to endure many lean years before one could make a living. We

131

decided we would have to start as general practitioners and hope to get part-time jobs in hospital.

About ten days after we arrived at Taranto my name was posted as in charge of a troop train and I parted from Mavor again. These troop-train journeys during the war were always very miserable. This journey took three days from Taranto to Boulogne. We had one hot meal each day. Our first stop was at Faenza in Northern Italy and here we were royally treated. I don't remember the name of the British officer in charge, but he deserved great credit for his work. We were marched from the station to a large hall where all ranks were given a sit-down meal of three courses served by Italian waitresses, and I think the men also had a glass of beer. We returned to the train in great form. The next meal in France was the usual hand-out of tins of stew from a boiler.

We arrived at Boulogne at 4 p.m. on the following afternoon, Saturday, having had no food all day. I was told that we would have to walk about three miles to the camp and the men would have to carry their kit bags as well as their rifles and all their other equipment. With the help of a sergeant major I managed to get them to fall in and make off in some kind of order. Their kit bags were all very heavy, full no doubt of souvenirs, and I felt very angry indeed that we had no transport. We had several halts, but after we had gone about 1½ miles the men refused to fall in again on command. They just sat on the roadside and refused to move. I did not know what to do at first, but finally I got up on a high bank at the side of the road and addressed the company. 'I think this is bloody treatment to give men coming home from the Great War,' I said, 'but after all we are a bit late in getting home, the war has been over for a year now and they have forgotten all about us. All I know is that there is a chance of getting some supper if we can reach the camp. You can all stay here if you like, I am going on myself for my supper.' They fell in silently and followed me. We arrived very weary after a few more halts.

I got my papers and tickets the following day to go direct to my home, and left the following day by channel steamer. Mavor, who followed me a few days later was given charge of a party to take to Bishopton, near Glasgow, so that I actually got off easier than he did and was home before him.

London was very crowded in November 1919. I had crossed with several officers who had been in the 19th Brigade in Persia and we arranged to meet at 7 p.m. at the Piccadilly Grill and have our dinner together. We arrived in London about 2 p.m. and I got a taxi and spent two or three hours going round the hotels looking for a place for a night's lodging. When I was just about giving up and taking my kit to Euston Station left-luggage office, an officer in an hotel who heard me asking for a bed and getting a negative reply said, 'Look here, old chap, you can share my bed.'

His bed was actually in a boarding house quite a distance away. However, I found it and dumped my kit. I made my appointment at the Piccadilly Grill where we had a happy evening and did not break up till after midnight. When I got to the boarding house I found my good friend sound asleep in bed, and there was a strong smell of alcohol in the room. I got in beside him, but when I got up next morning about 8 a.m. to catch my train, he was still sound asleep. I left a note on the table thanking him very much for his hospitality.

And so I came home to Glasgow after five and a half years, and the first great war was over so far as I was concerned. It was about the end of November. There was a cold spell of weather at the time, with 12 degrees of frost on the night I arrived. I did not like it at all.

BOOK TWO

XII

General Practice in Govan

I arrived home about the end of November 1919. I found my mother
and sister well and still living in our old house in Dumbreck. My sister
was trained as a teacher, but had given up teaching in the past year
to be with my mother and they were living on a comparatively small
income.

Shortly after I came home I started writing my thesis on typhus
fever for an M.D. degree. I had kept careful notes of all my typhus
cases during the epidemic in Baku and I had some quite interesting
material. I had seen one case of typhus fever at the Western Infirmary
which I had admitted as a pneumonia when I was a resident there pre-
war, but typhus by this time was an extreme rarity in the British Isles.

In December a vacancy for an assistant physician in the Glasgow
Military Hospital, in Bellahouston Park near my home, was advertised
and I applied for it. This carried a salary of £500[21] a year and would
have suited me very well. It would have enabled me to accept a post
in one of the voluntary hospitals, which were unpaid, and to start
my career as a junior physician, which was my ambition. I was not
successful in getting this appointment, although I was told unofficially
that I was the second choice and very nearly got it. I therefore began
to look around for a practice in or near Glasgow to earn my bread and
butter and wait for an opportunity to get an appointment as a junior
physician (unpaid) in one of the teaching hospitals.

Early in January 1920, Osborne Mavor told me that he had
arranged to take over Douglas Russell's general practice in Langside.
Russell was a senior visiting physician at the Victoria Infirmary, and
he was giving up general practice. Mavor had arranged to go into the
maternity hospital at Rotten Row for a fortnight to get a refresher
course in midwifery, and would I join him? He was taking on the
practice and at the same time he had been appointed junior physician
in Dr Ivy Mckenzie's wards.

21. About £19,000 at today's values (Bank of England inflation calculator).

134

This was a very good arrangement, and in fact it was the usual way at that time by which junior hospital staff made their way. It meant hard work of course. The morning was spent in hospital and the afternoon and evening were devoted to general practice.

I accepted Mavor's offer to go into the maternity hospital for the refresher course. It was always a joy to be his companion anywhere, and we went into the student residence at the hospital. There were no other students at the time and we were alone in the residence. Although we were paying a fee for our course, none of the staff took any notice of us. We were not even called when a birth was expected and we had to make the enquiries ourselves about them or hang around waiting. After several days spent like this we decided that the course was no good and that we would just have to learn obstetrics the hard way by experience. I was not very worried about this because I had spent six months in my last year at hospital doing only obstetrics after failing in my final. Mavor was different, however, and in fact did very little midwifery during his time in general practice.

After making our decision we went along to the North British Hotel and ordered a vodka. The waiter looked at us a bit queerly, but eventually produced it. Vodka was not such a common drink in this country then as it is today. We had dinner and a bottle of wine and I decided that I also would look for a general practice.

The opportunity came quite soon. A practitioner in Govan, an industrial district near my home, was found dead one morning in his chair. He had been making up his list of visits for the following day and his notebook had fallen by his side. He was small in stature but had been a very active man and a popular practitioner. His name was Brown, but he was called affectionately by his patients 'Wee Broon'.

His neighbour, a man called James Cumming, took over his work. Cumming heard that I was unemployed and called on me to see if I would take over the work and later on, if satisfactory arrangements could be made, take over the practice. I agreed and started work at once as I could do so from my own home.

After a few weeks I took over the practice from the doctor's widow. I got the practice cheap. I paid £1,000 for it but I think I paid about £1,250 for the house. It was a nice house for the district in which it was and I think that Mrs Brown was more sorry to part with the house than the practice. Owing to the fact that I had been abroad most of my five years of service I had not spent much money,

135

and with my gratuity I had about £1,100. I borrowed the rest from my mother.

We sold the house in Dumbreck and my mother and sister came with me to Govan. The house faced onto a small park, the Elder Park, and was a comfortable house, but I was appalled at the conditions of poverty and misery in some parts of the practice. The houses near my home were occupied almost entirely by better-class tradesmen ship-workers, such as joiners, platers, plumbers etc., and their houses were well-kept and clean, but in the poorer parts of the town, where the more casual labourers lived, the conditions were very bad. Although I had lived not far away all my life I had no idea that such conditions existed, but I was soon to know all about it.

Govan, where I now settled in general practice, is a place of consider-able antiquity. In 1920 it was the centre of a great shipbuilding and engineering industry and had been extremely busy during the war years. The building of iron steamships really started on the Clyde, and the population had increased at a great rate. T.C.F. Brotchie, in his book *The History of Govan*, says that between 1864 when Govan was made a burgh and 1905 when he wrote his book, the population increased tenfold, in forty years increasing from 9,000 to over 90,000. This seems probably as great as any American increase in population. Writing in 1905, Brotchie states, 'Fairfield [one of the largest ship-building yards in Govan] laid down, built and launched a steamship of 5,000 tons in 88 days. Such a performance is amazing. It is an excellent example of brilliant administration and capable workman-ship. They can build, launch and equip a vessel in Govan of 10,000 tons in nearly half the time taken abroad and at a third less cost. The design, workmanship and finish are also much superior to foreign work. Therein lies the secret of the success of the Clyde.'

In its earlier days Govan was a very picturesque village, and in pre-historic times was the site of a monastery founded in the earliest days of Christianity by one of St Columba's missionaries. It had always a close connection with the Church. King David, about 1147, granted the whole land of Govan to the Church of Glasgow. The land on which my house there was built was what is called in Scotland a free-hold, and my only obligation, according to my lawyer when I bought the house, was that I had to deliver to the Archbishop of Glasgow so many salmon and capon each year. Although Govan had once had a very prosperous salmon fishing industry, there were now no salmon in the Clyde at Govan and my obligations were therefore nil.

As always during a war, the heavy industries like shipbuilding and engineering had been extremely active and Govan had been a very busy place from 1914–1918. There was a short boom after the end of the war, but the heavy industries were the first to suffer when the recession came and by the time I started practice in 1920, the slump had already struck Govan, although the post-war boom continued in other parts of the country for another year.

During the war wages had doubled, but the cost of living had increased even more. When everyone was working, however, this was not noticed so much. Very soon it appeared to me that nearly one third or more of the men in Govan were unemployed, although this level of unemployment only affected places like Govan and was by no means general throughout the country.

Shortly after I took over the practice, unemployment benefit at the rate of fifteen shillings[22] a week was started. Benefit could only be drawn for fifteen weeks in any one year, and one week only could be paid for every six weeks' contributions paid. One can understand that this was not much good in a place like Govan. It was 1922 before the benefit was raised to twenty-five shillings,[23] and dependants' allowances given and an uncovenanted benefit, 'the dole'. This dole was at first given for five weeks and then stopped alternately for five weeks. What the men and their families were supposed to live on during the second five weeks I never quite understood, but any savings which they had were soon used up, and furniture in the houses became very scarce. Everything went that could be realised. Even the blankets on the beds became fewer.

These conditions of unemployment and semi-starvation continued more or less for the thirteen years, 1920–1933, that I was in practice in Govan. There was a slight improvement in 1924–25 when shipbuilding improved for a time, but this was followed by a slump which was even worse. In fact these depressed conditions continued in Govan till shortly before the Second World War.

The housing conditions in Govan were by no means good, and had deteriorated in the older parts because nothing had been done

22. Roughly £28 at today's values.
23. About £47 at today's values.

to them during the war years. The houses in the older parts of the town in those days were high tenements, built strongly of sandstone. Some of them, for example in old Queen Street, now demolished but occupied in my time, were four storeys high with, I think, four houses or more on each flat. They had no baths but had one W.C. for each storey of four houses, always in a deplorable state. I remember calculating that between 100 and 150 people entered or left these houses by one narrow entrance, or close as it is called in Scotland. Although I thought that this street was the worst slum, some other streets like Albert Street and Hamilton Street were little better. Some of them had what were called 'back lands'. This was another smaller tenement which was built later in the space at the back. The people living there had to enter through the same congested close. Very little light got into these back lands, and there was no place for the innumerable children to play except in the middens or small back courts, or in the street.

A few days after I started practice in Govan I was called to see a little girl in one of these back lands. She was about seven or eight years old and was lying on the floor on a straw mattress in a tiny room. Her mother told me, in front of the girl, that the parish doctor had told her that she was dying of consumption and that there was nothing they could do for her. They had told her to keep the child in this room as she might infect the others. The house was on the ground floor and the room appeared to me to be really only a cellar, about 6 feet by 6 feet. It was dark and damp.

Meantime the emaciated child was looking at me with large staring eyes. I did not know what to say, but I examined her lungs and found that they were riddled with tuberculosis as the parish doctor had told them. The mother said then, in front of the child, that she just wanted my opinion as to whether the child was dying or not. She did not wish me to go back to visit her if I could do nothing for her.

I tried unsuccessfully to get her removed to hospital. There was no accommodation at that time for incurable cases. I went back, however, to see her several times in the next few weeks before she died. I took her a few simple toys one day, and when I went back the next time she said to me, 'Will there be any toys in heaven, Doctor?' I told her that I was certain that there would be lots of toys there, and she seemed quite happy.

This incident, coming so soon after I started work in Govan, had an effect on me and I realised that I was back in the front line again, but in a different kind of warfare.

—

Shortly after this I went into a close one day in a street called Harmony Row. It was almost quite dark with only a flickering gas jet in the close when suddenly I was struck in the face by someone's arm. It was not a heavy blow but I was sure I was going to be assaulted and robbed. I stood back with my hands clenched, when there was a voice from further inside the close, 'Leave him alone, Jimmy, you bl—dy fool, can you no see that's the new doakter?' I had run into a bookie's party taking bets, and the man who stopped me was on the look-out. This kind of poor-man's betting was illegal at that time.

I was, however, very soon a well-kent figure, and saw all that went on without let or hindrance. Sometimes when my patients had no money to pay my small fee, they used to go along and borrow from the bookie.

I shared consulting rooms near the centre of Govan with Dr James B. Cumming who proved to be a great philosopher and friend to me. His father had been a sea captain and was later one of the Clyde river pilots. Cumming could not follow his father's profession because he was short-sighted, and became a doctor instead. What he did not know about practice in Govan was not worth knowing, and I went to him whenever I was in any difficulty.

For consulting rooms we shared a flat one up. There were two double-apartment houses and one single-apartment house on each landing. We had each a waiting room and consulting room, and the single apartment was used as a dispensary, where an unqualified girl dispensed medicines with the help of Dr Cumming and myself and took messages during the day. It was really quite a respectable set-up and much better than the average consulting rooms of that period.

When I took over the practice we were paid eight shillings and sixpence[24] a year under the National Insurance Act for each working person on our list. The women and children were not covered by insurance, but the old friendly societies, the Rechabites etc., still tried to carry on their system of support for the mothers and children.

Shortly after I took over the practice, several of these bodies which were organised locally came to me and asked me to come to

24. Roughly £16 in today's values.

an arrangement with them. As far as I can remember, their offer was about three shillings and sixpence[25] per patient per year and I was to supply all medicines also for this sum. My predecessor, Dr Brown, had had agreements with several of these societies but Dr Cumming advised me strongly not to take them on; he said it was better to keep my independence. He thought that 'Wee Broon' had killed himself with overwork. I took Cumming's advice.

Another piece of advice which he gave me was that I should always charge cash for a visit or consultation, or at least that I should always ask for my fee. He said that it was no good sending accounts. Most of these poorer patients could not pay accounts, and if they owed you money they simply went to another doctor and did not come back to you.

The Govan doctors had a local association, and during the prosperous years in Govan of the 1914–18 war they had made a mutual agreement that fees for a private consultation would be two shillings and sixpence[26] and a home visit three shillings and sixpence.

It became obvious to me very shortly after I started work that a large proportion of my patients could not pay this fee. When I asked Cumming about this, he said again, 'Always ask for it. If they don't pay it you don't need to go back again. If they are old patients and are decent people and your services are really urgently required, say that you will get the fee when you come back next time. When you go back they will almost certainly offer you the fee. If you think that they are very hard-up and really can't afford the three shillings and sixpence, tell them to put it in a box on the mantelpiece and you will get it when you come back again. If you think they are on the starvation level you can leave it there till you are finished visiting, but always take it before you leave finally.'

He advised me, however, to be careful not to let the patients make a fool of me, and told me about an incident that happened to him. He had been visiting a child in White Street, Govan. The house was very bare and there was obviously great poverty, so he did not accept the fee which was offered to him. He did another visit in the street and as he passed the Stag Inn, a public house at the foot of the street, a man who was washing the windows said to him, 'There's a couple of women inside, Doctor, drinking your health with your fee.'

25. Roughly £6.60 in today's values.
26. Roughly £4.70 in today's values.

All this advice was extremely valuable to me, and I must say that I carried out Dr Cumming's methods. For years it is true that I did a great deal of work for nothing, but I kept the respect of these people and many of them probably paid me more than they really could afford. At first I only used these methods for my poorest patients, the unskilled casual labourers. In a year or two, however, even the skilled tradesmen like joiners, engineers, plumbers etc. began to get into difficulties when they had spent their usually small savings.

Most of these were extremely decent, hard-working people who kept their small houses spotless. They had no unnecessary complaints and it was a pleasure to do anything for them. I remember one such family. The man was an engineer who had been out of work for many months. He had run into one of these periods when his dole was stopped and he had been unwilling to apply for parish aid, now called public assistance. He had finally applied but had so far not received anything. He had four or five children, and I was attending the youngest child for a broncho-pneumonia which was a very prevalent and deadly disease among children at that time. I had realised that they were in difficulties and had not accepted my fee for some time, although I was always offered it. When I came to the end of my visit this day, the woman suddenly burst into tears. She told me the whole story and said that she had had to spend my fee. She had nothing else in the house, it was a Saturday and the children were hungry. They had expected to get some parish money but had not received it. The husband had gone out to see if he could borrow some money from his friends.

The next visit I paid that day was to the grocer. I never gave my patients any money, but in such cases I used to send them in a parcel. I certainly knew who deserved it and needed it.

———

Fortunately I was comparatively well off myself for those days. National Health Insurance, although it only applied to the workers in those days and that was chiefly the men, gave the doctors in industrial districts like Govan an assured income. I had a very large practice with about 3,000 insured people. At eight shillings and sixpence a patient that gave me an income of over £1,200[27] a year. I had another £300[28]

27. About £45,600 at today's values.
28. About £11,400 at today's values.

or so from private practice and my mother who now lived with me had a small income of her own.

I had, of course, a great deal of work. In fact my work was never finished. I must have been responsible for 9,000–10,000 people at least. The sickness rate was very high, as it always is when people are badly nourished and suffer from anxieties and depression. The food they had was inadequate, not only in quantity but in quality. They lived largely on bread and carbohydrates. They were insufficiently clothed, especially in winter. Rickets among the children was still widespread although we now knew the cause and prescribed cod liver oil when they could get it. Rickety children are particularly liable to pneumonia and other infections. Tuberculosis was rife. Diphtheria, scarlet fever and whooping cough, when they occurred, were very frequently fatal. Even measles was often a fatal disease. The health of these people, particularly the women and children, was terribly neglected. However hard I worked I realised that I could do very little; good food and clothing could have done far more.

Motor cars were luxuries in those days, and for the first two and a half years in practice I did all my visits on foot. The houses were nearly all tenements and the practice was very concentrated; it was not much more than a mile from one end of the town to the other. I usually started off with an umbrella, but oftener than not it came home before me. I usually forgot about it and left it at some house, and the patients brought it home. One wet day I came in for my lunch and my mother, noticing that my coat was very wet said, 'Your umbrella has not come back yet, that's rather unusual.' When I came in for a cup of tea, as I usually did before I went to my consulting rooms at 6 p.m., my mother reported again that my umbrella had not been returned. When I got to my surgery and rang the bell for the first patient, a little fellow in bare feet darted in and laid something on my desk, saying, 'My mither said to give you that ticket.' Then he disappeared as quickly as he had come in. It was a pawn ticket for my umbrella. I did not make any further enquiries. I thought it was very decent of them to return the pawn ticket. It only cost me five shillings to reclaim the umbrella and I was grateful to get it, as it was the only one I had at the time.

I have already explained, I think, that when I started work in Govan in 1920 Lloyd George's National Insurance Act had already been law for some time. It actually started just before the first war.

This insured all the people who were working but not the families. I think they got fifteen shillings[29] a week sick money.

When unemployment became so bad in the heavy industries on the Clyde the sickness rate began to go up steadily and the doctors, especially in Glasgow, began to receive complaints and exhortations from the Department of Health that we were too easily influenced by our patients and were giving sickness certificates too easily. This was what the authorities called 'bad certification'.

It was not long before I began to realise that this 'bad certification' was not such a simple thing as it appeared to the lay authorities. I found older men by the dozen suffering from chronic bronchitis, heart troubles and many other conditions, who had been working to the best of their ability so long as there was plenty of work, but as soon as work began to get scarce they were the first to get their books (discharge). They naturally felt depressed at losing their work and began to be more conscious of their genuine disabilities. When these men came to me I had no alternative but to sign them unfit for work. They *were* unfit for work, and should not have been working previously.

The Department of Health for Scotland were getting very anxious about the situation. Articles were written in the papers condemning the 'slackness' of the doctors' certification, and in 1922 or thereabouts, a lady statistician from the Health Department was sent to Glasgow to lecture to us about our sins. Apparently she had been making a special study of the situation. One of the large halls in Glasgow was booked for the occasion and we were all called to the meeting. We were shown by means of graphs etc. the great rise in the rate of certified sickness.

Several of the practitioners present spoke and all said that there was undoubtedly a great rise in the sickness rate, and that so far as they were concerned their certificates were genuine and not given without careful consideration.

The lady speaker, whose name I cannot now remember, was a very able person and she had comparative figures for all the different districts in Glasgow. One old doctor who was sitting near me got up and said that he came from the Springburn district of Glasgow. He knew all the practitioners there and he was certain that none of them would give a certificate that was not genuine and given for a very

29. About £28 at today's values.

143

good reason. The lady referred to her notes and said, 'Springburn! Springburn is the second worst district in Glasgow.' At this the old doctor got up and walked out of the meeting and I followed him. I had a lot of work to do that day and I thought I was better to be getting on with the job.

I never attended a medico-political meeting after that day for many years. In fact I have only once attended this kind of meeting since: that was in 1948 prior to the introduction of the present all-inclusive National Health Service. I know this has been very wrong of me, but I have left other people to do all the dirty work. Later on I was chiefly concerned with the hospital side of the service, and so I was necessarily concerned a lot with the administration of that instead.

As a sequel to this certification trouble, in 1923 the Department of Health set up a special referee service where patients about whom there was any doubt about their incapacity for work could be sent for a second opinion. This new officer was called the Regional Medical Officer, and his department has steadily grown and taken over other duties since its inception.

To begin with it was a simple referee service, and it was not long before I was in trouble myself. The first man I had whom the referee certified as fit for work was suffering from chronic bronchitis. I continued to issue sick certificates and appealed against the decision. The patient and myself were then brought before a special tribunal. The tribunal consisted of a citizen of some distinction such as a city councillor, an officer from the Department of Health, and the medical referee. The patient's doctor was also called to state his case. In my case Mrs Violet Roberton, a Glasgow City councillor, was the chairman of the tribunal. Mrs Roberton gave the decision in my patient's favour, and he was continued on the sick list.

My next patient to be referred was a rather pathetic spinster woman who earned her living by sewing-machine work. She suffered from sciatica and had been on the sick list for a considerable time. At that time sciatica was not so well understood as it is today: it was thought to be a simple neuritis and its relationship with spinal strain was not then appreciated. At any rate I was of the opinion that she was suffering from a considerable degree of genuine pain. Mrs Violet Roberton, who was again by coincidence chairman of the tribunal, again decided in the patient's favour. The department official, however, explained that she was now no longer eligible for benefit and her sick money would be stopped. Apparently it had to be accepted that when the referee first saw her she was fit, though Mrs Roberton and the medical referee himself agreed that on the day of the tribunal she was unfit. So long as her sickness had been continuous she would have remained in benefit, but her contributions were now insufficient and this break in her illness had put her out of benefit. Mrs Roberton told me that she had made a protest against this decision, but apparently it was according to the Act and she could do nothing about it. I said that I was very dissatisfied with this extraordinary decision.

The next time I was in trouble with the Department of Health was somewhat different. A young man in his early forties came to me one day and told me that he had taken a very severe pain in his chest. He explained that he had lost his job in Govan but got the chance of a job at Port Glasgow which is over twenty miles from Govan. He had been cycling to work and back every day, and that night cycling home against the wind, he had taken this very severe pain in his chest. He got off his cycle immediately and sat at the side of the road for over half an hour before it eased off, and he came home slowly, still suffering some discomfort. After his supper his wife had sent him to see me. He had four or five young children.

Although we did not know what a coronary thrombosis was at that time, and called this sort of heart pain angina, I realised that this was at least a serious form of angina and said that he must stop work and have a rest. In any case I said that he should not continue to cycle all that way to work. Very unwillingly he agreed to follow my advice.

After about a fortnight he received word to go before the referee. He was a very independent type of man and this annoyed him greatly. I expect that when he went before the referee he would have told the referee that there was nothing wrong with him. At any rate he was certified fit for work, and started work himself immediately, against my advice.

A few days later I was called to his house. He had just arrived home and was taking his supper when he was seized with another chest pain. He was lying on top of his bed with his clothes on and was in great agony, looking deathly pale and perspiring profusely. I gave him a quarter of a grain of morphia but the pain did not ease, and after half an hour I repeated the dose, still without any apparent relief. He died in my presence after about an hour. I certified death as due to angina pectoris; today we would have diagnosed this attack as a coronary thrombosis.

I was naturally very indignant at this occurrence and at my advice being disregarded, and I wrote a letter that night to the medical referee, who at that time was Dr Gilmour. Dr Gilmour had several assistants, and it was one of his assistants who had seen my patient. I gave him a history of this last patient and also my two previous patients, and said that I was convinced that the referees were trying to do an impossible job or at least that they were doing it very badly. I said that I would like to hear his comments, but that meantime I was preparing a full report to send to the local newspaper (the *Glasgow Herald*) and hoped that they would give it publicity.

I received a telephone message next morning from Dr Gilmour. He said that he was extremely sorry about what had occurred, and he would be very grateful indeed if I would come and see him. I did so that afternoon. When I went into his office he had a cup of tea sent in, and then he said, 'You realise, Dr Glen, that this is a very difficult job we have got to do here.'

'I don't think anyone could realise that more than I do,' I replied, 'but I think that you come to your conclusions much too quickly. I am not satisfied with the way your work is meantime being done.'

After some further discussion, he said, 'We are only finding our way meantime, and no doubt we will have to make changes in our methods. Would you be satisfied if I say to you today that we will never question any of your certificates again?'

I agreed not to do anything further meantime, and for the next nine or ten years that I remained in general practice, none of my certificates was ever questioned. I think also less drastic methods were gradually introduced, and the patient's doctor's opinion was given more consideration in many cases.

Tribunals of this kind are very seldom used today. It is not always realised, I think, by the public or by the politicians, what a difficult problem these certificates of fitness for work present to the doctor. I have been a witness on a number of occasions in my life when such cases, mainly connected with compensation, were argued interminably by learned counsel before a judge for hours on end, while I waited impatiently in an anteroom for my time to give evidence. The general practitioner is expected to give such decisions after a few minutes' consideration in the middle of a busy surgery.

XIII

Elder Cottage Hospital, General Practice, Maternity Work

There was a small hospital about a hundred yards from my new home in Govan, the Elder Cottage Hospital. The hospital had been built by Mrs Elder, the wife of John Elder, the great Govan shipbuilder. She originally had intended it for women patients only, but during the war it had been changed by its trustees into a small general hospital. It had only forty beds, twenty medical and twenty surgical beds, but it was substantially built and was well-equipped for a hospital of its size, having good X-ray equipment.

It was not long before I found my way into the hospital to see what was going on there, and met Miss Macdonald the matron, a remarkable woman. The set-up of the staff was rather unusual. The surgeon, Mr Renton, at that time a junior surgeon in the Western Infirmary and a very good surgeon, seldom visited oftener than twice weekly; on Mondays when he operated, and on Thursdays when he saw out-patients. Dr Youll Anderson, the physician, was a general practitioner who lived some distance away but attended two or three times weekly. There was no resident physician, but Miss Macdonald was a very capable and experienced nurse and rarely had to call on her consulting surgeon or physician for emergency visits.

I told Miss Macdonald that I was living practically next door and that I would be available any time she wanted me. I think she had been feeling the strain somewhat during the war and gratefully accepted my offer. She told Mr Renton and Dr Youll Anderson about the arrangement, and they were also very satisfied. We soon became good friends and remained so as long as she lived.

Soon a good deal of the work devolved on me. I visited all Mr Renton's cases post-operatively and reported complications to him, and I visited the medical wards on the days Dr Anderson did not come and often accompanied him when he did visit. I did the routine test-room and laboratory work which a resident physician or surgeon would have dealt with and which had not previously been done. I found an excellent oil-immersion microscope in a cupboard which did not appear to have been used since it had been purchased, and was able to do blood-counts and cellular pathology etc.

This work was, of course, additional to my general practice, which was pretty heavy and more demanding owing to the conditions I have already described. I was a bachelor, however, and my mother and sister were very indulgent to me. No matter how busy I was, however, I have always tried to keep regular hours for my meals. I used to leave whatever I was doing and go home at the right time if at all possible.

My day started with breakfast about 7.30 a.m. I was off doing visits soon after 8.30 a.m. The shipyards in those days started at 6 a.m. and the men worked until 8 a.m., when they came home for breakfast. I did visits till about 11 a.m., and then I went to my surgery in Govan Road. Often I was kept there till 1 p.m. and at that time I went home for lunch. After lunch I saw a few patients, mostly local women and children, in my house, where I had a well-equipped consulting room and study. I had usually made appointments for those patients whom I saw at my home. They were often patients whom I had first seen in my Govan Road surgery and wanted more time to examine, or perhaps perform some minor operation.

I remember seeing a girl in her early twenties at my surgery who complained of a pain over her heart. I examined her heart and lungs carefully but could find no cause for the pain. As she was very insistent about the pain and looked rather ill, I asked her to come with her mother to my house on the following day. After examining the girl again and talking to her mother, I came to the conclusion that something was worrying the girl that she would not tell me in front of her mother, so I asked her mother to go into the waiting-room for a little.

I then said to the girl, 'Tell me now what it is that is troubling you, because I think this is the cause of the pain in your heart.' Thereupon she told me that she was going with a young man and that they were very much in love with one another and wanted to get married, but she was an only child and her mother was a widow and she did not wish to leave her. She said that this was the only worry which she had, but she could not make up her mind what to do.

I asked, 'Do you mind if I bring your mother in and tell her about this?'

She hesitated at first but after thinking it over, agreed. 'Maybe, Doctor, that would be the best thing to do.'

The mother was a very understanding woman and was completely sympathetic. When she heard the story she said there was nothing she would like better than that her daughter should get married. She knew the young man in question and liked him. Next time I saw the girl, the heart pain had disappeared completely.

One reason perhaps why I remember the above incident is that by a remarkable coincidence I was presented with almost an exactly similar situation just a week later. This time the mother came with her daughter. She was again an only daughter, but this time I think there was a brother also. This girl also complained of a pain over her heart. I examined her and could find no cause for the pain. I looked at the mother and daughter and sized up the situation. With the previous case so fresh in my mind, I thought I would take a chance. So I said to the girl, 'You are not thinking about getting married, are you?'

Simultaneously they both exclaimed, 'How did you know that, doctor?'

I replied, 'Well, my experience is that when a girl takes a pain in her heart like this, she is usually very much in love and something has happened to disappoint her.' (I did not say, of course, that I had only seen this situation once before, and that was the previous week.)

In this case I soon learnt that it was the mother who objected to her daughter getting married. However when she realised that her daughter's heart trouble was due to her own objections to the marriage, she gave in immediately. She said that she had just thought her daughter was too young.

I began to appreciate then, as all doctors do sooner or later, what a large part anxiety and worry has in producing physical illness. It is true, I think, that we realise this truth more today than ever we did in the past. It does not make life any easier, however, for the doctor.

To continue with my description of my day's work. After I had finished these home consultations I continued with my visiting, sometimes going into the cottage hospital until 5.30 p.m., when I came home for a cup of tea before going to my surgery again at 6 p.m. This often went on till between 8.30 and 9 p.m., and then I came home for my supper which was a substantial meal. I had often to go out again after that to do more visits.

This was my routine on six days a week except on Tuesday, when there was no evening surgery. On Tuesdays I always tried to get a game of golf, either with my sister who was a keen golfer, or some of my medical colleagues in Govan. On Sunday I went to church when I could with my mother and sister, but more often than not this was not possible.

I graduated M.D. with commendation in June, 1920. M.D. (Doctor of Medicine) is a postgraduate degree for which one has to submit a thesis and undergo a clinical examination. I was still anxious to become a consulting physician eventually, and I applied twice during 1920 and 1921 for posts as dispensing physician at the Western Infirmary, and was a little disappointed, especially on the second occasion, that I was not successful. Sir Hector Cameron was the convenor of the medical committee at the Western Infirmary at that time and was largely responsible for making these appointments. I had had no contact with Sir Hector of any kind and had never been one of his students. Perhaps the fact also that I was practising in a place like Govan counted against me.

In 1921 the Governors of the Elder Cottage Hospital appointed me assistant physician to the hospital (unpaid of course), thus giving me an official status in the hospital.

—

I was beginning to get very busy. I began to be called upon a great deal for maternity work. The poorer people were attended at childbirth mostly by 'howdy wives'. These were unqualified midwives, mostly old women who had earned a reputation for being 'skilly with babies'. Some of them were reasonably good, but most of them were so ignorant they were a positive danger. They only called in a doctor when they were in trouble, and usually when they did they were in great trouble. We did not like to be called out for these emergencies, because they were always very difficult and more often than not there was no recompense.

If a high forceps delivery and an anaesthetic were necessary, we usually called in one of our local colleagues, and we helped one another very willingly. Sometimes the husbands of these maternity patients might be on our insurance list and to that extent we felt some obligation to help. Most of them, however, had been unemployed so long that they had run out of health insurance, and our only obligation was the duty of every medical practitioner to answer an emergency call. This still holds, and a doctor is liable to very severe censure by the General Medical Council if he does not do so. It did, however, put a very heavy burden on us in those days. The community has now recognised its responsibilities in this area, and there is now a service of trained registered midwives on whom every woman can call, and in fact a complete maternity service linked with the hospitals.

One of these maternity emergencies is very clear in my memory. I went to the help of Dr Ian Grant, who had started in practice in Govan about a year after I did. Ian Grant was the son of the Gaelic minister to St Columba's Church in Govan. His father, the Rev. Evan Grant, came to Govan from Ross-shire when I was still at school, and Ian was one of my early school companions. Ian went out to India as doctor to a tea plantation just before the First World War. He served in the Indian Medical Service during the war and spent most of it in East Africa. After the end of the war he came home and became partner to Dr John West in Govan.

Ian was a fine public speaker and from his earliest days in practice took an interest in medical politics. He was chairman of the Council of the British Medical Association and one of the best known and most respected doctors in Britain when he died suddenly in 1963.

On the occasion which I am going to relate Ian had been called out to a 'howdy wife's' emergency. Owing to the prevalence of rickets, a deformed bony pelvis was very common among the poorer classes at that time, and this caused obstruction to the birth of a child. He saw he was up against a difficult case and called me in to help. I gave the anaesthetic and Ian put on the forceps successfully, but failed to move the child.

After a while I took over from Ian to see if I could make any progress. It was one of these box beds in the kitchen which are quite common in Glasgow tenements. These beds are built into the house, with walls on three sides and are only open to the front. They are also usually quite high, and maternity work in them is always very difficult. I found when I tried to put on heavy traction I just tended to pull the patient out of the bed.

After a time I thought I might manage better if I got into the bed myself. I did so and was beginning to make some progress when there was a sudden crash. The wooden fixings of the bed had given way at the bottom where I was. There must have been a tub or a trunk under the bed, because it upended completely, landing me on floor level and the unconscious patient came right over on top of me. After I had extricated myself and cleaned up some of the mess we finished the job on the floor and delivered a healthy baby. We left the woman lying on the mattress on the floor, and she made an uninterrupted recovery.

There were many difficult obstetric cases like this. Dr Cumming showed me how to deliver a child by breech (i.e. legs first), after we had failed with forceps. In his lectures in obstetrics Murdoch Cameron had advised us against this procedure. It was, of course, very dangerous for the child and added to the strain on the mother. If the delivery took a long time, the child was liable to be suffocated owing to pressure on the umbilical cord, and there was, of course, danger to the spine and limbs of the child. It was also a very difficult thing to do in a contracted pelvis. Murdoch Cameron, of course, wanted us to diagnose the condition early enough so that a Caesarian section could be done. In these Govan cases, however, it was always too late when we were called in. The only alternative was to destroy the child. I thought Dr Cumming's method was preferable because it at least gave the child a chance. I did it successfully myself on at least two occasions, although on most other occasions the child did not live. When I took over the practice from my predecessor Dr Brown, I bought his well-equipped maternity bag. It contained a perforator[30] for destroying the child, but although I carried it for thirteen years in Govan I never used it.

In a few years I built up quite a large maternity practice among the families of better class shipbuilding tradesmen. They were nearly all delightful people to work with. Their houses were small but they kept them very clean. They were easy to satisfy and very grateful for what one did for them. The work was also very satisfying to me. The treatment of general medical cases in these days on the other hand was often very disheartening. We had none of the wonderful drugs which are available today.

Many of the young mothers that I attended in their early confinements became my friends for life. I was the only one who could look after their children when they took ill – 'I understood their constitution.' Some of them still come to me for advice of one kind or another, not always medical. I meet the children that I brought into

30. See p. 18.

the world in all sorts of places. In later years when I became a medical teacher I had several of them as medical students.

The number of these confinements increased until a few years later, when I had an assistant, we did about 150 in a year. This was an average of about three a week and was too many. We tried to cut down the number after that.

Babies are born more often than not during the night, and the work entails considerable loss of sleep. I remember one night Ian Grant and I had been at a farewell dinner and dance for some friends from Australia. The party broke up about 1 a.m., and Ian and I promised to see our friends off at the station next day at 10 a.m. When we got to the station in the morning we both looked tired and it turned out that neither of us had been in bed. We had both attended two confinements during the night. This was not an unusual occurrence. I found in these days that I could miss one night's sleep and carry on as usual during the day, but if I missed my sleep on the second night I was liable to fall asleep in a moment if I sat down in a chair. I have always been a good sleeper and can still fall asleep quite readily if I wish to do so sitting in a chair.

Besides being hard and time-consuming work, this maternity work had its anxieties and tragedies. We had no antibiotics in these days, and puerperal fever was always a hazard. Some of our patients developed fever, and if it was serious they had to be notified and sent to the infectious diseases hospital. I only lost one patient from this cause, and we found that the 'howdy wife' in this case, who had large septic ulcers on her legs, had been sleeping in the same kitchen bed as the patient.

I was called in one night by a howdy wife and found a very unusual condition. The patient was a multipara (a woman who has had many children) and I found that the unborn infant could be moved about the abdomen very easily. It was some minutes before I collected my wits and realised that this was a ruptured womb and the baby was floating about in the abdominal cavity. The woman was in a poor way but not so shocked as one might have expected. This is a very unusual condition and I telephoned the maternity hospital to get her admitted. I got the answer that they had no accommodation. I refused to take no for an answer, however, and she was admitted and actually had an abdominal operation, but did not survive.

I had another very unusual but tragic case. This was a woman about 45 years of age who had been married for twenty years but had no family. She seemed to be a well-built woman when she came to engage me for her confinement. Antenatal examination was not routine at that time, and I did not examine her. When I examined her in the house when labour started I found that although she had been married for twenty years she was *virgo intacta*, i.e. the hymen was unruptured. It was not only unruptured but was very much thickened, and would require to be cut surgically. There is always in these cases a tiny hole in the membrane, otherwise she could not have become pregnant.

At her age I knew that she might have a difficult confinement. As her husband was a senior tradesman I said that I would like one of the doctors from the maternity hospital to see her. I telephoned one of the senior doctors at the hospital who sometimes helped me. He advised me to let her continue in labour meantime and he would see her with me on the following forenoon. When he arrived the following forenoon we gave her an anaesthetic and he cut the hymen. When he examined her, he said that the pelvis was somewhat contracted but that the womb was fully dilated and he thought that we might deliver her with forceps.

I gave her the anaesthetic, but after a prolonged trial he decided that it was impossible and asked if I could get a pair of large scissors and he would perforate.[31] I knew that it would be a terrible disappointment to the woman to lose her child. I asked would he not try to turn the child? He said that I could try to do it myself if I liked. He took over the anaesthetic and after a struggle I delivered the child, but it did not breathe. When I was trying to resuscitate the child the specialist suddenly said that the woman had collapsed. We failed to revive her, and there is no doubt that she died from a sudden cardiac failure. I had the terrible job of telling the father that both his wife and child had died. I had also to take home the thought that if I had allowed the specialist to destroy the child, the mother might have survived.

This condition of pregnancy with intact hymen cannot be so very uncommon, because I had another similar case later. She, however, had no contraction of the pelvis and her confinement presented no difficulty.

All our difficult cases, however, were not tragedies. One night when I was busy at my surgery in Govan Road, a very urgent message

31. I.e. abort the baby using the scissors.

arrived for Dr Cumming that one of his patients in labour 'had suddenly started to bleed terribly badly'. As Dr Cumming had not arrived
at his surgery I answered the call immediately myself, taking my maternity bag which I always had available. Luckily I had not to go far, and
when I got there I found the woman *in extremis* and blood literally
pouring from her. There was no doubt that it was a *placenta praevia*,
i.e. the afterbirth was attached at the mouth of the womb instead of at
the fundus, and the descending child had ruptured it. Until the actual
moment of birth the placenta supplies the blood from the mother to
the child's circulation and it is an extremely vascular organ. The blood
instead of passing through the umbilical cord was pouring out of the
passage and there was the gravest danger to both mother and child.
Although the neck of the womb was not fully dilated I applied forceps
and put on traction. This immediately stopped the haemorrhage to
some extent, but it was extremely painful for the patient who was
'screaming the house down'.

As I could not let go my traction I got a neighbour who was in
the house to put chloroform on a mask and apply it to the woman.
Fortunately Dr Cumming arrived just then and took over the anaesthetic. We delivered the child successfully and we got it to breathe
after a little persuasion. The woman, although she had lost a great deal
of blood, made a very quick recovery.

There is rather an amusing sequel to this story. Two or three
weeks later I was visiting another patient in the same close and passed
this woman on the stair. She gave me a very stony stare and then
looked deliberately away from me. A few minutes later I asked my
own patient what could be the matter. She said 'Oh, that woman! She
is spreading stories about you that you are a terrible brute and gave
her no chloroform.'

I felt rather hurt, however, and told Dr Cumming the story later.
As usual he had the right satisfying answer. 'Don't worry about her,'
he said. 'She is not a very good patient. I am quite sure that she will
never pay her fee for the confinement, and this will be her excuse.'
(The fee we got from the better-class tradesmen at this time for a
confinement was two guineas, which included post-natal visits for
ten days or a fortnight.) He went on to tell me never to expect gratitude in medical practice. He said that I would receive a great deal of
gratitude in my work, but that I would usually get it when I did not
deserve it much and very seldom when I did.

155

Continuing with maternity stories that come to my mind: one Tuesday afternoon just as I was leaving for a game of golf which I had arranged with one of my colleagues, a message for a confinement came in. I had a car by this time, and I put my golf-clubs in the car along with my maternity bag, hoping for the best and that I might be able to join my friends on the course later. I found the patient doing well. She was a multipara. The womb was well dilated; there was no pelvic contraction and there was no justification to apply forceps. A few good pains should finish the job. I sat down to wait. A half-hour went past and she did not have a single pain.

I had a sample of a new drug in my maternity case called pituitrin. It is a very old and well-established drug today but at this time it was new to me. It was supposed to cause uterine contractions. I decided to give it a trial and gave the patient an injection. It was a warm sultry afternoon. There was a fire on as usual in the kitchen. There was no howdy wife, or at least she had not then arrived, and I was alone in the house.

I had lost some sleep the night before, and when I sat down again in the kitchen armchair I suppose in a moment or two I must have fallen asleep. I half awoke with the sound of a low groaning and I did not realise at first where I was. The groan gradually became louder until it was a scream, and as I dashed towards the bed the baby positively shot into the world. At the same moment a large cat jumped on to the bed and started spitting wildly at me.

After I had tidied up the mess I found that the baby was very well and the mother had not even a perineal tear. By this time, however, I realised that my friends would be well started with their game, and I thought perhaps a little sleep would do me more good, so I went home. Pituitrin is still used regularly today, and for a number of different purposes. In maternity work it is used more often *post-partum*, i.e. after birth, and perhaps in better regulated doses.

Some years after this, when I had an assistant, one of my neighbouring practitioners called at my house one Friday night and said that he had been called away unexpectedly for four or five days, and would I be good enough to carry on his work for him. He gave me a list of a few patients, and said that there was nothing very much happening but there was one confinement which was due.

He was not long away when I got a call from this confinement case. I found that she was a woman in her mid-thirties. She had had three previous confinements. In each case the labour had been very difficult and she had been sent to the maternity hospital. Each time the child had been born dead. She had told her doctor that whatever happened, she would never go to hospital again and she now told me the same thing. I tried my best to persuade her to go to hospital, and said that at this early stage she could probably have a Caesarean section and be sure to have a live baby. I told her that they had much better facilities at hospital and that in a case like hers there was a considerable risk to her own life if she stayed at home. She replied that she was prepared for that, but insisted that her doctor had left her in my care and that I would have to do the best I could for her. When I examined her I found that the pelvis was contracted, but not too badly. I thought that what must have happened at the maternity hospital was that they had been hopeful that they could make a successful forceps delivery but had failed each time to get a live child.

I felt that I could, after all, do as much myself, and I thought it unlikely that the woman herself would come to any serious harm. I made up my mind that so long as the mother's strength held out the right course was to be extremely patient and I explained this to the mother. She promised to cooperate as well as she could. The labour continued on Friday night, all day Saturday, Saturday night and all day Sunday. By Sunday night she was getting quite desperate and we were being sent for about every hour and told we must do something. Her strength, however, seemed to be keeping up wonderfully. Her pulse was not too quick and we could hear the baby's heartbeats.

Late on Sunday night the head was firmly engaged in the pelvis and I began to have hopes that we would be able to deliver with forceps. As she seemed pretty exhausted and very emotional, at midnight I decided to give her a quarter of a gramme of morphia and promised the howdy wife and the patient that she would get relief for an hour or two and that we would positively deliver her next time we came back.

My assistant at that time was Dr James Anderson, a local Govan boy who had recently qualified. We went home to my house and in the hope that we might possibly get an hour's sleep we tossed a coin to see who would get the couch and who the big chair in my sitting-room. Anderson won and lay down on the couch. I awoke in the chair suddenly feeling cold and miserable and with a crick in my neck. A glance at the clock showed it to be 5 a.m. I was thoroughly alarmed and woke Anderson immediately. A ¼ gramme of morphia should not have lasted all that time. The most I had expected was about an hour's respite. Was it possible that she had sunk into a coma and the howdy wife had mistaken it for sleep?

We went quickly to the house and found a very happy state of affairs. A large male baby was sleeping in a basket. It had an unusually long-shaped head. The mother was asleep also but awoke and gave us a happy smile when we arrived. A minute or two reassured me that everything was all right. It appeared that the baby had been born quite suddenly and naturally about quarter of an hour after we left and the midwife had no time to call us. When she found everything to be all right she decided not to call us as she knew we had lost a lot of sleep.

When the patient's own doctor arrived home a few days later I told him quite casually, 'By the way, that confinement that you mentioned came off all right and they are both doing well.' He looked, I think, a little surprised, but I said no more and we never mentioned the subject again. I expect he heard all about it from the midwife and the mother.

Mitral stenosis (valvular heart disease) is a great hazard at confinements. It is caused by rheumatic fever and is much less common in these days of antibiotics than it was in the 1920s. Sir James MacKenzie, who started practice as a general practitioner in Burnley, Lancashire, lost one of his early confinement cases very tragically from mitral stenosis during her labour. This was one of the occurrences which gave him the impetus to study heart disease, and it was while he was still in general practice that he wrote his first book which revolutionised our knowledge of heart disease.

Although a young woman can get about fairly well with this type of valvular heart disease when going about normal house duties, when she becomes pregnant a much larger burden is thrown on the heart, not only from the extra work it has to do but because of the embarrassment to the heart's action by the abdominal swelling associated with the pregnancy.

I was called by a howdy wife to a case like this in the early hours one morning. The woman's husband was at sea. I found the woman's condition to be grave. She had congestive heart failure. Her legs were swollen and oedematous. She was blue and cyanosed,[32] and her heart was fibrillating (i.e. beating very irregularly). As there was no one else

32. Suffering from lack of oxygen.

about I sent the midwife over to the Police Office, which was not far away, to telephone for one of my colleagues to help me and to give an anaesthetic.

Fortunately the labour was well advanced and I thought it would be fairly easy to terminate it and give the young woman relief. I had started to give her anaesthetic myself to relieve her somewhat when she suddenly became worse. Her breathing became sterterous and her face started to twitch. I was afraid that she was dying, and I thought the best thing I could do was to deliver the child. I put on forceps, but as I was trying to deliver the child the woman's whole body went into a violent convulsion for a minute or two. When the convulsion ceased I quickly delivered the child, which was alive, and then gave my whole attention to the mother.

She improved after a while and consciousness returned, but I found that she was paralysed all down the right side. What had happened was that a clot had formed in the heart owing to stress and dilatation. This had moved into the carotid artery which supplies the brain, and formed an embolism blocking the circulation to one side of the brain.

The woman eventually recovered but was left with a practically useless right hand and forearm. Her leg recovered completely and she was able to walk and speak normally.

Nowadays a patient with a heart condition like this would not have been allowed to go on to full-time labour. Pre-natal examinations are always carried out. The pregnancy is terminated early or Caesarean section is arranged in good time and the patients are sterilised to prevent further conception. These valvular constrictions are now frequently operated on, and great improvement in the heart function brought about.

I could tell many stories about the maternity work in Govan. It was difficult and anxious work, but so long as I was physically fit and not too tired, I liked it. After bringing two or three children into the world a doctor begins to have a very close and real relationship with the family. He begins to have a personal interest in them all and they develop an extraordinary faith and confidence in their doctor. One day Dr Cumming told me the following story. He said that his door bell had been rung about 4 a.m. the previous night by two young apprentice lads, one of whom had a cut over his eye which required stitching. It appeared that they had been having a fight over the merits of their respective doctors while on night duty. One of them had said

159

that Dr Cumming would not come out when called at night. The other stoutly defended Dr Cumming and in the ensuing fight had caused the cut in his opponent's eye. Afterwards he challenged his opponent to go to Dr Cumming's house and see if he would attend to him. Dr Cumming stitched the eye and advised them to make up their quarrel.

XIV

Victoria Infirmary, Studies in Diabetes

Two appointments for junior assistant physician became vacant in 1922 at the Victoria Infirmary. The first was as junior assistant to Dr Douglas Russell. Mavor was very anxious that I would apply for it and I was anxious myself to get it. I actually interviewed Dr Russell, who said that he would like to have me, but when I contemplated the work I would have to do in addition to my large practice I turned it down.

Later in the same year another similar appointment to Dr Ivy McKenzie at the Victoria Infirmary was advertised. This time I decided that I would get an assistant. With Osborne Mavor's recommendation. Ivy McKenzie accepted me and I was appointed by the governors. This meant that I had to spend the forenoon at the hospital and my assistant would have to do morning surgery for me.

The first person offered to me as assistant was Dr Elizabeth Young. She was the daughter of an Ayrshire farmer. She said that it would suit her very well to stay at my house for five nights during the week and go home at the weekend. This suited me also as I could manage the work at the weekends myself and my mother and sister would not have a stranger in the house for the whole time. Dr Young, however, was an extremely capable and agreeable person and very soon became very much a friend of my mother and sister.

A salary of £200 a year went with my appointment as junior assistant physician. This was quite a new development. At this time the Victoria Infirmary had increased its connection with the University of Glasgow and these new junior appointments were part of an attempt to create a teaching hospital at the Victoria. Previously any medical teaching had been very limited, although Mr Parry the surgeon had a very popular clinical class in surgery on Saturday mornings which I had attended myself as a student. The chief in each ward was now appointed an honorary lecturer in medicine or surgery by the University. A meeting was held at the hospital to launch the scheme, at which Principal MacAllister of the University and Sir James MacKenzie, the general practitioner from Burnley who had revolutionised our conception of heart disease, spoke.

Medical teaching, however, has never been a great success at the Victoria, chiefly because the hospital is too far away from the University, but partly also for academic reasons, which are not of sufficient general interest to discuss here. The classes always remained small, but from the student's point of view this had many advantages. All the time I was on the staff of the Victoria, the unit to which I was attached had students each session. Sometimes there were only six or eight students, sometimes as many as twenty-four. The payment of £200 a year to the junior assistants, however, only lasted for a few years and was then discontinued due, I think, to the hospital's financial difficulties. I was later paid £25 yearly as 'cab money'. The chiefs of a unit were paid £50 yearly as 'cab money'. This was supposed to be for transport to and from the hospital.

My new chief, Dr Ivy McKenzie at the Victoria, was a very able and rather unusual person. Although he was in charge of general wards at the Victoria Infirmary, he specialised as a neurologist first, and had also charge of mental observation wards at Duke Street Hospital. McKenzie had suffered from 'infantile paralysis', now known as poliomyelitis, in infancy and had a marked limp. He had been a brilliant student at Glasgow University and had received promotion to charge of wards in the Victoria at an unusually early age.

The anatomy of the brain and the different nerve tracts in the brain is an extremely complicated study. McKenzie knew this anatomy better than any physician I ever met. The study of the brain was his chief pastime. He read it at home at night for pleasure and he employed a very able technician histologist called Boot (I forget his first name) at the Victoria Infirmary all the time he was on the staff, at his own expense. Boot was an exceptionally good technical histologist and was very faithful to McKenzie all his life. When McKenzie finally retired from the Victoria, Boot followed him to Duke Street Hospital, where McKenzie continued to work for some years.

McKenzie's routine was to go round the wards rapidly each morning. Sometimes he only stopped a moment or two at each bed, but he knew all that was going on. Robert Marshall, his senior assistant, was also a very able neurologist. He was consultant neurologist to the Glasgow Corporation and was responsible also for all the mentally defective and spastic schoolchildren, and had to decide to what extent and how they were to be educated. When they came to an unusual neurological case in the ward round, he and McKenzie might argue over it for half an hour or so. McKenzie would then go down to the laboratory to see Boot and his latest sections, and often spent an hour or more there.

This anatomical work in which McKenzie was so interested was really scientific work and only remotely connected with patients in the ward, although occasionally it had a direct relevance. McKenzie had a great many friends among famous anatomists and often spent weekends in London and Cambridge visiting them. The aim of McKenzie's research was to map out the different areas and tracts in the brain which were connected with different functions. One cannot carry out experiments on human beings and the only way to study these tracts is to study the effect which local disease of the brain has on function. This was where Ivy's study was so useful to the anatomists.

I remember one morning Sir G. Elliot Smith, a great Australian anatomist, coming to the Victoria to help McKenzie to section a brain post mortem. This patient had shown very unusual symptoms during life, and they were hoping to prove that a certain small ganglion in the brain had been affected. I remember that they took about an hour to decide how to do it. I was so fascinated that I could not leave them to get on with other work which I knew was waiting to be done. Sometimes on days like that I was called on by the sister of the wards to go round the patients again and talk to them and satisfy their questions and anxieties.

A day or two after I started work at the Victoria, McKenzie asked me if I had read Sir James MacKenzie's book on heart disease which had recently been published. I answered no, and he told me, 'Get it as soon as you can and read it.'

I did so, and although it was a difficult book to read I was tremendously interested. He had in many ways changed our whole conception of cardiac function and I had to relearn again a great deal that I had been taught as a student. Some of the cases which had originally stimulated his interest had been maternity cases suffering from mitral stenosis like the one I had come across early in my practice in Govan and have already described, who took a cerebral embolism when I was trying to do an emergency delivery. James MacKenzie had a case like that in practice who died during labour.

Ivy McKenzie had bought one of James MacKenzie's polygraphs, and I was given the job of trying to make it work. It was a very complicated instrument which took simultaneous tracings of the heart and jugular vein impulses on smoked paper. I spent a lot of time on that job and was not, I am afraid, very successful. A few years later the use of the galvanometer to take electrical tracings of the heart muscle made cardiac investigations very much easier.

⸺

One group of patients which I found at that time to be very much neglected was the diabetics. The only treatment for them was dietary. A few of the older ones did fairly well, but most often younger diabetics died in a few weeks or months. A few outpatients were attending the wards at regular intervals to have their diets adjusted and I was given charge of these. They were a pathetic group, but just about that time there was beginning to be new hope for them. In 1921 Banting and Best had isolated insulin. In January 1922 the first sample of crude insulin was given to a boy.

I learned that they were using a fairly simple method of testing blood sugar in the Physiology Department of Glasgow University and I went across one day and saw it done. The method only required a small quantity of blood which could be taken from a finger pricked with a needle. I got the necessary apparatus and was soon doing blood sugar estimations at the Elder Cottage Hospital.

The following year, 1923, the Western, Royal and Victoria Infirmaries got their first small supply of insulin simultaneously and I gave the first dose of insulin to a patient in the Victoria. The results were truly amazing. One little girl about nine years of age and weighing only two and a half stones doubled her weight to five stones in exactly a month. She is still alive and well after 48 years, is married and has a child. There are several others amongst these early patients who are still alive and well today. Insulin supplies never failed after they started, but we had to choose our patients carefully for a few months.

My outpatient group of diabetics grew rapidly, and soon I had to make special arrangements for their accommodation. Each year the British Medical Association in Glasgow chose one of the large hospitals to give a clinical demonstration. This year, 1923, it was the turn of the Victoria Infirmary to give the demonstration. Naturally they wanted a demonstration on insulin. There was an extra-large turn-out, probably about 150 medical men, because, I suppose, of the interest of the subject; and I had to give the demonstration. I did the best I could, but I was not experienced at this kind of thing and if it had not been for the great interest of the subject itself I am sure my listeners would have been very disappointed.

In Easter 1924 I told Ivy McKenzie, my chief, that I was going through to St Andrews for a week's holiday with my mother and sister. He said that he would like very much if I would take certain microscope slides through to Sir James MacKenzie who was now working at his institute at St Andrews. Ivy McKenzie and James MacKenzie were not related in any way so far as I am aware, but they were good friends.

I was very pleased to do so, especially as it gave me a chance to meet Sir James MacKenzie. I went along shortly after 9 a.m. on a Saturday morning to the institute. I did not expect to meet him so early; I thought I might be able to make arrangements to meet him later. He was already at the institute when I arrived. It appeared that he had been to London, and had just come off the London train. I was shown into his room immediately, and he rose to shake hands with me. I gave him my message and he asked about Ivy McKenzie and what he was doing. He told me that he had just come back from London where he had been seeing a patient. He said that he had made up his mind some time before that he would not do any more private work, but these people had been very insistent and had finally said that he was to come and name his own fee: it did not matter how much it was. He said that he thought the institute could do with some money, and he had wired back that his fee would be £1,000 for the St Andrew's Institute. The answer by return was, 'Come immediately'.

He then had a look at my slides and said, 'I can't give you any opinion about these, laddie, but take them to Professor Hertring [the professor of physiology at St Andrews at the time], he will be interested. Come and I will show you something I do know about.'

He took me into a small lecture room where there was a blackboard and took a human heart out of formalin solution. He told me, 'This is the heart of a man who died last week. I attended him for several years with complete heart block. It shows an old infarct which is involving the "Bundles of His".' (This is the band of muscle and nerve fibre which form the connection between the auricles and ventricles of

165

the heart and transmits the impulse which makes the ventricle beat following the auricular contraction.)

MacKenzie pointed out the small scarred area where a coronary branch artery had been blocked by a thrombosis. He then went on to the blackboard and gave me a demonstration on the heart which lasted about half an hour, answering many questions which I put to him. This subject is quite well understood now, but at that time we were only beginning to understand it. I thought it extremely kind of him to take such great trouble to explain it to me. Sir James MacKenzie died the following year from angina pectoris himself. I did not know at that time that he had been suffering from it for several years.

In 1925 Dr Young left me to get married and Dr James Anderson became my assistant in my practice. He became my full-time assistant and relieved me very greatly, because with all the hospital work I was now doing I was finding my practice a very heavy burden.

Unemployment had been very severe all through these years since the end of the first war in 1918, but in 1925 it began to get much worse again owing to a recession in shipbuilding. 1926, however, proved to be even worse, and for me it was a particularly tragic year.

The mining industry which had been controlled by the Government during the war was decontrolled in 1921. It was difficult to make a profit at that time, and I suppose that the miners' wages were progressively reduced as were most other wages. Many of the shipbuilding workers, joiners, engineers etc. had also had their wages reduced, some of them to about half what they had been during the 1914–18 war. Although the cost of living had fallen considerably, it had not fallen as much as that.

Early in 1926 the miners went on strike; I think they were threatened with further wage reductions. The strike continued, and in May the General Strike was called. This collapsed very soon, but the miners remained on strike and coal began to get very expensive. I think it went to 9 shillings or 10 shillings a bag, which was unheard of at that time.

One day when the weather began to get colder, I went in to see an old-age pensioner in whom I was interested. He was an Irishman called Savage. He had been a jobbing gardener for my father for many years, and I had known him since I was a boy. He used to give all the plants and shrubs etc. their Latin names. As far as I knew he was self educated. I knew his wife had died the previous year.

I found him sitting at the kitchen table reading the Bible in Hebrew. There was no fire in the grate and the house was very cold and he looked ill. When I said to him that he really ought to have a fire, he answered, 'How can I get a fire, Doctor, with coal at nine shillings and sixpence a bag and a pension of ten shillings a week?'

I agreed that it was not a very easy problem to solve, and when I went out I got the first coalman I saw to take him in a bag of coal and the grocer to send him some provisions.

When I went in to see him a few days later, he asked me, 'Was it you, Doctor, who sent in that bag of coal and these other things?'

I admitted that I had done it, and he replied, 'You should not have done that, Doctor. I have still got a little money, but I am keeping it for emergencies and for my old age.'

He was then probably 80 years of age, because he had been a pensioner for a number of years. He then requested, 'Would you put your hand behind that bookcase, Doctor?'

I did so, and brought out a small parcel which he opened in front of me and counted about £340 in notes. He then produced a bank-book for the local Trustees Savings Bank in Govan. There was over £700 in the book, and he asked me to take it up to the bank for him and get them to add the interest.

When I did so the banker looked at me and asked me if I knew this man. I explained what I knew of Savage, and he said, 'This is the most remarkable book we have in the bank. The account was opened on the day the bank itself was opened.' He told me the date but I cannot remember it. Almost every week since then there had been a small deposit made of a shilling or so, but no money had ever been drawn out.

When I took back the bank-book to old Savage I tried to explain to him that this was one of the emergencies for which he had been saving, and that now was the time to spend it. I tried to persuade him to put the £340 into the bank where it would be safer, but he refused to do that. He said that something might happen to the bank. He promised, however, to spend some of the money on himself.

He died the following winter in hospital, and some far-off relative in Ireland got the money which he had saved.

I have found this kind of miserly saving quite often in very decent old people, perhaps most often in women. I think it is because they have a great feeling of insecurity; some money saved gives them the sense of security they want and they do not know when to stop.

That year there was an influenza epidemic in the autumn. When these epidemics occurred, which they did several times shortly after the First War, the number of calls for visits increased astronomically. I remember one morning after surgery going in to see Dr Cumming about this time. I said, 'I am afraid there is no time for a smoke this morning, Cumming, I have probably about sixty visits on my list.'

'Sit down, Glen,' he replied, 'and have your smoke, this is the very morning you need it.' I sat down for about ten minutes.

One of the troubles during an influenza epidemic is that everybody takes it, and the doctor himself is one of the first victims. As a general rule he carries on feeling miserable for a day or two, but I think this sort of thing tends to shorten his life. Another trouble is that when you visit a house it is not one patient you see but usually at least three or four. All of them have to be carefully examined to make sure that they are not developing complications like pneumonia.

In one of these houses one day where I had multiple patients, I noticed a peculiar sweet sickly smell. I examined all the family and found nothing unusual except the usual influenza symptoms. When I got down to the foot of the close (it was one of those three-up houses), I suddenly realised that it was acetone[33] I had been smelling. One of the patients must have been an acute diabetic. I retraced my steps up the stairs to the house, and after further observation traced the acetone smell to one of the daughters, Minnie McVicar, aged 17. She was reeking of acetone and I realised that she must be a diabetic.

I took her into the Elder Cottage Hospital that afternoon. She was semi-comatose by that time and her blood sugar was 0.8%. This is an unusually high figure and I gave her an exceptionally large dose of insulin. About two hours later Miss Macdonald, the matron, telephoned me to say that she had regained consciousness for a short period but had again become unconscious and was sweating profusely. This looked extremely like hypoglycaemia (i.e. her blood sugar had

33. Acetone is produced during the breakdown of fatty acids in the liver. In diabetes this can result in ketoacidosis, a dangerously high and then often fatal accumulation of organic acid. Acetone if at high levels can be smelled on the breath of a person with diabetes.

gone much too low). This condition also causes unconsciousness and can be very puzzling at any time, but in these early days of insulin it was particularly so.

When I tested her blood sugar I found, as I suspected, that it was extremely low. We gave her large quantities of glucose by mouth and by rectum. At that time we had no prepared ampoules of sterilised glucose for intravenous injections, and I made my solutions up in those days from large jars of commercial glucose used for jam-making. An hour or so later Minnie McVicar had again gone into diabetic coma with high blood sugar.

By this time my other work was completely disorganised, but Dr Anderson, my full-time assistant, was fortunately able to take over the rest of the caseload. I spent the night at the hospital, and by morning had Minnie stabilised on small hourly doses of insulin and small quantities of glucose and milk. We found that her liver was much enlarged and she was running a high hectic temperature (i.e. a temperature with large swings from high to low). Her liver, as well as being enlarged, was very tender, and Mr Matthew Whyte who followed Mr Renton as surgeon at the Elder Hospital agreed with me that she might have a liver abscess. After watching her for about ten days he operated and found that the liver was infected by miliary tuberculosis. This had been caused by an abdominal gland infected with tuberculosis bursting into the portal vein, which takes the nourishment absorbed from the intestines into the liver.

This is a very unusual occurrence and, in fact, it is the only time I ever saw such a thing happen. That it should happen in a diabetic was another extraordinary coincidence, but it taught me a most important fact about diabetes which at that time was probably only known to a few research workers, that the liver acted as the sugar store, and was a buffer which helped to regulate the blood sugar. When the sugar in the blood got too high, it could be stored in the liver, and when it got too low it could give up its store and so prevent the blood sugar getting too low.

Rather miraculously, after her operation, Minnie McVicar gradually recovered. Her temperature gradually settled and after three months she went home and was treated for some years as an outpatient on a moderate dose of insulin. I am sorry to relate that she later developed pulmonary tuberculosis and died from this disease in a sanatorium. In these days we had no cure for tuberculosis such as we have now.

It was about this time that I decided that I would require to get some assistance in the laboratory at the Elder Hospital, especially with the biochemical tests. I knew that I could do a great deal more if I had someone who could carry on the routine technical work in my absence. I therefore advertised and got a young man from the Veterinary College in Edinburgh who was anxious to get into hospital work. He was an Aberdonian named Gordon Pirie and I worked with him for many years, both at the Elder Hospital and later at the Victoria Infirmary. I paid his salary, which was £4 a week, myself. Miss Macdonald, the matron, and I decided that if we asked the governors of the hospital officially, our request would be turned down owing to the state of the finances, so we said nothing about it.

My sister Mollie was married in the autumn of 1926. I think she hesitated for some time before she agreed to get married, no doubt because she was unwilling to leave a helpless person like myself alone with my mother, who latterly had not been too robust.

For some reason or other, I never knew why, when she was in a playful mood she used to call me 'Metaphysics'. One day she said to me, 'Metaphysics, have you never thought of looking for a wife yourself?' I said sometimes I had but I had been too busy and a bit too shy so far to do any courting. She then asked me if I had any particular person in mind. When I told her, she said that there was no one whom she would like better as a sister-in-law but she said that I had better hurry up and pay her some attention or I might be too late.

A month or two after her marriage my sister became pregnant, but she began to suffer from exceptionally severe hyperemesis or sickness of pregnancy. It became so bad that the local doctor who was looking after her called in a specialist who advised that the pregnancy should be terminated. Personally I was strongly against this procedure. I was present when the consultation took place and I argued against it strongly. There was no doubt that my sister was getting very exhausted and weak, and the fact that seemed to weigh most with the specialist was the story of my older sister, who had been very sick during her pregnancy and had gone into coma and died immediately after her child was born. I argued that she had had a very rough sea voyage just before the child was born and had been very sick as a result of that.

The specialist, however, was adamant, and as her brother I felt that my judgment might be biased and I very reluctantly consented. She was removed to a nursing home. She was given a chloroform anaesthetic and the uterus was emptied. She went into a coma shortly afterwards, and in spite of all we could do she died in twenty-four hours. I saw her die and then I had to go home and tell my mother. This was, I think, the most difficult and tragic job I have ever had to do.

For some time I had been working on post-operative sickness at the Elder Hospital. I had been acting as resident medical officer for several years at this hospital and saw all the patients before and after operation. I had been struck with the amount of post-operative vomiting which occurred. Miss Macdonald, the matron, used to say that she could recognise the patients who were liable to be sick even before their operation. When we tested their urine on admission we found that a certain percentage had a trace of acetone, and these were the patients who afterwards suffered from vomiting. They were usually intelligent and sensitive patients who were apprehensive about coming into hospital.

I saw several cases of what was called then delayed chloroform poisoning. The patient continued to be sick and unable to take food after the operation. They became slightly jaundiced. Urine secretion diminished until there was only a trickle of thick syrupy urine and then the patient died.

The liver is the chemical laboratory of the body and there was no doubt in my mind that in those cases it was overwhelmed by the amount of waste products and poisons it had to deal with, and that chloroform was the chief sinner. It seemed to be particularly harmful when the patient had a tendency to nausea and sickness, e.g. in gall-bladder cases and, of course, in hyperemesis[34] of pregnancy. Strangely enough, in normal confinements when the patient practically never suffers from sickness and vomiting, it was well tolerated.

I knew that James Hendry, who had been at the University when I was there but was several years senior to me, had done several years as an assistant in the physiology and biochemistry department and had now started practice as a gynaecologist, was interested in this subject

34. Excessive vomiting.

and I went to see him after my sister's death. He agreed almost entirely with my views on the subject. James Hendry was afterwards Professor of Midwifery and Obstetrics in Glasgow University.

———

My sister died in December 1926, and so ended a tragic year for me and for a great many other people. As I have said, it was the year of the General Strike and the miners' strike which lasted about nine months.

XV
Marriage, Hospital and General Practice Continued

I was married in October of the following year, 1927, to Elizabeth Wallace Agnew. I had known her since we played as children together. Her father, who had a brilliant career as a shipbuilder, had died when comparatively young and my father had been one of her mother's trustees. She has been a wonderful wife and helpmate and companion to me throughout the years. A doctor's wife has a great many extra duties to perform which I do not think are fully appreciated. The doctor's home is his office. His wife has to act as his secretary and keep notes and remember innumerable messages. She has to put up with irregular meal hours and all sorts of frustrations too numerous to mention. Besides nourishing and sustaining me, my wife has looked after all these things and has looked after the social side of our life and kept an open house for friends as well as patients.

We went on our honeymoon to the French Riviera for three weeks. We had intended to stay in London for a few days on our way home, but the morning after we arrived there my assistant telephoned me to say that my mother had taken suddenly ill during the night and had become unconscious. We travelled home that day. She was deeply unconscious when we got home and died the same evening. She had failed greatly after my sister's death and complained frequently of severe headaches. I think that she had a cerebral aneurism which had ruptured, causing a cerebral haemorrhage.

My mother had a very sympathetic nature and the patients who lived near my house in Govan had soon got to know that. They used to come to the door for all sorts of advice. She would advise poultices and castor oil, and promise that she would see that I came along immediately. She rather surprised one day when a caller asked for a 'wee drop of whisky' for someone who had fainted. She gave him an unopened bottle of whisky, but the bottle was never returned.

Another day a man called and said that Dr Glen had told him to call at the house and get a pair of boots. I wore shoes at that time and my mother gave him the only pair of boots I had, old army boots which I was very sorry to lose. There were many incidents like that, and my sister and I got a lot of fun out of them, but my mother continued to be very easily deceived.

She did not sleep well latterly and when I got a night call she always used to get up and make me a cup of tea. I remonstrated with her for doing this, and one day I told her, 'If you do that again, mother, I will not take the tea.' The same thing happened a few days later and I will never forget the look she gave me when I said that I could not take the tea. I realised afterwards that it was very wrong of me, because I think she slept very badly and it was a relief to her to get up and have a cup of tea herself. After that I frequently took her a cup of tea myself when I came back from a night call.

My mother was extremely fond of motoring. In these early days the motor car was a revelation. Most of us had really never seen Scotland before except from the windows of a railway carriage. Before I was married, my mother and sister and I travelled widely in Scotland. One year we went to Lossiemouth in Morayshire for a holiday. We started early in the morning and went by Callander, Loch Earnhead and Loch Tay. The roads were narrow and the surfaces were rough and the tyres at that time were very poor. By the time we got to Pitlochry I had had three punctures which I had mended on the road. I got a new tyre and inner tube there.

The question was, should we attempt to cross the Grampians that day? It was a bit of an adventure, but we started off. The weather was good. The road to Inverness at that time was a winding single-track road with narrow hump-backed bridges. One can see some of these old bridges and traces of the old road today. We made Kingussie that night and reached Lossiemouth the following day.

Another time we went to London, staying at the English Lakes, Stratford-on-Avon and Oxford on the way, and came back by the East Coast, stopping for the night three or four times. The Great North Road at that time was a pleasant country road, and in many places single-track also.

My sister learned to drive a car very shortly after I got my first car, and used to drive me round my practice in Govan. It was almost a necessity to have someone in charge of a car at that time. Cars were rarities and an extreme object of curiosity to the children. If the car was left alone, they would climb on top of it, scratch letters on the paint, loosen the tyre-valves and let the tyres down.

When I left the car outside my own door the same things used to happen. One day I warned some children that I would chloroform the next one I caught interfering with the car. Sure enough I caught a boy a few days later standing on top of the bonnet. I said 'I am going to chloroform you this time,' and carried him into the house screaming at the pitch of his voice.

My mother quickly arrived on the scene and asked, 'What on earth are you doing to the boy, Alick?'

'I am going to chloroform him,' I replied. 'I caught him on top of my car.'

My mother responded, 'I am sure he won't do it again, if you let him off this time.'

So I restored him to the crowd of anxious youngsters at the door. Things were much better after that, at least in front of the house. The children frequently stood in a row looking at the car but did not touch it. When I got into the car I sometimes overheard them saying, 'You had better not touch Dr Glen's car or he'll "chloroform" you.' I don't think they knew what chloroform meant, except that it was something dreadful.

Children are extraordinarily sensitive to what other people are thinking. I would just be thinking that something they said was funny. I was not aware of showing it on my face, when they would simultaneously burst out laughing and often I had to laugh also.

Some years later I got an Austin 7 H.P. car. It was the first very small car that had been built, and it was very tiny, although it was an excellent car. One day a small boy said to me, 'Hey, Doctor, is that car a sample?' Another time one small girl solemnly explained to another in my hearing, 'That's Dr Glen's baby Austin; he keeps the babies under the back seat.' I meant to send that one to *Punch* at the time, but never got round to it.

———

During the next few years I became very interested in diabetes. I soon began to notice that there were different kinds of diabetes, and that although insulin helped all my patients, some, like Minnie McVicar whose story I have already told, were much more acute and reacted differently. I began to think that in young people it was not so much deficiency of insulin in their body, as something else which was neutralising the insulin which the islets in the pancreas was producing, and so more insulin was required to balance the metabolism.

These ideas started me on a trail of research work which kept me occupied in my spare time for many years. I now had the help of a first class laboratory technician in Gordon Pirie at the Elder Cottage Hospital. I bought a second-hand microtome (i.e. an instrument for cutting very fine sections of preserved body tissues) and began to study the histology of all the endocrine glands, especially the pituitary, the thyroid, the pancreas and the adrenals. These glands deteriorate very quickly after death as they are digested by their own secretions; one must therefore perform the post-mortem examination and fix these tissues as soon as possible after death.

I was able to get permission to do this on several occasions at the Elder Hospital within an hour or two after death while the bodies were still warm, and I was able to produce some very fine microscopic slides, particularly of the pancreas and pituitary. Dr Anderson, pathologist at the Victoria Infirmary, who examined them with me and helped me very greatly in this work, said that they were the best he had seen up till that time.

The histology of the endocrine glands had never been very carefully studied and there was a very poor literature on the subject. Owing to the discovery of insulin, however, more interest was beginning to be shown, and I was able to get hold of some new microscopic stains which showed up the structure of the glands much more clearly. This was particularly true of the pituitary gland, and we had some good specimens which differentiated the three different types of cell in the pituitary very clearly and in a way which Dr Anderson said that he had never seen before.

Anderson himself was rather a remarkable character and very much of an individualist. He had a high-pitched squeaky voice and when not in his presence the staff of the Victoria usually referred to him as 'Squeaky'. This did not mean any disrespect, because we all respected him very much. He never was very strong and suffered a good deal from various physical ailments, chiefly bronchitis. He always insisted on doing all the hospital post-mortems himself. For obvious reasons the mortuary is never heated and in wintertime it was like an icehouse. In his latter years I used to think it was a pathetic sight to see him on a winter's day struggling with the aid of his mortuary assistant to perform several post-mortems. He often looked far from well himself, with a bad cough and a drip at his nose.

When we went into the mortuary, usually with a few students and assistants, he would say in his high-pitched, squeaky voice, 'What do you expect me to find today, Dr Glen?' It used to give him great pleasure when he found our clinical diagnosis was wrong; I think he felt then that he was being of some use.

When he retired eventually and became more or less bed-ridden I was his doctor, and he proved to be a very good patient. His wife told me a story about him which I remember. She said that they were at one of the orchestral concerts in Glasgow's St Andrew's Hall when he turned to her and said, 'How many people do you think will be in this hall tonight?' She replied that she thought there might be about 2,000. He then observed, 'I suppose I will have done at least double that number of post-mortem examinations.'

———

One day in these earlier years when I was studying the histology of the endocrine glands, he had done a post-mortem on quite a young man who had died very suddenly on the golf course. He found at the post-mortem that death had been due to a cerebral haemorrhage caused by the rupture of one of the cerebral arteries. As I was studying the appearance of normal endocrine glands at that time, he gave me the endocrine glands from this post-mortem to study.

A few weeks later when the microscopic section had been prepared and I had found time to study them I discovered a small cluster of unusual cells in the middle of the thyroid gland about the size of a lentil. Although the cells had some resemblance to thyroid cells they seemed very different in some ways. When I pointed out these cells to Dr Anderson he suddenly got excited. 'Where did you get that thyroid gland, Glen?'

'You gave it to me as a normal thyroid, sir,' I replied.

'What's the patient's name? When did I give it to you?'

I gave him the particulars and he said, 'I've still got his brain.'

He went down on all fours under a bench, and from a number of porcelain pots, some of which I knew had lain there for years, produced a pot which contained a brain preserved in formalin and proceeded to explain it to me. 'This fellow's cerebral haemorrhage was in rather an unusual place, but I thought it must have been due to a small aneurism although I could not see one. I kept the brain to have it sectioned, but I have been too busy and had no time to do it. There is no doubt that it is a primary carcinoma that you saw in his thyroid, and that he died because a tiny secondary tumour in the wall of his cerebral artery caused the rupture of the vessel.' When he later examined his sections he found this to be true.

—

Osborne Mavor started practice in Langside early in 1920 about the same time as I started in Govan. I visited him frequently during 1920 and got to know his mother, who was keeping house for him in a house at Langside Drive which Osborne had taken over from Dr Douglas Russell along with his practice. Mrs Mavor was a very kind and hospitable person, and one felt after meeting her once or twice that one had known her for a very long time.

After I joined the staff of the Victoria, however, in 1921, I saw much more of him. Mavor entered into his medical work with enthusiasm. In addition to his general practice and his Victoria appointment he became a dispensing physician at the Sick Children's Hospital. He took part in a psychotherapy unit for shell-shocked ex-soldiers which he called the 'bogey-bogey' clinic. Some of these mentally disordered soldiers took a long time to recover after the First World War. We treated these cases much more efficiently and with more understanding during the Second World War and they did not take so long to recover.

In 1921 Mavor became a fellow of the Faculty of Physicians and Surgeons of Glasgow. About this time also he published his first book, *Some Talk of Alexander*. The title of the book is taken from the old song 'The British Grenadiers', and it was the story of our adventures in Persia and Russia. He compared our journeys and adventures there with those of Alexander the Great. Every chapter begins with a stanza of poetry, but to me the whole book reads like poetry. He did not make any money out of it but I have always been very proud of the fact that he dedicated it to me.

Mavor went on drawing caricatures of his patients or anyone he fancied, and it naturally followed that he began to draw his people in words; thus he wrote his first play, 'The Switchback'. He showed it to one of the authorities on drama in Glasgow at that time, Alfred

Wareing. He said it was clever but not suitable for production. Osborne put it away in a drawer. It was to appear again later.

We did not have very many holidays at that time, but I remember spending one weekend with 'Muckle' McCall Smith at Lochgilphead, where he had gone into practice. I drove my car down and Mavor sang opera in Russian practically the whole way without stopping. He had a fine voice.

McCall Smith had met his wife at Amara when she was nursing in Mesopotamia. After the war in 1920 he went back to Persia with his wife and started medical practice. Things were very disturbed there at that time, and in 1921 during a local revolution he had to flee with his wife and newly born son in very difficult circumstances.

Following this, in 1921 he started practice at Lochgilphead. Six months after his arrival there he woke up one morning after returning from a confinement case and found both his legs paralysed. He spent a good part of the next year on his back and some of the time he spent in the Victoria Infirmary. He then went back to Lochgilphead and continued practice there with callipers on both legs, and managed amazingly well considering his disability. In 1929 he was appointed Superintendent at the Victoria Infirmary so that our ways crossed again.

Mavor and I joined the Southern Medical Society in 1920. This was an interesting old society and I think that the whole set-up appealed to Mavor. The Society had been founded in 1844 by five local doctors in the south side of Glasgow. The first meeting was held on the banks of the old Paisley and Glasgow canal, and attended by five practitioners, one of whom had apparently got into some kind of trouble and the meeting was held to see if anything could be done to help him. They decided there and then to form a society, and meetings of the Society have been held regularly since that time. A remarkable fact is that all the minute books of the Society are still complete and are kept for safety in the Victoria Infirmary.

At the time Mavor and I joined the Society it occupied rooms in Carlton Place on the south bank of the Clyde. The rooms were used as a club, and alcoholic and other refreshments could be had. Some of the members used to meet in the evenings and play cards. A clinical meeting, which was always well attended, was held once a fortnight in a large kitchen in the basement of the house, which had an old fashioned fireplace. There was always a good fire and a kettle on the hob, and some of the older members used to sit near the fire and make toddy.

The Society, however, about this time had run into debt and some of the more responsible members had decided that the club had to be closed. There was great opposition to this suggestion, naturally. Mavor was secretary of the Society at the time, and largely through his influence it was arranged that although the club would be closed the Society would be able to continue its clinical meetings at the Victoria Infirmary. I was treasurer of the Society at this period and was very much in favour of this arrangement. It was the Southern Medical Society which had originally campaigned for the establishment of a general hospital on the south side of Glasgow and called the first meeting of local people who were interested, so that perhaps in this way the Victoria Infirmary was repaying a debt to the old society. The arrangement to meet in the hospital was a good one from any standpoint. It brought the local practioners more into contact with the hospital physicians and surgeons and the society has prospered greatly in consequence.

In 1923 Osborne Mavor married Rona Bremner. He gave up general practice and moved to the west end of Glasgow. He was appointed to Stobhill as physician under Glasgow Corporation. There he had large wards under his care and I know that he enjoyed that work. It also helped him financially, because he was paid a salary. In 1927 he became Professor of Medicine at Anderson College. About this time also (during 1927) he graduated M.D. of Glasgow University with commendation. Although he had all these other appointments, Mavor remained on the staff of the Victoria Infirmary as an assistant physician. This is not a bad record, and yet there were some people who could never quite believe that O.H. Mavor the dramatist was a good doctor. Any interview with Mavor was an experience, and perhaps in a medical consultation with him there was so much of interest besides the medical advice that the medical advice was apt to take second place.

XVI

Retirement from General Practice

About this time – I forget the year exactly – I decided that I would put myself forward, as Mavor had done, as a candidate for the Fellowship of the Faculty of Physicians and Surgeons of Glasgow. This is a very ancient body. It was formed in the year 1599 by a charter of King James VI of Scotland in favour of Maister Peter Lowe, Surgeon, and Robert Hamilton, Professor of Medicine, conferring on them and their successors power to exercise jurisdiction over all the practitioners in the city and surrounding country. The Faculty has a long and interesting history, but for a long time apart from its very valuable library and other facilities it has only concerned itself with the granting of higher medical and surgical degrees. It is now the Royal College of Physicians and Surgeons of Glasgow.

The examination in my time for the Fellowship in Medicine consisted of an oral and clinical examination in the forenoon, followed by a written paper in the afternoon. I did a good deal of general medical reading in preparation and made a special study of the central nervous system, because I had always felt, in company with Ivy McKenzie and Robert Marshall, who were experts in this subject, that my knowledge of the anatomy of the central nervous system was deficient. I got a preserved brain from Dr Anderson the pathologist and dissected it carefully in association with my textbook studies.

I did not tell McKenzie or Marshall that I was sitting the examination. I was examined at the Western Infirmary by Dr Barclay Ness of the Western and Dr John Henderson of the Royal Infirmary. I was the only candidate that day. They first took me into a side-room and asked me a great many questions about the work I was doing and where I had been educated etc. I told them that I was in general practice in Govan and was assistant to Ivy McKenzie at the Victoria. I thought that they did not seem very impressed. They then took me to a case of thoracic aneurism and said they would leave me for a short time to write a few notes on the case. After about half an hour they came and questioned me about what I had found. I had experienced no difficulty and I think my findings were probably reasonably correct.

They then asked me to look at a child in the same ward. The child screamed as soon as I took the bedclothes down to examine it and continued to scream, disturbing the whole ward. It was quite obvious from a very superficial examination that it was a congenitally defective child with very marked mental defect. There appeared to be also some defective limb development. I did not continue my examination but sat down and waited for my examiners. When they came along shortly afterwards they asked me what my diagnosis was. I said that it was a congenitally defective child, probably a cerebral diplegia, but that the mental changes appeared to be very marked. They then asked me if I knew the name usually given to this disease. I said that I could not remember the name. One of them then asked if I had ever heard of Little's Disease. I said that I had forgotten the name and that this would probably be described as a case of Little's Disease. They then asked me if I knew the cause of the disease. I said that I did not know the cause. I was then asked if I had ever heard that injury at birth was a likely cause. I said that I was quite sure that this had nothing to do with the cause of the disease.[35] I was then told that my clinical examination was finished.

I could have told them a good deal more about the disease if I had been given the opportunity. I had seen many of these cases in Ivy McKenzie's wards. Robert Marshall was particularly interested in them, because he had charge of the defective children in the Glasgow schools. I had never heard McKenzie or Marshall refer to the condition as Little's Disease but we had often discussed the possible cause of the condition. I brought up a child to hospital one day to let McKenzie and Marshall see him: I had delivered him with forceps through a contracted pelvis. He had a large depression in his fronto-parietal region, like an inverted saucer, but he was a perfectly normal child despite this.

I remembered also being annoyed when I sent a spastic child whose birth I had attended over to the Sick Children's Hospital for a consultation. One of the first questions the doctor asked the mother

35. Little's Disease is now known to be a congenital defect of brain development with a recognised biochemical basis – i.e. not the result of birth injury caused, for example, by a forceps delivery.

was, 'Was it a normal birth or was the child delivered with forceps?' The mother replied that it was a forceps delivery. Naturally, I am sure she always felt afterwards that I was probably responsible for her child's spasticity.

When I reported at the Faculty in the afternoon I was told that there was no need for me to sit a written paper, as I had failed in my oral examination.

When I told Ivy McKenzie the following day of my experience he seemed to be very amused and laughed quite loudly at first. Later, however, he said that I had been unfortunate and should try again when there might be different examiners. I never did try again, however. I could not raise enough interest to do so.

In an unguarded moment Mavor once told my wife that I was very stubborn. When she wishes to get her own way she sometimes reminds me of what Mavor said. Mavor had a very extraordinary understanding of human nature and I expect that in my case he was correct as usual. I think in the case of the Fellowship examination I was wrong not to try again, but I think I have more often been stubborn when I was right.

In 1931 my brother-in-law James Agnew joined me in the Govan practice. Before the war he had spent several years as an apprentice in shipbuilding, following his father's footsteps. He survived the war and continued his studies as a shipbuilder. He qualified as a ship-builder's manager after a year and immediately afterwards entered Glasgow University to study medicine. He said that during the war he had changed his mind about his future work. He passed through the medical course very easily and among other distinctions he was President of the Student Union. He joined me in 1931 and went into my house in Govan. I moved to a house in Dumbreck very near to the house where I was born. It was convenient for my work in Govan and also for my hospital work. By this time my oldest son was about two years of age. In 1971 I still occupy this house in Dumbreck on the south side of Glasgow.

I continued to be very busy and worked long hours. I tried to share the work of the practice, day as well as night, as equally as possible with my partner. As I was at hospital every forenoon, this meant that I worked late at night. I was beginning to get the reputation of having special knowledge about diabetes, and doctors in the south side of Glasgow began to send private patients to me occasionally for my opinion and advice. In these days the consultants in Glasgow lived in a particular area in the West End of Glasgow, and it was very unusual for a general practitioner like myself to carry on a consulting practice from Govan. It was out of the question for me to move to the West End. Although diabetics require a lot of medical attention, there are not really very many of them, and I was almost entirely dependent for my living on my general practice in Govan. I compromised by taking consulting rooms in the West End and was one of the first junior consultants to do this, although it is now the common practice for all Glasgow consultants. At this time they actually lived there. I went to my rooms at first two or three afternoons a week or when I had a patient to see. Mrs Pirie, the mother of my technical assistant at the Elder Hospital, came when required and helped me. I did blood sugar examinations and biochemical work, which was sometimes very time-consuming.

Early in 1933 we had an influenza epidemic, and Ivy McKenzie, who usually kept very fit, went down with it badly. He developed a pneumonia and became seriously ill. I was called to look after him. Pneumonia at that time was still a deadly disease. We had no sulphonamides or antibiotics, which shortly afterwards transformed the whole character of the disease. At that time the best recognised treatment was the injection of anti-pneumonoccic serum intravenously at eight-hourly intervals night and day. Dr McKenzie remained at home and had day and night nurses. This treatment meant that one of these injections had to be given in the early hours of the morning, about 2 or 3 a.m.

After about a week he turned the corner but his temperature continued to be irregular and he later developed the complication of empyema and was off duty for over four months.

A few weeks after Ivy McKenzie took ill, Robert Marshall suffered a cerebral haemorrhage and was never able again to undertake his professional work. This left me with complete charge of the unit at the Victoria. There were about twenty medical students that year, an unusually large number for us. In addition to this work at the Victoria I had my practice in Govan, the Elder Cottage Hospital and my private consulting practice, which increased considerably owing to the illness of my two senior colleagues. How I got through the next few months I do not remember, but I could not have done it without the generous help of my partner in the practice in Govan, James Agnew.

I knew very well that I had been doing too much, and when Ivy McKenzie came back to duty in the spring, I began to consider seriously what I was going to do about it. The senior physician at the Elder Cottage Hospital had died, and I had been appointed physician to this hospital in his place. I had medical beds there under my own care, and with the help of Gordon Pirie, my technical assistant, I was developing quite a useful laboratory there of the kind which suited the work in which I was most interested. I could not see any hope in the near future of being able to give up my Govan work which was the main source of my livelihood. I was too junior in the Victoria to be able to make a living as a whole time consultant, and there did not seem to be any likelihood of promotion to physician in charge of wards there for a very long time. I decided that I would have to give up my work at the Victoria.

I remember very clearly the circumstances when I finally decided to send in my resignation to the Victoria Infirmary. I was sitting in a patient's house at a confinement in the early hours of the morning. The patient was a young woman, a *primipara*.[36] She belonged to a family which I had attended since I had first come to Govan thirteen years before. Things were going slowly. The patient's mother and the midwife were in the kitchen with the patient. I myself was in the sitting-room at a comfortable fire. I had sent the young father off to his bed, as he had to be up at 6 a.m. I remembered the advice that my first chief William MacLennan had given me when I was resident in the Western Infirmary. He had said to me, 'Don't be a consultant. It is a terribly hard, competitive life. I see very little of my family. I would have been much happier, I am sure, in general practice'. That was his advice to me when I told him I wanted to be a medical consultant. Perhaps I thought also that night about Sir James Mackenzie, who had done most of his best work on the heart when he was in general practice. I was in some ways in a better position than he was. I was physician to the small local hospital and had opportunities for doing useful work there. Besides, I liked working among people whom I knew well. As a consultant I would only see patients once or twice. I would never get to know them well and would have no opportunity to study their illnesses over prolonged

36. A woman giving birth for the first time.

185

periods. By the time the baby was ready to be born I had made up my mind.

The next day I wrote my resignation from the Victoria and handed it to Dr Otto MacGregor, the superintendent. Dr MacGregor was quite a character. In those days he was responsible for the radiology of the hospital as well as being superintendent. When he had read my letter, he said, 'Do you really mean this, Glen?'

I answered, 'Yes, I have given the matter quite a lot of consideration. The reason is quite simple. I am very happy in my work here. I haven't quarrelled with anyone. I find that I have not time to carry on my general practice and work at the Elder Cottage Hospital and spend all forenoon at the Victoria also.'

He replied that he would be very sorry if I had to give up my work at the hospital, but said that he would put my letter before the governors of the hospital at their next meeting.

About a week later I received a telephone message from Dr John Cowan, who was convenor of the medical committee, to come over and see him in the evening. Dr Cowan was one of the senior physicians at that time in the Glasgow Royal Infirmary, and was very much respected by all his colleagues. He had made a special study of diseases of the heart. He had a very precise way of speaking and he gave one the impression that everything he said was the final word on that subject. I believe that when he served in an army hospital in the first war he was called 'Lord John' because of this mannerism. I had taken his class as a student and he was the medical convenor of the Elder Cottage Hospital as well as the Victoria, so he knew me well. In spite of his lordly manner he was really a very simple and sincere man. I remember one night when I had taken my young sons to the local circus seeing him in the gallery enjoying himself in the cheapest seat among the poorer section of the audience.

He got me to tell him all that I had been doing since I qualified in medicine. He wanted to know if I had made a special study of any subject, and if I had ever written or published anything. I replied that I had never published anything, but that I had a lot of notes, especially about diabetes and my study of the endocrine glands. He said he wanted to see my notes, and the following day I handed in to his house quite a parcel of them, including histological descriptions of a great many endocrine glands in diabetic cases. A few days later he asked me to come again to see him.

As soon as we sat down, he said, in his lordly manner without any preliminaries, 'You will retire, Glen, from your general practice in Govan. You will start a proper diabetic clinic at the Victoria Infirmary, and you will get a permanent nursing sister to take charge of this clinic. The hospital requires a biochemist and you will be appointed part-time biochemist to the hospital with a salary of £200 a year. You will bring your technical assistant Gordon Pirie from the Elder Hospital to assist you with your biochemistry.' That was all he said and he waited for my answer.

'Thank you very much, Sir,' I replied, 'for the consideration you have given to my position. Your offer is very tempting to me, but at the present moment I cannot see how I could accept it. I would like a week or so to think it over and will let you know my decision later.' He agreed to that.

When I told my wife about the proposal, she said that she was agreeable to anything which I wanted to do. My chief trouble was finance. At that time my consulting practice at Woodside Terrace was doing little more than pay its way after paying the rent etc, so that at first I would have little more than my £200 a year as biochemist as my professional income. I had a little capital which might last me for two to three years if I had to be wholly dependent on it, and my wife had about the same amount. We decided to accept the offer. My partner and brother-in-law, James Agnew, took over the practice. We continued to live in the same house in the South Side, which, as I have said, was rather an unusual thing for a consultant in Glasgow to do at that time. As it turned out my consulting practice did remarkably well. I earned £700 in my first year and the following year I was able to pay my way.

In the following year I wrote up my study of diabetes, particularly with reference to its effect on the different endocrine glands. I titled the paper 'Diabetes Mellitus: A Broader Basis of Interpretation'. It was turned down by the *British Medical Journal* and the *Lancet* but was published by the *Glasgow Medical Journal* in 1934. I was, of course, rather before my time, and the histological method was the most difficult method I could have chosen to prove my thesis. In fact, very little progress has been made in our knowledge of the histology of these glands. It is now recognised, however, and has been proved by biochemical methods, that insulin antagonism plays a large part in the causation of diabetes, especially in younger subjects.

The biochemical work in the Victoria Infirmary began to increase very rapidly. It is very time-consuming work, and I soon realised that it was really a full-time job. Professor Carl Browning, who was now the convenor of the Medical Committee in the Victoria, suggested that I could take on this job myself. I knew, however, that my knowledge of chemistry was not good enough to cope with biochemistry in medicine, which at this time was advancing very rapidly. My own idea was that the biochemist did not require to be a medical man, and that the combination of a pure scientist with a physician might be the best answer to the problem.

I went to London and interviewed the biochemists to the large hospitals there. Most of them were fully-qualified medical men but many of them agreed with me that an honours science graduate could do the work very competently, and would get on well with the medical staff. The governors of the Victoria Infirmary, however, turned down my idea, and in 1935 Dr James Eaton was appointed biochemist to the hospital. Dr Eaton had been six years as a full-time chemist with Imperial Chemical Industries before he started medicine.

—

In 1933, the year I gave up general practice, Douglas Russell had retired from the Victoria and Osborne Mavor had been appointed in his place as senior physician in charge of medical wards. In 1937, Ivy McKenzie was also due to retire. I decided to apply for the vacancy as a senior physician to the hospital. I felt I was entitled to do so because, although the only other applicant, Angus Scott, was a year senior to me in service to the hospital, I was a year older than he was and had been doing consulting practice for three years while Angus was still in general practice.

A few days before the governors of the hospital were due to make the appointment, Dr McCall Smith, the superintendent of the hospital approached me and suggested that I should withdraw my application for the appointment. He added that he was speaking also for several other members of the staff. He said that if I did so I would be assistant to Osborne Mavor and be in the same unit. He went on to say that he knew that we would be very happy working together and that it would really made no difference to me, because Mavor was not doing any private consulting practice. His spare time was now fully occupied with his dramatic work.

I was rather taken aback. I answered that of course there was nothing I would like better than to work with Osborne, but I was looking forward to the possibility that we might both be senior visiting physicians to the hospital. I ended by saying that I would give him my decision the following morning.

That night I pondered for a long time what I should do. I knew that Mavor was now being recognised as one of Scotland's greatest dramatists, as those of us who knew him well knew that sooner or later he would be. He was producing two or three plays every year, and great plays like *The Anatomist* and *The Sleeping Clergyman* seemed to come very easily from his pen. A hospital ward is full of human situations: anxiety, tragedy, hope and even comedy are its daily fare. Contact with real people was Osborne's main inspiration. I could relieve him of a lot of the routine and he could get on with the great work he was doing. Personally I knew that I would never grudge him that help, but other people might criticise him and in the end it might not be good for either of us. I decided that I would not withdraw my application.

If I had known the result of that decision I am sure that I would not have made it. When I told 'Muckle' in the morning, he appeared to be terribly disappointed. So much so, in fact, that I did not understand his reaction. I was soon to know, however. When I was leaving the hospital that morning, he told me that Mavor was resigning from the hospital to make way for both Angus Scott and myself.

It appeared that Mavor had previously indicated that he wished to resign, but had been persuaded by several members of the staff to let this proposal be made to me. When he was told of my decision he laughed loudly and said that he knew that I would turn it down, that was why he let them try it. I was very distressed, however, and Mavor apologised for playing the trick on me. He said that he had made up his mind that he was going to resign. A number of the staff were trying very hard to prevent him, so he thought that he would let me make the decision for them.

Of course we were all terribly sorry to lose Osborne Mavor as one of our colleagues. Was it wise that he should have retired from his medical work at this time? I have often thought about that, and I am still not sure. It is true that he had been living an extraordinarily busy life. Only someone who was very fit physically could have done what he was doing, and it was no doubt wise that he should take things easier. Mavor's play-writing, however, was only a part of his life. He was also an artist, a physician and a man of action. He would never have been the great dramatist that he was if he had sat at his desk all his life in the country making up imaginary plays about imaginary people. Mavor's plays were about real people. His characters were all people whom he had met and spoken to in real life. It was the people themselves who were important, not what happened to them. Some of his critics said that he did not write proper plays and that he did not finish them. Mavor's answer was, 'Only God can write last acts, and he seldom does.'

Mavor now retired from all his medical appointments and moved out to Drymen, where he lived among beautiful surroundings. He had a secretary. His output of plays and books continued high, but not any higher, I believe, than during his medical career. So far as possible I have noted the dates of his publications, and they work out as follows. From 1928 till the time of his retirement in 1937, nine years, he wrote 16 plays and one book. From 1937 till his death in 1951, fourteen years, he wrote 27 plays and 11 books. I have no doubt, however, that a quieter life was better for him in many ways, and that he could not have continued as he was doing for very much longer.

'Muckle' and I did not see much of Mavor now. We occasionally met him for lunch at the Art Club, where he was a great favourite among all the members. The other place where we met him was at the Baku Club Dinner. Mavor himself was responsible for starting the club and he was the self-appointed secretary. The meeting was held once yearly and in a different town in Scotland each year.[37] We arranged always to stay the night in the hotel where the dinner was held. All the officers of the field ambulance who were at Baku attended regularly. Occasionally we had guests like Walter Elliot and Eric Linklater, who had been at Baku at some time or other. We tried to recapture the spirit of Baku. We started off with vodka and caviare. The dinner progressed very slowly, as Russian dinners always do, interspersed with songs and dances. Drummie would sing 'The

37. Copies of the minutes of the first seven years of Baku Club meetings initiated in 1932 are now in the Glasgow University Library Special Collections, reference Scottish Theatre Archives 724. These are light-hearted minutes of meetings intended to recapture the spirit of Baku by those who were there in 1919. They were summed up by a reporter from a local paper who described them as 'Just meetings amongst yourselves'.

Drook from Astrakan', Tomory would dance the Lesginka, and the Deacon and Johnnie Murray the dentist supplied the comedy.

Later on some of the villagers and local people were often asked to come. Sometimes the local press came to make a report about the meeting, but no one ever understood what it was all about. These dinners continued except for the years of the Second War up till the time of Osborne's death. Mavor as secretary kept the minute book of the meetings, and Ronald Mavor, his son, now has this minute book.

XVII
Second World War

Although I have confined myself to a description of my medical experiences since I returned from the First World War in 1919, many things had been happening, particularly in the 1930s, which made one fear the possibility of the recurrence of war with Germany.

Adolf Hitler had been appointed Chancellor of Germany in January 1933. A month later the Reichstag was destroyed by fire. This was the year in which I retired from general practice. In 1934 Hitler murdered five or seven thousand of his political opponents. Concentration camps were already in being in Germany. To quote from Vol. I of Churchill's *Second World War*:

> Adolf Hitler had at last arrived; but he was not alone. He had called from the depths of defeat the dark and savage furies latent in the most numerous, most serviceable, ruthless, contradictory and ill-starred race in Europe. He had conjured up the fearful idol of an all-devouring Moloch of which he was the priest and incarnation. It is not within my scope to describe the inconceivable brutality and villainy by which this apparatus of hatred and tyranny had been fashioned and was now to be perfected. It is necessary for the purpose of this account only to present to the reader the most fearful fact which had broken upon the still-unwitting world: GERMANY UNDER HITLER, AND GERMANY ARMING.

After 1934 something terrible seemed to happen every few months. Italy attacks Abyssinia . . . Dr Dolphus is murdered . . . Hitler leaves the League of Nations . . . Hitler occupies the Rhineland . . . Civil war in Spain . . . The rape of Austria . . . Munich and the annexation of Czechoslovakia . . . The attack on Poland and the Second World War.

It was remarkable how slow the British people were to realise the truth. This was particularly true of the younger people. In 1933 the

Oxford students declared by a large majority, 'This House refuses to fight for King and Country.' I was astonished at the attitude of some of my junior assistants in hospital for a good many years after 1933. 'We could do with a Hitler to set our own country in order . . . Mussolini could at least get the trains to run to time,' were common remarks. Gradually, however, towards the end of the 1930s, they began to understand, and it is fair to say that my own assistants were among the first to volunteer for service when the war did come.

Hitler wrote *Mein Kampf* when he was imprisoned in a fortress after staging a revolt against the Bavarian Government in 1923. National Socialism, as he called his creed (later to be known as Nazism), was an ill-digested compilation of fragments of the old ideas of the German philosophers of the First World War. It contained all the worst ideas of that philosophy, such as, Man is a fighting animal; a country which ceases to fight for itself is doomed; the fighting capacity of the race depends on its purity, therefore it is necessary to get rid of all foreign defilements such as Jews, who are a universal race and therefore pacifist; pacifism is the deadliest sin because it means the surrender of the race in its fight for its existence; intelligence in case of the individual is not of the first importance, will and determination are the prime qualities; only brute force can ensure the survival of the race, hence the necessity of military organisation.

Mein Kampf was not published in full in this country until 1939, and we were only able to read occasional extracts from it until then. In fact there seems almost to have been an attempt to conceal the true facts from the British people and to present National Socialism as an admirable and efficient kind of political creed. The German people must have known better than anyone else the real truth. Hitler, of course, was a deliberate liar. He was always protesting that he was a man of peace. To a considerable extent he deceived the German people, but they must have liked his ideas and been very willing to be deceived, because they gave him steadily increasing support at elections, so that by 1932 he had a majority in the Reichstag and became Chancellor. From 1933 Hitler's party became the only legal party in Germany, and complete dictatorship was established.

This is not the place to recount the history of these years, but I will never forget the days of Munich when poor Neville Chamberlain was so deceived by the despicable liar, Hitler. I listened on my radio set and heard Chamberlain speak from the door of 10 Downing Street, waving a scrap of paper which he said meant 'Peace with honour, peace in our time'. He had bargained away the freedom of Czecho-slovakia for this peace. A few days earlier he had said, 'How horrible, fantastic, incredible it is that we should be digging trenches and trying on gas-masks here because of a quarrel in a far-away country between people of whom we know nothing.' When I heard the cheers of the people at Downing Street through my wireless set I felt terribly distressed and ashamed of my country. I felt that all the sacrifices of my comrades in the First World War had gone for nothing and we would have to fight that war all over again.

Next morning I had to pay a visit to see the child of one of my neighbours. Although nearly all my work was now consulting work, I still attended a very few of my old friends as family doctor, and this was one of these visits. I found that the child was not seriously ill, but after I had finished my examination the mother said to me, 'Wasn't it wonderful last night to hear Mr Chamberlain say that he had brought home peace with honour?' I replied that I entirely disagreed. It cer-tainly was not peace with honour, and I did not think that it meant peace at all. She became very excited and hysterical and said that she had lost her only brother in the last war and that nothing could be worse than war. Finally she showed me out of the door and said she never wanted to see me in her home again.

I tell this story as an example of the state of mind we were all in at that time. She was a very intelligent, kindly type of woman and I had great sympathy with her attitude to the prospect of another world war. It so happened that I never did enter her house again because she moved to another town shortly afterwards. About a year later, however, when the war started, she very generously wrote me a letter apologising to me for the way she had treated me at that time.

On 1 September a year later, the Germans attacked Poland. The following day it had become evident that war was inevitable. I had finished my work and correspondence near midnight on 2 September and was sitting contemplating the prospect of another war even more terrible that the first great European war. I was 49 years of age. More than half of my life had been shadowed by the First World War and its aftermath. Was the second half of my life going to be the same or worse?

The telephone bell rang. It was McCall Smith speaking from his home at Langside Cottage near the hospital. He said, 'Mavor is here. He wants you to join us. He is going to stay the night.'

I had not seen Mavor for months, and I wanted to hear what he and Muckle thought about it all. Bessie, my wife, had gone to bed but I went up to her room and told her that I was going to meet Osborne Mavor and Muckle at Langside Cottage. She understood that I would be very anxious to go but told me to be very careful in the black-out and not to stay too long. I promised to be back in two hours. This was the first night of the complete black-out. The headlights of our motor cars had been completely covered over, and only a slight glimmer from the slits in the metal covering slanted down on to the road. Although it was a very dark night I knew the road well and I had no great difficulty in finding my way. I was very soon to have plenty of experience of this kind of night-driving.

Mavor was in a somewhat subdued mood. None of us had any illusions. We all knew what war meant. Osborne and Muckle had both spent two years in the front line on the Western Front in the First War. We had an idea that this war would be much worse, especially on the home front. All three of us agreed that there was no alternative to war. In fact we seemed to have a feeling of relief that we need no longer feel ashamed of our country. We drank a toast, 'To Hell with Hitler and his bloody Germans'.

Osborne said that he could not stay at home and write plays and that he would join the army again. I was a member of a Territorial Army Hospital Unit but Muckle said that he would strongly oppose me leaving the Victoria, and that my place was on the home front. I agreed that he was probably right. I left within my two hours feeling more contented and much less resentful than I had felt for months.

Next morning, Sunday 3 September, 1939, on my way to hospital I went into a newsagent for my Sunday paper. The newsagent told me that Neville Chamberlain was going to broadcast to the nation at 11 a.m. I went along to McCall Smith's office at the hospital when the broadcast was due, because I knew that he had a radio set there. James Russell, the senior surgeon, was there as well as McCall Smith and a well-respected local practitioner named Fraser. Chamberlain announced that we were now at war again with Germany. He had given the Germans till 11 a.m. that day to stop their advance into Poland. He had received no answer from them and we were now at war.

None of us spoke a word after the broadcast, but as Fraser went out with me to the hospital door he said, 'I am going to lift my hat to the first dog I meet on the road'. I never knew what he meant by his remark and I did not ask him. My heart was too full to talk.

There is no doubt that it was fear of what another war would mean that made successive British Governments so unwilling to oppose Hitler in the earlier years before he became so strong. If we had only had the courage to oppose him then we might have prevented the Second War altogether.

After Hitler's brutal attack on Poland, nothing seemed to happen for a while. Hitler apparently was not quite ready for all-out warfare. He had such a low opinion of us that he did not expect us to go to war over Poland. We were also far from ready. We could do nothing about Poland ourselves although we had gone to war to help her.

The evacuation of primary school children out of the cities took place immediately after the declaration of war. This was a stupendous operation and in many ways was efficiently carried out, but the after-effects were incalculable and perhaps we are suffering from them still. The children were taken away from their own parents, although in some cases the mothers went with them.

The city schools were all closed at first. The Glasgow Academy primary school which my elder son was attending moved out to Whitecraigs on the south side of Glasgow, about seven miles from the centre of the city. A patient told me of a house which had been vacated there, quite near the school. As my consulting work and hospital work was all on the south side of the city in convenient distance by car, I rented this house and occupied it with my family for a few months. As the expected bombing did not occur, many of the city primary schools opened again by the end of the year. Many of the children returned home, although a great many did not and were separated from their parents for years.

In the spring of 1940 the Glasgow Academy opened its primary school again in the city and we returned to our old home. The war then began to start in earnest. Hitler invaded Denmark and Norway and Osborne Mavor, who was now in the army, was heavily bombed in a hospital ship off Norway. A great many casualties had been expected in the cities, and sanatoria in the country were emptied and the patients sent home. As it turned out this was a very bad decision and we had to pay dearly for it in increased incidence of tuberculosis. New hospitals were hastily built in the country to accommodate the expected casualties, and I was put in charge of the medical side of one of these large emergency hospitals as they were called which was attached to Hairmyres Sanatorium, and was not very far from White-craigs where I stayed during the winter of 1939–40.

At first I had no patients there, but I was told that my duty at that time was to help and advise with the equipment of the hospital. In many ways the equipment which was produced for these hospitals was completely out-of-date. I remember great crates of chloroform anaesthetic arriving. Anaesthetists at that time had practically given up using chloroform, and I think the authorities must have been using ancient army hospital schedules of equipment. When we found that there was a great deal of sickness among the general population we opened some of these wards to the general public and many of the tuberculosis cases were re-admitted.

Early in the summer of 1940 we also began to admit soldiers for sickness and for boarding purposes. Even after the hospital was opened I had great difficulty in getting simple medical equipment such as blood-counting apparatus. I found that these were still available in medical instrument shops in Glasgow. I was not, however, allowed to buy them there. I bought some apparatus myself, however, which carried me on for several months till the official supplies arrived.

By this time, April 1940, my two senior assistants had joined the army and I now had to take full charge of my wards at the Victoria as well as the outpatient work which had previously been done by my assistants. The only help I had was my very recently qualified resident assistants who, however, all rose to the occasion. I was allowed to take one senior resident who had done his year at hospital after qualifica-tion to assist me at Hairmyres. I chose Tom Semple, who stayed with me for two-and-a-half years and was of the greatest assistance to me. At the end of that time he insisted on doing his spell on active service.

I remained in charge of these wards in Hairmyres throughout the war. Sometimes I had large numbers of patients under my care there. One night about 7 p.m. in June 1940, I received a message to go out to the hospital. A large batch of 200 medical cases was arriving. Nei-ther the Superintendent of the hospital, Dr Johnston, or myself had any idea where they were coming from. In these days there seemed to some of us that there was a good deal of unnecessary secrecy. We waited patiently at the hospital for the arrival of the patients. Meantime terrible news was coming through the radio. On 10 May Hitler had invaded Holland and Belgium and the historic defeat of the allies in Northern France had followed. The evacuation from Dunkirk was over and on this night, 22 June 1940, as we waited for our patients we heard that France had asked for an armistice.

The first patients did not arrive till about 1 a.m. We were expecting British hospital patients evacuated from France or even French patients. I went out to the first ambulance that arrived and found it contained Australians. It appeared that about a division of them had been in the liner *Queen Mary* for about four months. They went first of all to Suez and stayed there for a week or two on board ship, and then they came all the way round South Africa and had arrived at Greenock on the Clyde. Many of these Australians had come from the back country and had never had many of the common illnesses such as measles, mumps, chickenpox etc. They had developed all these during their confinement on board ship, and there were many cases of pneumonia among them.

By about 5 a.m. on a lovely June morning we had them all examined and bedded down as we thought. Hairmyres is an extensive place built of hutments, and it was quite a walk to the new emergency wards which had been allotted to the Australians. We found practically none of them in bed. They were washing their clothes and hanging them up on ropes stretched between trees and strolling about enjoying the morning sunshine. I recognised one man whom I remembered having examined and found that he had pneumonic consolidation at the base of both lungs. When I told him that he was quite seriously ill and should be in his bed he said, 'I want to see Scotland. I have never been here before.' They were a tough lot.

Next morning more than half of them had disappeared from the hospital. Dr Johnston, the superintendent, was seriously concerned and was in doubt whether he should report the position to the authorities. I advised him, however, against this. I had fought alongside the Australians in Gallipoli and knew a lot about their ways. It was no good trying the heavy hand with them. They were all right if you treated them as man to man and showed good reason for anything you wanted them to do. Sure enough they were nearly all back by the evening. Most of them had walked to the nearest pub which was in the village of Eaglesham about three miles away. They had thoroughly enjoyed themselves and many went back the following day. Others went into Glasgow but they always came back. Fortunately, about the same time we got some regular army sisters (red capes) who had been evacuated from hospitals in France. They were very good with the men. The Australians called one of them a 'battle-axe', but usually did what she asked them to do.

I entertained some of the officers at my home and enjoyed their company very much. Their division went later to North Africa and did some very fine work there. It was their division which held Tobruk when it was surrounded by the Germans and Italians for several months. The owner of one of the licensed inns at Eaglesham, Mr Jamieson, told me that many of them corresponded with him for a long time after the war.

—

As the war went on, my professional work became heavier and was more than I could undertake. I very gratefully gave up my work at the Elder Cottage Hospital and one of my colleagues at the Victoria, Angus Scott, took it over. I usually arrived at the Victoria about 9 a.m., not infrequently doing a home consultation on my way there. If it was not an outpatient morning at the Victoria I left for Hairmyres about 11 a.m. and spent two hours there. On outpatient days I omitted Hairmyres in the forenoon and made up with extra visits at the weekend. On weekday afternoons I did private consulting at my rooms in the West End from 2 p.m. till 5 or 6 p.m. Most of my home consulting work was done in the evenings or at weekends.

In those days the consultants at the Victoria did a large part of the consulting work for the South West of Scotland. I frequently went as far as Dumfriesshire and Wigtown and Galloway, following the Ayrshire coast, leaving home about 7 a.m. and getting home often long after midnight. In the wintertime this work was very trying because we had no proper headlights on our motor cars. I later used to get one of my old Govan patients, a taxi driver, to drive me on those long winter runs.

I remember one day being called to Greenock to see a shipbuilder, George Brown. I knew that my wife was friendly with his family, and after the professional part of my interview was over I introduced myself and said that my wife was a daughter of George Agnew, a

Govan shipbuilder. He was very interested and we had quite a long talk. He told me that many years before, they had a shipbuilding and engineering club in Govan composed of young men. Among the members were himself, George Agnew my wife's father, my own mother's brother Andrew Munro and the three Mavor brothers: Henry (Osborne Mavor's father), Sam and Ivan. He said that all the Mavor brothers could write well and he was not surprised that O.H. Mavor was a success as a dramatist. He remembered that they used to read lectures to one another at their club, and that the Mavor brothers usually sent them to the *Syran*, the shipbuilding magazine, and got them published.

He asked me what sort of man O.H. Mavor was. I replied that he was very versatile and could be great fun at times. He said, 'He will be like his uncles. I remember one weekend the club had a trip to London. It was a most successful and almost riotous weekend, largely due to the Mavors.'

He then told me that my uncle Andrew Munro was the first lecturer in Naval Architecture at the Technical College, Glasgow. He said that he himself was offered the lectureship first but he made a number of qualifications which the College would not accept. It was then offered to Ivan Mavor but he accepted instead a post in a Newcastle shipyard. My uncle Andrew Munro was the third choice. This was probably the first lectureship anywhere in Naval Architecture. There is now of course a Professorship in Naval Architecture at Glasgow University. It was interesting to me to learn that my uncle and Osborne Mavor's father had been friends in their youth.

Osborne Mavor was at this time in charge of an Army psychiatric hospital in Northern Ireland, and I did not see him for a considerable time afterwards.

By this time my private income had increased considerably and my income was over £5,000 a year. All of this was earned from private consultations, except £600 annually which I was paid for my emergency hospital work at Hairmyres. Income tax at that time was ten shillings in the pound, and with surtax I was only able to retain less than half of my earnings. I however began to save some money and got a part-time secretary at my consulting rooms at Woodside Terrace which was a great help to me. What I was able to save in these war years I did not invest very wisely. I put most of it into War Loan. I never at any time charged high fees. Perhaps my previous general practice experience made me reluctant to do that.

I remember one day seeing a widow lady in consultation with a practitioner. Her house was neat and tidy but it was in a poor class district, and I was sure that she could not be very well off. At the end of the consultation I said to the practitioner, 'I don't think I should charge a fee here. She is a widow.'

He replied, 'Oh yes you must charge a fee. In fact it was she who insisted that I should get you to see her in consultation and she gave me £2.2.0d. to give you as your fee. Will that be sufficient?' I said that it was more than sufficient and accepted two guineas from him.

Although I had never liked doing so, I had sometimes accepted the fee in this way from the patient's doctor. Usually this was when I knew the doctor very well. On one occasion I was seeing what seemed to be a very poor patient with a doctor whom I greatly respected. I grew suspicious, and said to the patient in front of the doctor before we left the house, 'The doctor has paid me your fee, I hope that is all right.' The patient answered, 'He must have given you the fee himself, doctor, because I didn't give it to him.' I gave the fee back to the doctor and told him that if he wanted me to see any of his patients in future he was to let me be the Good Samaritan, and I think he did that occasionally afterwards.

In the case of the widow whom I have mentioned above, a very unusual thing happened. I received a letter from the widow asking me if I would send her a receipt for my fee as she was going to get the fee paid by one of the Trades House Incorporations. I sent her a receipt for £2.2.0d. and she wrote me to say that it was £4.4.0d. that she had paid me. I was very angry and telephoned the practitioner and asked him to come to see me immediately about a very important matter. I am sorry to say that he was a Jewish doctor. I say that because with my diabetic work I had over many years a great deal of contact with the Jewish people and always found them very honest, particular about paying their professional accounts, and very grateful for anything I did for them.

The doctor confessed what he had done. He promised me repeatedly that he would never do such a thing again, but I was extremely angry and said that I had no alternative but to report the incident to the General Medical Council. The following day I received a letter from him asking me if he gave up his practice in Glasgow would I say no more about it. By this time my anger had cooled somewhat and I agreed if he did that I would consider the matter closed. He went to London and I have never heard any more of him.

—

During this time things were getting very difficult at the Victoria owing to want of staff. Dr Cameron, the pathologist who had followed Dr Anderson, became ill and had to give up his hospital appointment. All his juniors had gone into the army. There were several very able technicians, but no qualified medical man to take charge. Hamish Munro, who at that time was my resident, volunteered to take temporary charge, and when he finished his six months term with me as resident continued in charge of pathology for a considerable period. Hamish was a man of exceptional ability and although he was very young we very soon realised that we were getting a much better pathological service than we had been having for some years. Hamish stayed on for a year or two after we got a new pathologist, but he had decided on an academic career and became a Professor of Biochemistry in Glasgow University. He is now (1966) in charge of the Department of Nutrition at the Massachusetts Institute of Technology.

Dr Eaton, our biochemist, was still with us at this time and he and Hamish Munro continued to help with my diabetic clinic. We had kept very careful notes about these diabetic patients since the start of the clinic in 1933, and Eaton and Munro, who were both very energetic workers, started to gather up a ten-year survey of these patients even during these busy war years.

One thing that impressed us was that the incidence of new diabetic cases seemed to have fallen during the war. There might have been several reasons for this, but one possible reason was the reduction of the sugar intake owing to rationing of sugar. I wrote to the Food Ministry to see if I could get any exact information on this point. I received a very cautious letter from Dr Drummond of the Ministry to say that he was very sorry that he could not give me the information as it was secret, but he thought that I might get approximate information from wholesale merchants dealing with sugar which might suit my purpose. I did so and found that we were probably consuming, for all purposes, somewhat less than half the quantity of sugar we were using pre-war. I was surprised at the quantity we were still using; I think it was about half a hundredweight per person. The Dr Drummond who wrote to me on this occasion was the Dr Drummond who along with his family was later murdered by a peasant in the South of France.

It has often been claimed that diabetes is a more common disease among the Jewish race than it is in other races. I was rather intrigued with this problem because we seemed to have a great many Jews in my clinic at the Victoria. This question is probably of interest to the general reader as well as to the medical profession and it may not be out of place if I tell how we tried to deal with it. There were several possibilities which we had to consider. There might be a specially large population of Jews living in the south side of Glasgow near our hospital. The Jews are known to be very careful about their health. Many people, especially in the older groups, suffer from a mild form of diabetes which they may have for years before it is discovered. Perhaps the Jews found out much earlier that they were suffering from the disease. Was it because of a different diet? Diabetes gets much more common in old age and it was in the older patients among the Jews, especially the Jewesses, that we seemed to have an excess of patients. If Jews lived to be older than gentiles in Glasgow this might account for the increase. I found, however, that there were no vital statistics for Jews. At that time they had no statistics of their own. They were always mixed with other races.

Noah Morris, a very able Jewish doctor and at that time biochemist to the Sick Children's Hospital, said that the only way he could think of to get Jewish vital statistics was to go to Riddrie Cemetery, where most of the Jews who died in Glasgow were buried, and look at the ages on the tombstones. I was due a few days' holiday, and as there was no chance of getting away from home I decided that I would spend a day or two looking into this matter of Jewish vital statistics.

I went to Riddrie Cemetery and found a very helpful superintendent there. He said that as accurately as possible he had entered the age of every person buried in the Cemetery in his register. He had the ages of all the Jews who were buried there, but he made one extraordinary statement which interested me greatly. He said 'Jewish children practically never die. It is the rarest occurrence to bury a Jewish child, but we bury plenty of Scottish children.'

I got the ages at death of 3,000 Jewish people and compared them with the ages at death of 3,000 gentiles and found that the Jews appeared on average to live about ten years longer. I went to Craigton

Cemetery where most of the Govan people were buried, and found that the proportion was even more adverse there. There was a very considerably larger proportion of children buried there. This difference in ages at burial was enough, according to our figures, to account for the larger number of Jewish diabetics. I never published these vital statistics concerning the Jews but I think that they are of general interest and worth recording here.

—

The War ran its course. This Second War was bad enough but it did not turn out to be so bad as most of us expected. That, however, is a matter of history and has not much to do with my story.

On 6 June 1944, D-day, the British and Americans landed again in France. The British casualties were heavy and Osborne Mavor's elder son Robert was one of those who died there. The Germans surrendered eventually on 7 May 1945 and the Japanese on 2 September after the dropping of the atomic bomb.

The British nation under Churchill fought the Second World War against Hitler and National Socialism. In this case it was the people who believed in the War. The diplomats had not so much to do with it. This last war was not fought to make the world better but to prevent Hitler and his Nazis from making it a worse world. Although it must be admitted that the world today is still not a very happy place, it would have been a much worse one if Hitler had not been beaten: the War was not fought in vain.

XVIII

The National Health Service

For many years even before the Second World War, the Voluntary Hospitals had been working under increasing difficulties. Medical and surgical treatment had been becoming increasingly more complicated and expensive. In order to get money, great collecting campaigns were organised. Workmen willingly agreed that a few pence would be taken off their weekly wage. There is no doubt, however, that the Voluntary Hospitals did rise to the occasion and kept themselves up to date. In many ways there were no better hospitals in the world. By the end of the Second World War, however, most of them were in financial difficulties, and in the last few years of the War most of them were receiving grants of some kind from the Government. In 1946 the yearly income of the Victoria Infirmary, to which I was attached, was £120,000. The expenses were over £200,000. In addition to income for upkeep, large sums were required for new buildings and new departments to keep up with our advances in knowledge.

In the last years of the war and in the early years of peace our depleted staff at the Victoria had formed a small committee which met weekly in the evenings to consider the changes in staff and equipment which were required when peace came. Although this was really the job for the Governors of the hospital, we knew better than any what the deficiencies were and hoped our advice would be valued. After the defeat of Churchill in the 1945 election and a Labour Government came into power, it became clear that we were going to have a State Medical Service and this required our very serious consideration. There was a great scarcity of hospital staff and generous grants were given to men returning from the forces who wished to attach themselves to hospital for postgraduate work and study for higher degrees.

It soon became clear that the Labour Government with Aneurin Bevan as Minister of Health was determined to have a complete State Hospital Service as well as a complete State General Practitioner Service. Everyone from the richest to the poorest in the land were to be included, and they were to get everything free, the highest medical and surgical skill, all kinds of surgical appliances, spectacles, wigs, artificial teeth, down to the humble laxative pill. Most experienced medical men who had worked with people all their lives and understood human nature were sorely troubled at the prospect. However many of the younger doctors returning from the Army to civil life welcomed the promise of a good steady job. In spite of many protests, nothing would make Bevan modify his proposals and the Conservative party, also no doubt for political reasons, offered no serious opposition. The Voluntary Hospitals, the growth and development of which was probably one of the noblest chapters in British history, were doomed.

My own opinion, and that of many of my contemporaries, was that it would have been much better to leave the Voluntary Hospitals as they were. They were well-governed by competent businessmen, with representatives from many of their contributors as well as working men representatives from the trades unions. They were independent bodies and could encourage individual members of their staff if they wished to develop in any particular line. The Voluntary Hospitals pioneered most of the great advances in medicine in this country. The local government hospitals on the other hand, which had been built to implement the work of the Voluntary Hospitals, were static, poorly developed and poorly equipped places which had always been starved for finance. Their chief equipment was beds. The great training schools for medical students and nurses were all connected with the Voluntary Hospitals. When the State took over the hospitals in 1948 the cost of a patient in the Victoria Infirmary per week was about £5.10.0d. It would have been much cheaper to have paid the hospitals £5 or £6 or even £10 a week for every patient which they looked after. In this way the well-managed hospitals would have received more patients and would have prospered. I am afraid that the local government or statutory hospitals at that time would not have been very popular. Today, under a state system, the cost of a patient per week in the Victoria is £36, and in many London hospitals it is nearer £50. Gradual development in the way I have suggested would have been much better and more in line with our greatness as a nation.

Great and costly administrative machinery was set up directly under the Ministry of Health in England and Wales and the Secretary of State in Scotland. The country was divided into regional areas with a controlling Regional Board, and the individual hospital boards of governors came under the jurisdiction of these Regional Boards, which themselves were under direct political control by the government of the day through the Minister of Health in England and the Secretary of State in Scotland.

I was appointed by the Regional Board to the new board of the Victoria Infirmary. Previous members of the governing board of the Victoria were re-appointed if they wished to stay, and it was understood that they would be allowed to continue on the board for as long as they wished. Other representatives were appointed on the recommendation of various bodies such as the University, the Trades House, the Trades Unions, the Local Authorities etc.

At the first meeting the chairman and convenors of the various committees were appointed. I noticed that the Medical Superintendent of the hospital, Dr McCall Smith, whose presence had always been considered necessary at all meetings of the old governing board, was not asked to be present. This seemed to me rather extraordinary, because from his position he knew more about the running of the hospital than anyone else.

At the second meeting of the board, the chairman read over an order from the Regional Board, RHB (5) (48) 8 which we were asked to accept. This stated that in future the Superintendent of the hospital would only be responsible for supervising the work of the medical and nursing staff, and that all other administrative duties of the hospital, clerical, catering, plumbers, electricians, painters, porters etc. would come under the care of the Secretary of the Board, who was a chartered accountant and occupied offices in town. To my astonishment the new chairman of the board, Dr James Coutts, said, 'I suppose that we will just agree to the change.' Nobody appeared to have any comment to make.

It must be remembered that a large proportion of the members of this board had been newly elected. Most of them knew nothing about hospitals or their administration and were unwilling to comment so soon on something about which they had little or no knowledge. As it appeared to me from the chairman's remarks that he thought we had no alternative but to accept this order I was forced to speak myself. I said, 'I entirely disagree, Mr Chairman. This is a revolutionary proposal and requires a great deal of consideration. It should not have been put before us at our very first working meeting without any warning or previous discussion. A large part of the catering of a hospital is composed of special diets – surely this is a medical matter and should be under medical control. Most of the hospital secretarial staff work with the medical staff, and surely their distribution and control is a matter for the Medical Superintendent. The decision as to when a painter or electrician is to work in a ward full of sick people is surely a medical matter. If the Superintendent is under the administration of a Secretary in town who is never in the hospital I can see endless complications. I move that we reject this order or instruction from the Regional Board.'

Dr Coutts said he was very unwilling to divide the board so early in its existence, and asked if I had a seconder. Someone seconded my motion and it was put to a vote. The voting was exactly equal and the chairman gave his casting vote in favour of acceptance of the Regional Board's instructions.

Fortunately the opposition from the other hospital boards in the region was so strong that we were told at our very next board meeting that R.H.B. (5) (48) 8 had been withdrawn. At this next meeting strong opposition to the exclusion of the Medical Superintendent from the board meetings was expressed by several members and he was asked to attend future meetings.

This was our first experience of what remote bureaucratic control meant. We have heard a great deal about it since that time. We are all now well aware that the hospital service in this country is controlled by politicians and administered by civil servants in London and Edinburgh and in the Regional Boards. These men are able and well-meaning but they have never been connected closely with hospital work. The majority have never been inside a hospital and do not understand the complicated human problems inherent in such a service. If I wished to do so I suppose I could write a volume on this subject alone, but I propose to recount here as briefly as possible only my own experience of the National Health Service.

I was appointed Senior Visiting Physician to the Victoria Infirmary in 1937. In 1936 it was already considered that the accommodation for outpatients and for the laboratories had become quite inadequate. That year and the following year plans were prepared for these new departments. We had the money to proceed with these plans. The financial position was satisfactory. Endowments totalled £300,000. General funds were £140,000 and there was a surplus of £8,000 a year on maintenance.

The outbreak of war, however, in 1939, deferred the project. At the end of the war, in 1946, the financial position was not so good, but the governors of the hospital launched a scheme to get more funds. James Bridie wrote an excellent brochure for the hospital when it launched the scheme, and I have no doubt that it would have been successful if we had been allowed to carry it through. Permission to build, however, could not be obtained, and the hospital was taken over by the Government under the National Health scheme in 1948.

For the next ten years no new building or construction of any kind was undertaken at the Victoria Infirmary, not one brick was laid. This had never happened before in the history of the hospital. There had never been a year in which some addition to building or internal construction had not been carried out. When I retired from the hospital at the age of 65 in 1955, the plans of the new outpatient department which I had helped to prepare in 1937 lay gathering dust. By 1955 the numbers of outpatients attending the hospital had increased more than threefold; conditions had been getting more and more uncomfortable and difficult for everyone concerned in every department of the hospital.

As I write this in 1966, eleven years later, the new outpatient department, which was only started two years ago, is still uncompleted. It is now eighteen years since the hospital was taken over by the Government. Even after they do make a start under the National Health Service they seem to be an extraordinarily long time in completing the job. The other day, when I went along to see how the building was getting on, I only saw three or four workmen on the job.

The excuses that the ministries and bureaucrats put forward for this incredible slowness in action are many and varied. 'There is such a great deal to do . . . Other hospitals have prior claims . . . The costs of running a hospital are rising astronomically . . . The Treasury will not advance the money.'

No doubt a large part of this great increase in costs is due to the general rise in wages, but a large part of it is due to faulty administration and bad planning. Instead of spending what money they had on the established hospitals which had been coping with the work for generations, in Scotland at any rate, they appear to have looked at the matter geographically and spent large sums of money in upgrading hospitals all over the country at great expense. Many of these hospitals had been efficiently staffed previously by the local practitioners. When they got into special difficulties they called in consultants from the large city hospitals or transferred their patients there. It was not necessary that all of these hospitals should be kept absolutely up to date and fully staffed with specialists. There is frequently not sufficient work for these specialists and they get disgruntled and lose their enthusiasm. Medical advances are so rapid that a new department is hardly built before it is out of date. It is only possible to keep a few hospitals fully equipped and the old pattern which had grown up over very many years should not have been disturbed. Men sitting at desks in London and Edinburgh cannot be expected to understand these things. The men on the spot understand them much better.

When the government took over the hospitals and the medical service of this country in 1948 they took over something of very great value. No doubt the hospital buildings and equipment as a result of two world wars required renewal, but apart from that they were in good shape.

In 1948 I went for a holiday to Sweden, and when in Stockholm I took the opportunity of visiting one of their most famous hospitals, the Karolinska Hospital in Stockholm. Inside the entrance there was a great hall. All round this great hall were the offices of the hospital. There were shops where newspapers, sweets etc. could be bought. Refreshments could be had. There was a large department where children could be left and amused while their parents were visiting their friends and relatives. The Swedes, of course, are very keen on physical development, and in a prominent place there was a very large picture of a nude female figure. It was shortly after the Second World War and there were underground shelters which could accommodate very quickly all the patients and staff of the hospital.

I went round the hospital in company with an American doctor who was a visitor like myself. We were shown a medical outpatient department where the patients were waiting in great comfort in large lounge chairs. Their examination usually took all day and they were provided with meals during that period. A staff of three physicians, assisted, of course, by the X-ray department and laboratories etc., told me that they only examined about 25 patients daily. The patients were all seen by appointment and I asked one of the physicians if they have to wait long for their appointments. He said that sometimes they had to wait a good many weeks but that helped to get rid of what he called the 'rubbish', patients who had not much wrong with them.

In the wards the nursing system was very different from our own system. The nurses did not live in the hospital or belong to any particular hospital. They lived in a hostel or at home and the hospital applied daily or weekly for the number of nurses that they required from a central authority. The sister of the ward seldom left her own room. She was in touch with every patient by telephone and when the patients required anything they just lifted the telephone and spoke. When any nursing procedure had to be carried out the patient was always whisked out of the ward, which was usually quite small and contained only 4–6 beds. The beds were all easily moveable on wheels. The staff who moved the patients about did not appear to be fully trained nurses and they took the patients to the nurses. In spite of the very modern buildings the patients did not appear to me to be so clean or well attended as the patients in our own old hospitals.

As we came away the American doctor said to me, 'These are wonderful hospitals, Doc. The hospitals in your country are like slums compared with them, but if I take sick I am getting the first plane back to your country. I know that I will be well nursed and cared for there.'

The system of nursing in the Voluntary Hospitals of this country has always been that the nurses lived in the hospital or more usually in a Nurses' Home attached to the hospital. They are always strictly disciplined. The younger probationer nurses, as they are called, attend classes under the sister tutor. If they are out on their day off they have to report in by a certain time. This is necessary because they have to work very hard and study hard also. If they make a mistake of any kind they do not get off easily. Strict discipline is necessary because they have a very responsible job and they have human life under their care. They must not make any mistakes in the medicine or doses of medicine which they administer. They must be constantly watchful and on the alert so that they can report any change in a patient's condition. Neglect to report a change in a patient's condition may

211

mean the unnecessary loss of a life. I have always felt that the fight against disease is like a battle. It is like constant warfare. Emergencies are always occurring. The nurses are the soldiers and they must be strictly disciplined.

The extraordinary thing is that once they have got over the first month or two and settled down to hard work they are extremely happy. I know no happier persons than probationer nurses, so there is no need to be sorry for them or think that they are too strictly disciplined. During the Second World War, as soon as the nurses in the Victoria finished their training they were lined up and given their red capes and commissioned as Army Nursing Sisters. They were already disciplined and responsible people and did not require any further training. Since the National Health Service took over the voluntary hospitals the period of nursing training has been reduced from four years to three years and a nursing grade with an even shorter period of training, 'Assistant Nurse' has been introduced. I am not grumbling about this, it may be necessary in our modern affluent state; but one cannot agree that it indicates an improvement in nursing standards.

In England a number of the larger teaching hospitals have a governing board which is responsible directly to the Ministry of Health, and these have a little more authority than any of the Scottish hospitals which are all under Regional Boards. The powers of the Scottish hospital boards are therefore very limited. They only deal with minor matters. They cannot initiate any change of any consequence. Many of the members feel that their attendance is a waste of their time. Apart from the occasion on the second meeting of the board when we resisted the order limiting the powers of the Medical Superintendent, I can remember only one other occasion when the board successfully resisted the Regional Board and the Department of Health. This was on a medical matter and connected with the duties of the nurses in relation to tuberculosis cases.

At the end of the Second War it was soon realised that there had been a great increase in pulmonary tuberculosis. This was true of the whole country, but the increase in tuberculosis was particularly marked in Scotland. At the beginning of the war sanatoria had been evacuated for the expected bombing casualties which never occurred. In addition, housing conditions in Scotland were particularly bad and movement of the population due to evacuation of children had also increased the hazard.

The Secretary of State for Scotland quite rightly decided to start a campaign to get the disease under control. In the new National Hospital Service, Mearnskirk Hospital, which had previously been under the Glasgow Corporation, was put under the same Board of Governors as the Victoria Infirmary. Mearnskirk at that time was a hospital for surgical and pulmonary tuberculosis. There was a shortage of nurses, and one of the plans which the Department of Health conceived was that the Victoria Infirmary nurses should spend some time during their training nursing these tuberculosis cases.

Professor Carl Browning, who was convener of the Medical Committee of the Victoria Infirmary and was Professor of Bacteriology at Glasgow University strongly opposed this suggestion, as did many other members of the board, including myself. The Department of Health, however, continued to press the Victoria board to accept this suggestion and the Secretary of State attended a meeting of the board himself one day, accompanied by several officials. He addressed the board, saying that he was very surprised that we were refusing to co-operate and that the matter was very urgent. He was quite sure that it was not the fault of the nurses and that they would willingly volunteer for the work. Professor Browning, however, was adamant. He said that so long as he was Convener of the Medical Committee and a member of the board he would never be party to such an arrangement. These probationer nurses were particularly hard-worked. In addition to their hospital duties they had to study in their spare time. They were at a very susceptible age and it would be quite wrong to put them in close nursing contact with acute cases of pulmonary tuberculosis. It was like putting the most inflammable material nearest the fire. If they were short of nurses they should employ older nurses and pay them a sufficient salary to attract them. It was quite wrong to employ probationer nurses who were really undergoing their training and were a form of cheap labour. He was quite sure that this was not the way to tackle the problem. I myself spoke in support of Professor Browning, but little more was said and the Secretary of State's party left very soon. We did not hear any more of this scheme.

A few years later new anti-tuberculosis drugs were discovered which have already almost eliminated the disease, and the large sanatorium at Mearnskirk is now almost entirely occupied by general medical and non-tuberculous patients.

213

The sequel to this story is not so happy and does not do any credit to the National Health Service. I believe I am right in stating that an undertaking had been given to the members of the boards of the old Voluntary Hospitals that they would be allowed to continue as members of the boards for as long as they wished to do so. Professor Browning was one of the governors of this hospital before it came under the state. He had been convenor of the committee which looked after the medical staff for a considerable time and was trusted and greatly respected by all. Governors appointed since the state took charge are renewed, however, every three years. Although he was one of the old governors, Professor Browning was notified very soon after the incident described above that his services to the board were terminated. He was, not surprisingly, upset about this, as were all the governors and staff of the hospital.

I tried to find out who was responsible for this action. The secretary of the Victoria Infirmary Board assured me that the Regional Board was not responsible. Professor Browning was a nominee of the University and I actually interviewed the Principal of the University but he disclaimed all knowledge of the occurrence. The Department of Health in Scotland is finally in control of these appointments and they must bear the responsibility for this action. All members of hospital boards know that this is not an isolated instance and if they show too much independence of thought it is extremely probable that their services will soon no longer be required.

The hospital service therefore today is under direct government authority and is managed by civil servants who are in full control of policy and finance. The hospital Boards themselves only deal with very minor unimportant matters. The result is an enormously expensive, static and unwieldy hospital system. There is no doubt that it is today a good hospital service. It should be, considering what it costs. The old Voluntary Hospitals, if they had been paid by the state for each patient that they looked after would, I am sure, have been equally good and probably better and more varied in their services and development.

One great objection to a state service is that the civil servants and ministries are too distant to be in touch with real hospital problems. They have great difficulty in deciding what to do with the money which they have available and they have fallen dangerously behind in their hospital building programme. They dither for years over which hospital has to be rebuilt and where the new building is to take place. Naturally every region clamours for a new hospital for itself and the responsible authorities, not understanding where the real priorities are, have made great mistakes in their planning and too often have done nothing at all because they cannot decide what to do.

I have described the extraordinary delays in the new building at my own old hospital in Glasgow, the Victoria Infirmary. The Western Infirmary in Glasgow, which is the chief teaching hospital in the city, is suffering from similar difficulties. Its structure is very old and it requires complete rebuilding. The State hospital authorities have been talking about it now for ten years and they do not appear to be any further on now than when they started talking. The old hospitals knew their own problems and would have developed their hospitals in the most practical way with the money which was available. The objections which I have to a national state hospital system are its enormous expense and its bad planning and administration. We cannot afford to keep up this kind of system in this country and in the end we will be left with a dull, static and very mediocre state hospital service.

One of the greatest mistakes made in the National Health Services Act was the complete separation of the general practitioner service from the hospital service. The hospitals are administered by local regional boards. The general practitioner service, however, is administered by a completely separate body – the local executive council. It was possible, however, for a general practitioner by working part-time in hospital to get experience and training so that he could eventually become a whole time consultant. In my time a very large number, probably the majority of consultants, graduated in this way. There was a large pool of junior assistants available as a result for the hospital service. Many of them made the grade and became senior hospital physicians and surgeons. No doubt many of them gave up hospital work when they saw no prospect of promotion, but they made all the better practitioners for the experience. On the other hand those who did become consultants were all the better for their experience as general practitioners. They had worked in the homes of the people and understood many problems which their patients had to meet which those hospital assistants who had spent all their time in hospital could not appreciate and understand.

This was the road which I travelled, and although it was a hard road I do not think that it did me any harm. Before the National Health Service was introduced, most of the local hospitals in smaller towns were staffed by the local general practitioners. These were fairly quickly replaced by full-time hospital specialists at very much greater expense. This sort of action is typical of a nationalised service organised by people who are out of touch with practical problems. These junior hospital posts which used to be filled voluntarily by the general practitioners, who were keen and interested in their work, are now largely filled in most parts of the country by foreign students who look on those under their care as 'cases', from the study of which they can learn something, and not as Mrs Brown with a large family to look after at home who will require to get home as soon as possible.

This is no exaggeration. In fact the objections to this system are worse than I have described. The general practitioners are left dissatisfied with their way of life in many ways. Those keenly interested in their profession are frustrated. They have no opportunity for advancement. As they grow older there is no chance of increasing their income except by increasing the load of work. An experienced practitioner is paid the same for looking after a patient for a year as a newly qualified doctor. In private practice an experienced doctor used to be able to decrease his work and increase his fees to compensate. In the National Health Service private practice is discouraged in every possible way.

My old friend, the late Dr Ian Grant, who was a general practitioner and was Chairman of the Representative Council of the British Medical Association at the time of the introduction of the National Health Service Act, said that this division of the medical profession into hospital doctors and medical practitioners was a political manoeuvre to 'Divide and Rule'. Ian Grant said that Aneurin Bevan, realising that if he got the hospital staff on his side he could control the general practitioners, made a pact with the Royal Colleges in London and granted many of their demands. He knew that he could provide an emergency service with the hospitals alone if the general practitioners refused to cooperate. There is no doubt that he could have done so. Whether this story is true or not, there is no doubt that this division of the medical services into two completely separate parts has done great and probably irreparable harm to the medical profession in this country.

Recently, realising the increasing shortage of junior hospital staff, the Health Service authorities have made some attempt to reintroduce general practitioners into the hospital service. Under present conditions they cannot hope to be very successful. The junior hospital assistant must continue his hospital work from the time he qualifies in medicine. He can then take up general practice as part-time work. It is much more difficult – almost impossible – for a general practitioner to take up part-time hospital work, especially if he has been away from it for any length of time.

—

Some people will no doubt think that I am too severe in my criticism of the National Health Service, but I feel that I am at least well-qualified to criticise. I have practised among the richest and poorest people in the country for 52 years. I have had great experience of human nature and I understand sick people's requirements. I believe that the National Health Service as established in this country is going to be a very expensive failure unless the patient is given more responsibility for himself and the people are given more interest in and responsibility for their own hospitals. Health is a very personal thing. There is some analogy between a compulsory state health service and state religion. I do not believe that either is good for the state or for the people. There is no doubt that great and fundamental modifications will require to be made in our present National Health Service and they will require to be made soon, otherwise it will break down completely.

XIX

O.H. Mavor (James Bridie)

The National Health Service was introduced in 1948 and I have no doubt that the reader will have gathered from what I have written that the older members of the staff of the Victoria Infirmary were not very happy about it. We were disgruntled about many things, and from being one of the happiest hospitals began to be rather an unhappy one. Osborne Mavor, or James Bridie, the dramatist, as he was now known, had always remained interested in his old hospital, and one day in the autumn of 1948 he telephoned me and asked me how things were getting on. 'Not very well,' I replied. 'I don't like nationalised medicine at all.'

He answered, 'Come down and see me and tell me all about it. I am not feeling very well myself, anyway.'[38]

38. Earlier that year he had written:

Finnich Malise
Drymen Station
Stirlingshire

21st June 1948

Dear Alec,

Many thanks for your letter. I enjoyed your consultation enormously. Indeed, it made me feel very much better and even the haemorrhage from the lower bowel stopped within twenty-four hours. I don't think I shall take any of your bloody medicine and I can see at a glance that your asthma exercises are no bloody good. But the girl in the pictures is rather pretty.

I'll see what I can do. Yesterday I practised leg-break bowling against a tree and it did me a great deal of good. If I had a deck I would play deck quoits, as that is a very good exercise for a large belly. I took in three holes of my Sam Browne belt with it on the hospital ship – it was either that or an indefinite number of pink gins a day and no worries.

Come out soon again and give me good advice.

Ever yours
OH

When I saw him next day he asked, 'Are you sure I have not got a high blood pressure?'

I had taken it before and never found it raised, but I took it again and found it normal for his age. I suggested that he was not having enough exercise. As it was a fine morning we decided to have a walk. We climbed quite a steep hill which was part of the small estate which he was occupying at that time. I found that I was more out of breath than he was when we got to the top, and I told him that his idea about his blood pressure was all nonsense.

On Christmas Day 1949 I saw him again professionally. This time he had a temperature and had a pneumonic consolidation at the base of one of his lungs. He came into a private ward at the Victoria and had a course of penicillin. He got better very quickly and went home in a fortnight.

There is no doubt, however, that after this his health was not so good, and about the middle of December the following year he took a venous thrombosis of one of his legs. He came into his old hospital again and improved rapidly with rest and simple measures. After this illness he went for a short holiday, to North Berwick. On his way home from North Berwick I arranged that he should see Professor Sir James Learmonth of Edinburgh Royal Infirmary. Professor Learmonth was an old friend of both Mavor and myself. Mavor seemed quite well during his interview with Learmonth. Shortly after leaving the Royal Infirmary after he had seen Sir James, while he was being driven through Edinburgh by his chauffeur he took suddenly ill. He asked his wife Rona to take him back to the Royal Infirmary, as he was afraid he had burst a blood vessel in his head. His diagnosis was unfortunately correct.

He rallied for a while, but on 29 January Sir James Learmonth, under whose care he still was, telephoned to the Victoria and told McCall Smith and myself that things were looking very bad. Muckle (McCall Smith) and I went through to Edinburgh to see him. He was conscious and recognised us but could not speak. He had symptoms of acute respiratory failure. We stood for a minute or two by his bed and said our silent farewells and then came away. As we walked slowly along the rough flagstones of the old Infirmary basement, Muckle, who loved Mavor very much, said to me, 'Life will never be quite the same again, Alick, without Osborne.' He was 63 years of age. He died just when he seemed to be at the height of his achievement as a dramatist.

Mavor had a multitude of friends in all walks of life. I have never known anyone who was loved and appreciated by so many people. He had contacts with people in so many places. I knew very little of his friends in the theatre and the literary world and in art. I only knew him as a colleague in hospital. I served with him in the Army in Mesopotamia and Persia. I knew and admired him greatly when he was a student although I was not one of his close friends at that time.

Mavor's chief interest and study in life was his fellow man; not mankind in the abstract but man as an individual. These men or women might seem quite ordinary or even dull to other people but Mavor always found something interesting or even unique in everyone he met. It might be a fellow student or a professor, a patient in the general ward of a hospital, a private soldier in the army, an officer or a Lieutenant General, an actor or a waiter in a café; they were all interesting and extraordinary fellows and none of them was long in Mavor's company before they began to be infected themselves with Mavor's opinion. That was why, whenever Mavor appeared, he was immediately surrounded by a motley crowd. In the Students' Union in Glasgow University, in a hospital side room, in an army mess, in the Glasgow Art Club or in the Citizens' Theatre in Glasgow which he founded, it was always the same. They loved to hear him laugh and talk, and were ready in return to act the part and give their answers in keeping with the character which Mavor had discovered in them.

There is no doubt that Mavor with his great gift of understanding saw all sorts of things that others did not see. As a student he drew wonderful revealing caricatures with a few simple lines. He continued to do this all his life, and if he had concentrated on this art he could have been a great caricaturist.

When he grew older he drew a different kind of picture of people whom he had met and put them in his plays. It did not seem to matter whether they were good people or bad people, he liked them all. He seemed to find something good and interesting in even the apparently worst characters and I think that he was right in that attitude to life. He never showed any great desire to reform people. He liked them as they were. Nevertheless no one was more willing to give a helping hand when help was required.

Mavor was always a happy person, but in his later years he seemed to me to become more serious-minded. This showed in the plays which he wrote.

Rona Mavor, James Bridie's widow, gave me a book by an American writer, Helen L. Luyben. The title of the book is *James Bridie: Clown and Philosopher*. She divides Bridie plays into three periods, 'Songs of Innocence', 'The Clown Despairs' and 'Songs of Experience'. She says that in Bridie's work there is a philosophical continuity which can be traced through three stages of moral awareness and which, when recognised, goes far in defining Bridie's genius. Bridie, she attempts to show, was essentially a moralist and his plays are in a special sense morality plays. There is no doubt that Miss Luyben has written a most interesting and sympathetic book about Bridie, but in my opinion Bridie was not just a moralist.

Bridie's understanding of life was the result of his experience of life. I do not think that he read books on theology or philosophy. I doubt if he would have recognised himself as a philosopher and moralist. His books were about the men and women whom he met and talked to and tried to understand. I think he was saddened by the waste of life and goodness which he found in the world. He thought it was rather illogical. Perhaps that is why so many of his plays seem to be illogical.

—

Mavor had a happy home life as a child, as a student and family man, but like the rest of his generation he did not lead a sheltered life. He served in two world wars and did not escape personal tragedy when he lost his elder son in the Second World War. Mavor, as an Officers' Training Corps man, joined the army automatically as a Special Reserve Officer, as most of us did, at the beginning of the First World War and went to France with one of the first new divisions in the winter of 1914.

He gives a few of his first impressions of war in his autobiography, *One Way of Living*. He thought that Lewis Carroll had forecast aspects of it in *Alice in Wonderland*. After his first bombardment he declared that 'this business might easily become intolerable'. In the first book which he wrote after the war, *Some Talk of Alexander*, there are a few verses in the *Alice in Wonderland* vein which I think he must have written in these early days in France.

The history of a man-made shell
Is like a tree that grows in hell.

Around the grisly flats one sees
The budding of those sudden trees

Along the acres of decay
They spring and grow and fade away.

For me I like the trees that grow
As they were planted long ago.

(Just past the cottage by the well,
Better than those that grow in Hell.)

He spent about two and a half years on the Western Front with his division. He 'drifted from Ypres to Arras, from Arras to the Somme and back to Arras again'. Most of the time he spent with ambulance dressing stations and on several occasions he was battalion Medical Officer. Very few men, I think, can have seen more of the bloody side of the bloodiest of all wars, or stuck it for longer than he did. He was invalided from France with jaundice in 1917.

And yet he said very little about that side of war in his books or plays. When I shared a tent or billet with him in Mesopotamia, Persia and Russia, I used to try to get him to talk about those days in France, but he said that he had forgotten all about them. He said that he remembered only the men he had met in France and he had met some extraordinarily funny fellows. Then he would burst into a roar of laughter and recount some incident in which an M.O. called Duggie King very often took part. Douglas King was one of our medical contemporaries in the Officers' Training Corps who did not survive the war. Mavor's outlook seems to have been, on the surface at least, like Bruce Bairnsfather's Old Bill.[39]

There is one revealing incident in his autobiography. Talking about himself in the third person he says 'When a blinded, wounded

39. Captain Bruce Bairnsfather was a well-known humourist and cartoonist who created the characters of Old Bill and his pals and published regularly in the magazine Bystander during World War One. Bairnsfather served with the Royal Warwickshire Regiment in France from 1914.

officer said to him once "Who is that? My God, you have got gentle hands! You know your job all right," his tank was filled with enough vanity to keep him running through the war and for a long time after it.' Mavor had very gentle hands. When he percussed a patient's chest his hands just seemed to touch the chest, one could not hear him tapping at all.

Mavor accepted life in war at its grimmest and made the best of it. He accepted life as he found it wherever he was and enjoyed it to the full. Nevertheless those grim days must have had some permanent effect on his sensitive nature. When he came to write his plays they were always realistic and sometimes shocking to people who had lived a sheltered life.

One day when I was visiting him in 1950, shortly after he had written his play *The Queen's Comedy*, he autographed a paper-bound copy of it and gave it to me. I read it and re-read it many times as I have done most of his plays. Mavor calls the play 'A Homeric fragment, the scene is laid in Heaven, on earth and under the sea'. It is about the war between the Greeks and the Trojans. The gods seem to get a good deal of fun out of the situation – Jupiter favours the Trojans while Neptune favours the Greeks. Meanwhile on the war-torn earth, the poor muddy and bloody soldiers are fighting and dying on the battlefield for no very good reason that they can understand. They show high courage and many virtues but the tragic futility of war is very evident. In the last scene Jupiter talks to the other gods and some of the humans who have fallen in the battle.

He said that one day when he was a child and in a very querulous, impatient mood his mother pulled off a chunk of chaos from the round in the kitchen drawer and gave it to him to play with. He played with it and found that it got lighter and lighter as he moulded it and became like a balloon full of floating pebbles. He was very pleased with it and called his toy the Universe. He soon found that it was easier to make a Universe than to control it. 'It was full of mad meaningless fighting forces. I got most of them bound and fixed and working to rules and all of a sudden I felt lonely. I felt that I would rather my mother had given me the puppy dog or the kitten, so I thought of something else. I found that if I arranged the forces in a certain way I got a thing called life. Life is very interesting. I am still working on its permutations and combinations . . . Long ago I put a little swelling at the end of the primitive spinal cord of a sort of fish.

223

I am happy to say that in some of the higher apes this lump has taken on extensive and peculiar functions. One of these functions appears to consist in explaining me and my little Universe. I have no doubt at all that these explanations are very interesting and stimulating. Perhaps in time these little objects will attain to the properties and activities of the Immortal Gods themselves. Who knows? I have not nearly completed my Universe. There is plenty of time. Plenty of time.'

Mavor at heart was really a shy and reserved man. He seldom talked of religious matters and I do not know what his faith really was. I never had an opportunity to discuss the 'Queen's Comedy' with him again. When one met him there were always so many interesting things to talk about that no doubt I forgot to raise the subject. Shakespeare probably understood more about human nature than any other man and we have no idea what his faith was either. Mavor's friends, and they were legion, all knew that the man himself was greater than his works. With all his great gifts he was in essence a simple, kindly, loyal and courageous man.

Two years ago I was staying with one of my sons, who at that time was working in a hospital in Chichester, Sussex. We went to a performance at the Festival Theatre there. Alastair Sim had the leading part in Bridie's play *The Magistrate*. We were having supper afterwards in the restaurant attached to the theatre, and Alastair Sim and his wife sat down at the table next to us. I could not resist the temptation to speak to him. I said, 'I am an old friend of James Bridie and I know you were one of his friends. I would just like to say how much we have enjoyed the play tonight.' Alastair Sim answered, 'God bless you for speaking to me if you are an old friend of James Bridie. I loved that man. He was a great dramatist and a wonderful man. I have only one complaint against him. He died too soon. Next time I meet him I am going to tell him so.'

I met Lord Boyd Orr shortly afterwards and told him what Alastair Sim had said about Mavor. He enjoyed the story, and then he said, 'Mavor and I used to meet when we were students and drink to the two ugliest men in the University.' I am sure that would be Mavor's own idea. He always liked a bit of fun. They were both very unusual men, but I never thought of them as being ugly.

XX

A Senior Hospital Physician, Retirement from Hospital Work

In an earlier chapter I described the changes in the hospital service under the National Health Service and I also described general practice under nationalisation. I would like now to describe the changes which have taken place in a consulting physician's work under the National Health Service and to say something also about the work I have done since I retired from active hospital work in 1955, at the age of sixty-five.

—

Today the Victoria Infirmary draws its patients chiefly from the south side of Glasgow. In the pre-National Health Service days it drew patients from the whole south-west area of Scotland, including Lanarkshire, Renfrewshire, Ayrshire and as far south as Dumfriesshire, Wigtownshire and Galloway. A senior consultant rapidly became known to all the practitioners in his area. He reported to them about the patients he had treated in hospital and when they required assistance for their private patients he was the one to whom they naturally turned. Many of these patients did not attend the outpatient department of the hospital but were sent to the consultant's private consulting rooms. In the same way there were no free domiciliary visits and I visited private patients with their family doctors. Sometimes I might be called to a country town, possibly a considerable distance from Glasgow. After I had seen one of the doctor's patients, perhaps in a large country house, he would often say 'I wonder if you would be good enough to see one of my patients whom I am rather anxious about.' Consultants in those days were always willing to do that. Sometimes we saw several patients in that way and occasionally some of them were charged a small fee.

When the National Health Service was introduced in 1948 the whole pattern of consulting practice changed. The hospital belonged to the people. They were no longer accepting charity and were encouraged to come to hospital for consultation. There was the additional advantage from the doctor's point of view that he could do a better job for his patients if he saw them in hospital. Medicine was getting much more complicated and technical, and he could have X-ray examinations and laboratory tests more efficiently and easily done in hospital. Before the advent of the Health Service I did all my own blood tests laboriously in my consulting rooms, but now the patients went to hospital where technicians did them.

The National Health Service introduced domiciliary visits to patient's homes on the request of their practitioners. The year before the NHS was introduced I did between 700 and 800 of these privately in the Glasgow area for which I usually charged a fee of three guineas. In the first year of the Health Service these domiciliary visits were limited to 100 for each consultant. Personally I was placed in a very difficult position. I very soon used up my 100 consultations, and I had to say to general practitioners with whom I had worked for many years, 'I am sorry but I cannot do any more visits for you. You will have to get another consultant.' This arrangement of course suited the junior consultants and I did not grudge them that at all, because I remembered the many lean years I had endured as a junior hospital assistant. The result for me, however, was that after the first year of the NHS my income steadily declined until I retired in 1955, in spite of the fact that I was paid a salary.

I suppose that it was partly to compensate for this that 'merit awards' were introduced for consultants. Many of us were strongly opposed to these payments, and I was one of those. Only one consultant in Glasgow, however, the late Tom Newton F.R.C.S., a surgeon in the Western Infirmary, refused to accept his award. I would have liked to have refused mine, but my retirement from hospital was not far off and I was beginning to get somewhat anxious about my financial position.

In the old voluntary hospital days a consultant's career consisted of many lean years as a junior when he was learning his job, which culminated in ten to fifteen years when he was at the peak of his profession and his name was a household word in the area that he practised. My peak years coincided with the years of the Second World War and the few years following, when income tax was at 50%, so I had not been able to save very much.

These merit awards are decided by a secret body of consultants whose names are never divulged. In my day there were three grades of merit award, £500, £1,000 and £1,500 a year. If you did private practice you only received 7/11 of this amount, just as one only received 7/11 of one's National Health Service salary if one did private practice. We were supposed to work seven half-days a week, including Saturday and Sunday. I suppose Saturday and Sunday afternoons were considered as non-working days, but I was never quite sure how they arrived at 7/11. I got 7/11 of a £500 merit award. It would have been very much fairer to have given us a higher pension as some compensation for the loss of our private practice. In pre-National Health Service days a consulting physician continued to have a considerable private practice for some years after he retired.

The arrangements for pensions under the National Health Service were that we received 1/80 of the payment we had received under the National Health Service for every year of service. I served seven years under the National Health Service and a few months before I retired in 1955 I went to see the treasurer of the Regional Medical Board to see if he could give me any idea of the pension I would receive. After doing some calculations he said, 'You are very good. Much better than most of your contemporaries. You will get about £350 a year as a pension.' Actually, to begin with it was £352. By the time I retired private practice for a retired consultant had practically disappeared, and I was dependent on my pension and on what I had been able to save.

For some years after I retired I did work as a consulting physician on medical tribunals, which are final appeal courts under the Industrial Pensions Act. These appeal courts consist of a legal chairman, usually a Sheriff, a consultant surgeon, and a consultant physician. The pensioners had suffered from injuries at work or industrial diseases, and were dissatisfied with their awards. I was very struck by the efficient and rapid summing-up which these legal men made. One day I said to the Sheriff, 'I think we will have to give this man the benefit of the doubt.' The Sheriff replied, 'You don't give anyone the benefit of the doubt, Doctor, you make your decision in the balance of probabilities.'

It was very interesting to meet and work with these men, and I enjoyed also meeting some of my old surgical colleagues. I retired from this work at the age of 72, but I continued to do Regional

Medical Officer work with the Department of Health until 1970. This is the work which I had encountered in its early stages when I practised in Govan. I usually did two morning sessions a week with the R.M.O. I enjoyed this work also. It took me out of my isolation and I met medical colleagues and heard their views on many subjects.

This work also is interesting and often quite difficult. It calls for a good knowledge of medicine and also a knowledge and understanding of human nature. The medical part of it usually came easily to me after all the experience that I have had, but in assessing the patient's capacity for an occupation one has to consider a great many other factors. The chief one perhaps is the psychological factor. Many of these people are depressed, perhaps from long periods of unemployment, perhaps from social and family difficulties at home. Their intelligence may be low and they are inadequate to undertake many kinds of work. A superficial judgment could be unfair to them. I was surprised at the large numbers among the chronic sick who have social and family troubles at home. Many, particularly those who have the capability to only earn a small wage, are better off not working. One sees a complete cross-section of the community at these R.M.O. sessions, some of the best and most deserving members of society and some of the worst and least deserving. Perhaps we see an unduly large proportion of this latter group and may get a false impression of their relative numbers in the population, but I think that they indicate a serious sickness in our society today.

There are many anomalies also which discourage people from working. I will give one example. I saw a young man one day who had been handicapped since infancy as a result of paralysis of one leg due to poliomyelitis. He was on the disabled list. This is quite a useful arrangement and gives a disabled man a better chance of getting suitable work. Every firm has to employ a certain small proportion of disabled men so that more jobs are now available to such people. Unfortunately, however, the pay is usually low also. This particular disabled man had a wife who was recovering from tuberculosis, and when he was unemployed she got a special allowance from public assistance so that she could get adequate nourishment. Unfortunately when her husband was employed this allowance stopped, and their income was about £2 less when he was working than when he was unemployed. This couple had no family otherwise the discrepancy would have been still greater.

I would not like to give the impression that I do not appreciate the enormous improvement that has taken place in the social condition of what used to be the poorer section of our community since the end of the Second World War. The Welfare State has played a large part in this improvement, but it is by no means the only reason for it. The people of this country, probably the kindest and best people in the world, had a guilty conscience about what happened in the great depression after the First World War. I experienced and have described these conditions myself. The people, all of them, were determined that this would not happen again. As a result, the Welfare State was planned for a very much poorer population than the one we have today. It covers the whole population. There was never any necessity for this, and there is less necessity now than ever there was. In my opinion the great programme of state aid is sapping the independence of the individual in our country.

One of the other problems facing this country is dealing with crime. I have little sympathy with the sloppy sentimentality with which some people approach this subject. These mistaken people seem to think that understanding and kindness are all that the young criminal requires for reforming him, and that harsh treatment is wrong because for some reason the young criminal is not responsible. They equate this in their minds with the love of humanity. However, the father who loves his children the most is always very strict with them. It is the parent who does not bother about his family and does not love them much who lets them do what they like. He gives them more pocket money than they ought to get to salve his conscience. I think that this attitude holds also in public life. If you feel that young offenders should not be punished then I think you are deceiving yourself.

The older I have become, and the more experience I have had, the greater has become my respect for mankind and the ordinary man and woman. Life for most of them is a constant battle against difficulties. Those who have not to fight so hard to make a living and a home for themselves have often to fight even harder against temptations in their personal life. In spite of all these difficulties the great majority of men and women are cheerful, kindly, unselfish and helpful to others. This applies to all of them: even the outcasts and the jailbirds sometimes surprise one with their virtues.

XXI

Fifty Years' Progress in Medicine

A present-day reader will have knowledge of many of the advances in medical practice which I have described in these pages. What is not so apparent is the effect these momentous changes had on the physician and the practice of medicine. Equally the revolutionary National Health Service and the Welfare State have had a social impact.

These fifty years of my professional life have seen enormous advances in medicine as well as in the science of physics, chemistry, engineering and aviation. Joseph Lister had introduced his antiseptic surgery in Glasgow in 1865 and Simpson had started using chloroform as an anaesthetic in Edinburgh some years earlier. Therapeutics, however, i.e. the treatment of disease apart from surgery, had made no progress whatever. We had lost confidence in the old pharmacopeia. Professor Ralph Stockman, who was Professor of Materia Medica and Therapeutics during my time as a student at Glasgow University, was a sceptic as well as a philosopher. We had to spend many months studying the old pharmacopoeia, but he told us in his lecture that he could count all the drugs which were of any real value on the fingers of his hands. Morphia, digitalis, potassium iodide, chloral hydrate, mercury and thyroid extract, discovered at that time, were some of these.

Arsenic had long been used in medicine. It was poisonous to certain parasites but even more poisonous to the human host. About the time I was a resident doctor in the Western Infirmary, Paul Erlich, the German physician and scientist, had produced a form of arsenic, Salvarsan, which was strongly toxic to the parasite of syphilis and only feebly toxic to the host. It was given at first as a very dilute solution into the veins. This was quite a procedure and I spent a good deal of time as a resident physician doing this work. Very soon we got Neosalvarsan, an improved form of the drug, which we were able to give in a much more concentrated form in a large syringe. From that time onwards the great scourge of syphilis was at least partly under control. Later on, with the introduction of penicillin, it was almost completely eradicated for a while at least. This, however, was the first of the great new discoveries which were to revolutionise the whole of medicine during my professional life.

When I came back from the First World War and started in practice, the bottle of medicine was still the panacea for every trouble. The patient always got his bottle. The family doctor is nearly always, from experience, a very good psychiatrist, and his bottle of medicine was one of his best methods of treatment. Sometimes the doctor can do most good by simply listening to his patient's story of his troubles. That is one reason why the doctor today under the National Health Service is annoyed and frustrated and knows that he is not practising good medicine. His surgery is so full that he has not the time to listen to his patients. I remember very well once going to see a women patient when I was in practice. I had scarcely time to say 'Good morning' when she started telling me all about her troubles. I listened patiently for about half an hour and then came away without giving her a prescription. As I came away, she said, 'Thanks very much for your visit, Doctor. You have done me an awful lot of good.' As I went down the stairs feeling rather humbled, I realised that I had not said more than a dozen words to her. This is particularly true, I think, of people who live alone, often old people or those whose family life is unhappy or broken. The practice of medicine does not consist of handing out prescriptions or certificates in a crowded surgery, as any good doctor or clergyman will tell you.

After Salvarsan new therapeutic methods seemed to come in a flood, and at an ever-increasing rate. In 1921, the year after I returned home from the first war and started practice, insulin was isolated by Banting and Best. It was 1923 before it was being produced in a large scale in Britain. I have related in an earlier chapter how I was particularly interested in it. It completely transformed the whole outlook and future for diabetics. Instead of a short miserable, hopeless future they could now look forward to a long and useful life.

A year or two later I was in Edinburgh at the scientific meeting of the British Medical Association. At the end of a forenoon session on a subject I have forgotten, the chairman of the meeting said that he had received a letter from America which he would read. This letter said that two American physicians, Minot and Murphy, had found that if a patient with pernicious anaemia ate half a pound of raw calf's liver daily it would cure his pernicious anaemia in a few weeks. When the letter was read out, many of the doctors present laughed outright and there was a general murmur of amusement.

I had gone to Edinburgh with an Australian doctor friend who was staying with me temporarily. His father in Sydney, Australia, also a doctor, was suffering from pernicious anaemia and was only being kept alive by blood transfusions. He said to me, 'I don't care whether they are laughing or not, I am going to send a telegram to my father today and tell him to do this.'

He received a wire from his father in return, 'Think you must have gone mental but will do what you tell me.' In a few weeks he had almost fully recovered.

Pernicious anaemia or Addison's anaemia or megalocytic anaemia, as it is commonly now called, is quite a common condition.[40] At that time it was usually fatal in a year or two. It is a most distressing condition to watch. The patient died from want of oxygen. There were not sufficient blood cells to carry oxygen to the tissues of the body and in the final stages the patients were gasping for breath. On two occasions I saw patients break a window in their desperation to get air. This happened once in hospital and once in a patient's home. To look at them used to distress me more than to see patients suffering pain.

———

Pneumonia had always been the great killer of mankind, especially in northern climates like our own. It has been called the 'Captain of the Men of Death'. It seemed particularly to affect men in the prime of life. It was very accurately described by the ancient Greek physicians. 'There is thirst, dryness of tongue, desire of cold air, aberrations of mind, cough mostly dry, but if anything be brought up it is frothy phlegm with a florid tinge of blood. The bloodstained is of all others the worst.' This was an exact description of the patients I saw as a student in the Western Infirmary of Glasgow. The disease got steadily worse and the delirium increased until the ninth to the twelfth day, when the temperature, which had remained high throughout the ill-

40. The condition is the result of a lack of the vitamin B12 in the body. A derivative of B12 combines with oxygen in the haemoglobin of red cells. The vitamin is stored in the liver.

ness, fell suddenly and the patient sweated profusely. This was called the 'crisis'. When this occurred the patient usually recovered, although sometimes he collapsed and died just at the time of the crisis. The mortality rate was high, about 20 to 40% of all cases. In 1903 Osler said that 40,725 deaths occurred in England and Wales alone from pneumonia.

In these days our treatment was called 'expectant treatment'. This meant treating complications as well as we could with the means at our disposal. Nursing was all-important and very demanding. The patients were usually very delirious and noisy, liable to fall out of bed. We gave them stimulants such as alcohol and cardiac stimulants such as digitalis. Feeding was very difficult and required constant nursing attendance. In the late 1920s, a new treatment by anti-pneumococcal serum was introduced. This serum was produced through making a horse immune to the disease by injecting into its veins small doses of pneumococci. The blood of the horse was then drawn off at intervals and the serum injected into the patient's veins. This was very similar to the antitoxin which had been used in the treatment of diphtheria for over 20 years previously, and had reduced the death rate from diphtheria by about half. In the case of diphtheria the serum was injected under the skin of the patient.

The difficulty about serum for pneumonia was that there are a great many different types of pneumococcus, the organism responsible for the disease. It was necessary therefore to have at least half a dozen different types of serum available. The patient's sputum had to be examined or typed for the pneumococcus, and this took a day or two. The serum had to be given as early as possible in the disease if it was to be any good. It used to cost about £10 for serum to treat a private patient. The serum had to be given at eight-hourly intervals. That meant that one injection had to be given during the night or very early morning. As fairly large quantities had to be injected into a vein, this was a skilled procedure, and in those days very few doctors were qualified to give it and treatment usually had to be carried out in hospital or a nursing home. This treatment helped greatly and reduced the death-rate from pneumonia, but it was a very costly and laborious treatment. Fortunately a much better treatment was soon to be available.

Early in the 1930s the successor to Erlich in Germany, Domagk,[41] found that a newly synthesised red dye was effective when administered

41. Domagk received the 1939 Nobel Prize for Medicine for this work.

to mice with streptococcal infections. This substance was distributed by a German chemist, Bayer, and was called Prontosil. Good reports of this substance when administered to human subjects were recorded in the journals, but I was never able to obtain any for use myself. Very shortly afterwards it was found by French chemists at the Pasteur Institute that the active part of Prontosil was sulphanilamide, a more simple substance, which had been known for many years. Soon chemists in Britain and America, as well as in France and Germany, were producing various forms of sulphonamide and selling it under different trade names. The first sulphonamide we got in this country was called M&B 693.

I remember very well my first trial of M&B 693 when I received my first supplies. I put four typical cases of lobar pneumonia into a side-room and put two of them on to the tablets, which were soluble in water and very easy to give by mouth. The other two cases I continued on the old expectant treatment. The following day the nursing sister in charge said, 'These two cases you put on the new tablets do not appear to be very bad cases. They are not delirious and they seem to be fairly comfortable.' Next day she said to me, 'I don't think these men who are on the tablets have had pneumonia at all.' There is no doubt, however, that they had been typical cases of pneumonia. They had consolidation of the lung and all the typical signs of lobar pneumonia. There was no doubt that the disease had been arrested with the treatment, and in a day or two they were convalescent. Sulphonamide was easy to produce and in a few weeks we had ample supplies and we never again saw typical pneumonia. The students of medicine who started their studies after that time have never seen typical lobar pneumonia.

Until this time we had never really believed that we could find a drug which could kill bacteria and yet not poison the host. Now that we knew that it was possible, research chemists all over the world began to look for other and perhaps more effective substances. One of the difficulties with this research work was that these new substances were not always bactericidal in a test tube but only inside the living body. It was the reaction of the tissues which made them bactericidal, and when this was realised progress proceeded rapidly.

The story of penicillin is well known. Fleming, the pathologist at St Mary's Hospital, London, had noticed as early as 1929 that a patch of mould which had settled on one of the plates where he was culturing bacteria appeared to be destroying the bacteria. Fleming made some experiments and found that this mould produced a substance which could kill several kinds of bacteria. He found it did not seem to harm animal tissue and he thought it might be a useful dressing for wounds. He called it penicillin. Unfortunately it was difficult to produce in large quantity. He wrote a number of articles about it in the medical journals which I remember reading at the time. No one thought of injecting such a substance into the bloodstream; that was considered dangerous and useless.

In view of our experience with the sulphonamides, research workers began to consider trying this with penicillin, and in 1939 Florey and Chain at Oxford started this work. They produced a large quantity of penicillin, concentrated it 1,000 times and made it stable. They injected the substance into mice which had been experimentally infected, and found that the mice which had received even the most infinitesimal dose of this penicillin extract survived, while all the controls died within 24 hours. This proved that penicillin was by far the most powerful chemotherapeutic substance against these infections which we had ever possessed. The next stage was the production of sufficient quantities of penicillin to treat these diseases in human subjects.

This proved a very difficult problem. The war in Europe had now reached its most serious stage so far as Britain was concerned, and so Florey went to America to put all his knowledge at the disposal of the Allies in order that large quantities could be produced for use against the septic war wounds and gangrene which had been so prevalent and fatal in the First World War. It was found that penicillin was almost a specific in curing bacterial endocarditis, a condition in which the valves of the heart were affected by bacteria and which previously had always been fatal. We knew of the great value of penicillin in these cases, and the waiting time until we got our first supplies was sometimes a painful period. I remember one young girl who died of bacterial endocarditis just a few days before we received our first supplies of the drug. We had made frantic attempts to get hold of some for this particular patient during her short illness, to no avail.

Owing to the early use of sulphonamides and antibiotics like penicillin in cases of tonsillitis and other infections, many conditions like endocarditis, scarlet fever and rheumatic fever have almost disappeared today. These are late results of infection and do not now occur. Drugs have been found which are effective against tuberculosis and many other infectious diseases. Tuberculosis has been almost wiped out in Britain, and sanatoria and fever hospitals are now being used as hospitals for older people. The reduction in mortality is enormous. People are now living to a much greater age. The saving to the national economy because of less time off work and shorter stay in hospital is very great. It has been estimated that the use of anti-tuberculous drugs alone has saved the country about £55,000,000 a year, or about half the total drug bill of the National Health Service. There are still, however, very many unsolved medical problems.

The use of penicillin was of great value to the Allies in the Second World War and gave us a very considerable advantage over the Germans. In many other respects also, our medical services in North Africa were greatly superior to those of the Germans and Italians. Wounded soldiers received injections of penicillin very quickly after they were wounded. Our previous experience of war in the Near and Far East had taught us a lot. Our anti-typhoid injection was greatly superior to that of the Germans, and we produced sulphonamides which cured dysentery very rapidly while the Germans and particularly the Italians suffered very greatly.

The Japanese medical services were almost non-existent. They had spent practically no money on them, and after their first great rush forward in Malaya and Burma their troops became greatly handicapped because of diseases like scrub typhus, dysentery and malaria. This was in spite of the fact that in occupying Indonesia they had captured nearly all the world's supply of quinine. The British chemists had to set to and make substitutes for quinine, which in the event proved superior to quinine itself. Towards the end of the campaign in Burma, most of the Japanese soldiers were riddled with disease and had ceased to be an efficient fighting force. Some of those best qualified to know believe that medical services played a great part in winning these campaigns in the end. Perhaps this is one area where the philosophy of the German and Japanese aggressors failed them.

—

The pattern of medicine is quite different from what it was when I began my professional work about fifty years ago. The medical wards in hospitals in those days were full of young people and children, many of whom died. Now the medical wards are full of old people suffering from degenerative disease. Young people are exceptional. A great many diseases which used to require hospital treatment are now treated at home. The same description applies to the surgical wards, but perhaps to a lesser extent.

In more recent times, almost incredible advances have been made in our ability to control life itself, and perhaps even the further evolution of mankind. The artificial kidney machine today can take over the functions of the kidney and keep the patient alive for an indefinite time when these organs have been completely destroyed by disease. The function of the heart can be taken over, at least temporarily, by a machine, while the natural heart is being immobilised for an operation to the heart itself. It is well-known to everyone today that certain organs of the body which are essential to life, but which become diseased and useless, can now be removed and replaced by healthy organs from someone who has died suddenly in an accident.

Kidney transplants have been particularly successful. This is a dramatic procedure, but it has only limited application and there are many other recent advances in medicine which are of greater importance. In recent years, also, drugs have been developed which can control many kinds of mental disturbance, and enable patients suffering from these conditions to lead a useful life.

Most remarkable of all, perhaps, are the advances in our knowledge of molecular biology. We have learned a great many of the secrets of heredity. This is a complicated subject and difficult to explain to anyone who does not understand the cellular structure of living tissues. Perhaps a simple way to explain it is to say that every cell in the human body has inside it a pattern or diagram which can only be seen by the most high-powered modern microscopes. From the study of this pattern, however, the scientist can read a complete picture of the constitution and the physical and mental peculiarities of the individual from which the cell was taken.

A great deal of this knowledge is still only of academic interest; some of it, however, is already relevant to medical diagnosis and treatment. For example, by examining the cells which have been shed by the developing foetus into the fluid which surrounds it in the womb, it is possible at a quite early stage to tell whether the developing child is suffering from one of the serious physical or mental congenital abnormalities. This gives us some hope that we may yet be able to prevent them from occurring by methods of treatment. It is possible to tell whether the developing child is male or female. With abortion so freely available today, this may give the legal profession something to think about also. There is no doubt that these discoveries are of enormous importance to the future of mankind.

XXII
Vanity Fair (Post-War Britain)

I think I told you in one of my earlier chapters that during my childhood we used to hold family readings of Bunyan's *Pilgrim's Progress* on Sunday evenings. The characters in his allegory made a great impression on me, and I have read and re-read it all my life. Although it is now three centuries since Bunyan lived there is some similarity between his time and our own. The British people had come through a long civil war followed by ten years of austerity under Cromwell. The Monarchy was restored in 1660. After the restoration the people reacted against puritanism and Charles II's reign was notorious for its immorality and licentiousness. John Bunyan was arrested shortly after the Restoration for public preaching without authority and spent most of the next 12 years in prison. It was during that time he wrote *Pilgrim's Progress*.

To quote John Bunyan again:

> Then I saw in my dreams that when they were got out of the wilderness they presently saw a town before them and the name of that town is Vanity; and at the town there is a fair called Vanity Fair; it is held all the year long; it beareth the name of Vanity Fair because the town where it is kept is lighter than Vanity; and also because all that is there sold or that cometh thither is vanity . . . At this fair are all such merchandise sold, as houses, lands, trades, places, titles, countries, kingdoms, lusts, pleasures and delights of all sorts as, harlots, wives, husbands, children, masters, servants, lives, blood, bodies, souls, silver, gold, pearls, precious stones and what not and moreover at the fair there is at all times to be seen juggling, cheats, games, plays, fools, apes, knaves and rogues and that of every kind.
>
> Here are to be seen too, and that for nothing, thefts, murders, adulteries, false swearers and that of a blood-red colour.

If we bring these vanities up to date and describe them in modern language this is not an exaggerated description of our society today. What strikes me most forcibly about our society is the tremendous importance that is placed on money. Loyalty and service to others does not appear to count for much. In fact those who practise such virtues are looked on as being somewhat simple and half-witted. Take as much as you can and give as little as you can seems to be the accepted practice. This applies to all classes. The working people with whom I had the greatest sympathy in my early days in medical practice in Govan are now no exception. The trades unions which did such good work in those days in improving the conditions of the working people have now become extremely powerful. Some of those that are in a position to do so do not appear to hesitate to cause great hardship to the ordinary citizen, in depriving him of necessities such as transport, fuel and even food in order to gain what is very often an unfair advantage to themselves. There is no need for me to describe all our modern vanities, but I would like to say something about several others.

There seems to be an illusion in the minds of a great many people today that sex is the most important thing in life and that life can be built on sex alone. The newspapers are full of it. Television appears to be obsessed with it. Young people, as a result, are led to believe that unless they are experienced in sex and are constantly thinking about it that there is something wrong with them.

Michael Schofield, a Research Director of the Central Council for Health Education has produced what he claims was an accurate report about the sexual behaviour of Britain's teenagers. Schofield says that by the age of 19, one in three of the boys and a quarter of the girls are sexually experienced. He says that this premarital intercourse sometimes starts as early as age 15, but gets very much more common after 17. The boys are more promiscuous, but with the girls it seems to happen most often with the boys with whom they go steady, as they describe it. Most of them admit that their impulse originally was curiosity, but many of the girls said that they were in love with the boys and hoped to marry them afterwards. Less than half of the boys, 48%, and less than one third of the girls, 30%, said that they liked it. About 16% of the girls at age 19 said that they were engaged to be married, but only 4% of the boys said this.

Overall, from these figures, and I think they can be accepted as being reliable, only between one-quarter and one-third of the teenagers had this irregular intercourse and I think they must be looked on as the abnormal ones. The great majority, and no doubt the best and most natural and healthy-minded teenagers, did not do these things. In my opinion, curiosity, the bad example of older people, the great amount of publicity given to matters of sex on television and in the press today are to a great extent responsible for this abnormal minority.

Perhaps another cause of the change in the behaviour of young people is the freedom and equality with men which young women of today have compared with their mothers. During my generation women fought for and gained the vote but they gained recognition of their equality with men in a great many more important spheres than just the franchise. There used to be an accepted standard of sex morality for men, in certain classes of society at least, and a very much higher standard of morality in sex matters for women in all classes of society. Now, for a number of reasons of which contraceptive availibility is only one, the sexes look at one another as being more or less on a level. Are the young women of today going to claim the laxer standard tolerated by men, or are they going to raise the men to their higher standard? A large measure of responsibility for the permissive society may depend on them.

There is no doubt that this lax sexual behaviour does great harm to young people as individuals, psychologically as well as socially and morally. It also does great harm to society and to the community. It can do grievous harm to a young woman if she becomes pregnant. At the best it may mean a very early marriage when the parents are immature and unsure about many things and unable to undertake the great responsibilities which are involved in marriage. The Family Planning Associations are today greatly concerned as to whether they should make birth control advice available to these young people. In my opinion they should certainly do so. I do not think it is likely to make things any worse, and in any case the decisions of the young people should be made on higher grounds than on the availability of contraceptives.

Closely related to this subject is the problem of the deliberate termination of pregnancy. Like many of my medical colleagues I have been much concerned about the recent Act of Parliament which practically permits legalised termination of pregnancy (abortion) on demand. God's Universe, as astronomers describe it to us, is a wonderful and incredible creation, but life as it has developed on this planet, and man himself, the highest form of such life, is to those who understand these things even more wonderful and incredible.

There have been many advances in the scientific study of man in recent years. It seems that we are not really the same flesh as our parents after all. Every human being is a unique creation. There never has been anything like this new child before and there never will be again. The two infinitely small cells which come together at the time of conception contain within them the power to direct how the embryo is going to develop into an adult, and what kind of adult it is going to be. They appear to send on messages to the developing child. The new human being may have some of the characteristics of its parents, or even of some remote ancestor, but it may also have some characteristics that no man ever had before.

It seems an irresponsible act to destroy the developing child at any stage of its development. The only valid reason for doing so is that the life of the mother is at hazard. During my later years in practice, when I was a consulting physician, I had sometimes to give my opinion as to whether or not a pregnancy should be terminated. These were mostly cases of severe cardiac valvular disease with associated heart failure, and I had no doubt about the decision. Occasionally, however, when the abortion was recommended for more doubtful reasons I had grave misgivings.

No thoughtful and responsible gynaecologist or nurse likes to see this operation performed, especially if the foetus is at all advanced in its development. Many of them in fact refuse to perform it unless the indications are extremely urgent. These are surely the kind of cases where a previous knowledge and practice of contraception would be the lesser evil.

The Church of course is absolutely right in being so strongly against premarital and extramarital sexual intercourse. It is essential for a child to be born into a family where it is wanted and where it will be loved and cared for lovingly and well. This is the reason for the great importance which the Church places on the marriage ceremony. This is only one of the problems which confronts the Church today and about which the Church will have to make difficult decisions.

The last vanity about which I wish to say something is the most important of all. It is our apparent indifference to God and things of the spirit. We seem to have lost the faith in God which our fathers had. Our fathers accepted on trust a great deal of the religion which they were taught. For the last fifty years or more, most of us, or perhaps I should say the minority that think at all about these things, have been refusing to give credence to a great many things that our fathers believed. After all we know that the Bible, the Old and New Testaments on which our faith was founded, was written by men like ourselves who were liable to error. They wrote the story as it appealed to them and as it would appeal to their contemporaries. Today we find it difficult to accept the Bible story in the form that it was written many centuries ago. Because we cannot accept some parts of it we have made that an excuse for neglecting the whole and the most important parts which are not in doubt. Perhaps we are so concerned with worldly matters that we are glad to have some excuse for neglecting things of the Spirit.

One great cause of anxiety and uncertainty today among thinking people, and I think especially younger people, is nuclear armament. Perhaps this also has contributed to our loss of faith in God. We know that if a nuclear war were to start the civilised world would be destroyed in a very short time. Is there anything we can do about it? Many of our fellow countrymen sincerely believe that no matter what other nations do we should not arm ourselves with nuclear weapons. They are represented by C.N.D. (the Campaign for Nuclear Disarmament). However sincere they are, I believe that they are wrong in this. I am old-fashioned enough to believe in the Devil, or at least in the evil that is in the world. Man has discovered how to make nuclear weapons. The real danger is that good men may be afraid of them. If we show that we are afraid, evil men will destroy us with them. If we show that we are not afraid of them, the evil man, who is always a coward at heart, will be the first to surrender. President Kennedy will go down in history as the man who demonstrated this to mankind. This is just another phase of the continual battle between good and evil in this world of ours.

Whatever the reason, and I am not very competent to judge these matters, there is no doubt that the Christian Church in our land is being neglected today. People no longer attend church as a matter of habit. Perhaps that is not altogether a bad thing. They go when they want to go. The young people do not appear to be very interested, but the majority still like to celebrate their weddings in Church. The Church of Scotland today, I am told, is losing between 8,000 and 10,000 members annually.

I am confident, however, in spite of all these depressing facts, that sooner than most of us expect we will move on again from Vanity town to better things. In Bunyan's allegory, Faithful was beaten to death in Vanity town, but Christian escaped and went on his way. It is unlikely to be a puritan revival this time, but it may be something much better.

XXIII

Religio Medici

When we are young we believe all that we are told. In our adolescent and student years we begin to disbelieve everything and become very critical of all that we have been taught when we were young. We go through a stage later which might be called the rational period. We reason out everything, and any ideas which do not satisfy our reason we tend to reject altogether. Then there comes a period when life is so full that we have little time to think much at all. This is the period of experience. In our later years our convictions are formed not so much from pure reasoning but as a result of experience of life. We cannot explain why we believe them but we know that they are true. This perhaps applies to a greater degree than usual in a person like myself who has led a very busy life as a physician with very little leisure time. I have done very little reading apart from my professional work. My knowledge of such subjects as philosophy and theology, for example, is very deficient. I feel, however, that it is only right that I should put down in this last chapter a few of my own thoughts and convictions which are the result of that experience.

―

The contact with pain and suffering and with distress is part of a doctor's life. It is always with him and round about him. Fortunately we can do a great deal now to relieve actual physical pain, but this is the least part of our problem. We can do very little for mental suffering. The more civilised man becomes, the more sensitive and understanding his spirit, the greater is his capacity for mental suffering. This problem of human suffering has troubled all the saints and prophets and great thinkers since time began, and none of them have been able to give a satisfactory explanation.

For many years I attended professionally and was a personal friend of the Minister of the Church of Scotland in Glasgow to which I have been attached all my life. This was George Johnstone Jeffrey, who followed W. Macintosh Mackay about whom I wrote in one of my earlier chapters. Jeffrey was a Doctor of Divinity of Glasgow University and was Moderator at one time of the Church of Scotland Assembly. He was a great student and a man of great learning. The desk in his study was surrounded by books and he knew them all. He knew exactly where each volume was and could put his hand on each one in a moment, whenever he wanted to do so.

With all this knowledge he was one of the kindest and most sympathetic men I have known. He had a very happy home life and he enjoyed life very fully. He had played football in his youth and he loved to watch a game of professional football and used to get very excited on those occasions. I have been with him at a football match and when his favourite team scored a vital goal, he got up on his feet on his seat, waving his hat in the air.

He was one of these men, however, who was very much distressed when he came in contact with human suffering, and he used to get quite depressed at these times. I remember one such occasion. He had a habit of suddenly asking me questions on all sorts of subjects, but mostly I think about medical subjects. He was in bed and I was attending him professionally one day during the Second World War. He had just heard that a member of his congregation had lost an only son in action and he was very upset and saddened. Suddenly he said to me, 'Doctor, you are a kind-hearted man. How do you manage to carry on your work surrounded by so much suffering and distress? Does it not make you despondent and lose faith in God?' He knew very well the extent and limitation of my faith. We had talked about these things.

I hesitated a while before I answered, and then I said, 'It does make me a bit despondent sometimes, but if I think about it at all I sometimes say to myself, 'God can't help it. Life has got to be like this. It couldn't be otherwise.'

He did not say anything for about half a minute, and I began to think that I had said something terrible and hurt him badly. Then he responded, 'That's all right, Doctor. If it helps you to think that, I don't see why you should not do so, but that would not satisfy me. There is some explanation much more mysterious than that which we cannot meantime understand.'

'It really does not satisfy me either,' I said, 'but it helps me to forget and get on with the job.'

Nearly all of us learned the Lord's Prayer when we were children. Perhaps many of us do not say it very often now. It begins, 'Our Father which art in Heaven. Hallowed be Thy Name. Thy will be done in earth as it is in Heaven.' This does not mean that if something dreadful happens to us it is God's will. I will tell a story which may help to illustrate what I mean.

I was called out late one evening during the last war by a doctor to see two medical cases. The first case was a child who had a tuberculous pleurisy, and I decided it would have to go to hospital. The prognosis was quite good and the child was almost certain to make a good recovery, but the parents were not British, they came from southern Europe and they made a great fuss and there was much weeping when I told them that the child had to go to hospital. I did not think much about that, because I knew what to expect and it was their natural reaction to such a situation.

The second case was much more tragic. It was an only child and his father had been killed in the war a few months earlier. The child's mother and grandmother, his father's mother, were there. A glance at this child told me that it had meningitis. In those days the commonest cause of meningitis in a child of that age was tuberculosis, and it was invariably fatal. Cerebrospinal fever, or 'spotted fever' as it was sometimes called, was the next most common type. In a sporadic case like this in a child, it was also a very fatal disease. Probably about 50% survived in those days. There were a few other rare types of meningitis caused by pathogenic germs like the pneumococcus, but they were just as fatal at that time as tuberculous meningitis. This child had no rash and I very much feared that it was the tuberculous type. When I told the women that I was afraid that the child had meningitis, the mother wept quietly, but Grannie said, 'It's God's will, Doctor.' It was obvious that she was terribly distressed but she was quite calm.

I got the mother to wrap up the child and I took the two women and the child along to my own wards at the Victoria. I took some fluid from the child's spinal canal and to my great joy it was turbid. Spinal fluid from a case of tuberculosis is always quite clear. It was either cerebrospinal fever or one of the pathogens.

Staining and microscopic examination showed it to be pneumococcus. We had recently got new drugs to combat pneumococcus and I began to be hopeful. I had actually cured a case of pneumococcal meningitis in a young man about six months previously with pneumococcal serum, and now we had the sulphonamides, which were even better.

I gave the child a maximum dose of sulphonamide. In the morning the child was greatly improved and very rapidly made a complete recovery.

Grannie was quite right, of course, to say, 'It's God's will.' What she really meant was that she trusted God whatever happened. If the child had died it would be wrong, I am sure, to say that it was God's will. I would say rather that it was God's will that I should work to the utmost to save the child.

———

I have seen very many people die during my long life as a physician. Few people, I think, can have been in the presence of death more often than I have been. One thing that has impressed me, in spite of what we read in novels, is that it is extremely rare for men or women to know when they are about to die. One would expect that doctors, at least, would know when they are dying. I have looked after many medical men in their final illnesses. Many of them knew, of course, when they developed incurable diseases and understood at least that their days were numbered. As the days of their illness went on they appeared to care less and less about this aspect and concerned themselves chiefly about simple and family matters. When the day came for their departure from this life, they very seldom appeared to realise that they were going. Most often they became unconscious for a short time or passed away in their sleep.

Sudden or violent death is, I think, much the same. I doubt very much if those who are so stricken know that they are dying. None of the soldiers that I saw going into battle in the first war expected to die. At the worst I think they thought that they might get a 'blighty'. This was a wound that would take them out of the war for good. It seems illogical, when this was their outlook, that death should mean the end of their body and their spirit also. I think this was how James Bridie was thinking when he wrote his play *The Queen's Comedy*. Personally I have never been able to believe in the resurrection of the body, but I do believe that the spirit of those whom I loved on earth still influences me, although they are gone.

One of the things that has troubled me all my medical life, and still troubles me, is where to place in the world the child who is born mentally deficient and grows up without any understanding. It seems to me even more difficult to explain that problem than to explain pain and suffering.

One must admit that the natural world around us appears to be an amoral world. It is a beautiful and wonderful world, but it is also a cruel and wicked world. The natural world, the world of living creatures, does not appear to be concerned at all with ethical value and still less with spiritual value. Nevertheless, if the world instead were a moral world and all its creatures were naturally good, it would be a very poor world for men to dwell in. It is only in a neutral world like ours that there is a choice between good and evil, and man's character can develop and evolve.

Some psychologists would have us believe that our ideas of good and evil are only what we have learned by precept and custom since we were born into the world. I do not believe this. My experience of life does not bear this out. We may be taught what is right and what is wrong and the things we are taught may be right or wrong, but good and evil are different – they are external and spiritual things. They do not change.

I have met many degraded and hopeless people: men who had been in and out of jail many times; men and women who seemed to have a grudge against society; men and women who have been brought up under the most miserable and unhappy conditions in childhood. Even the worst of them responded a little to kindness and sympathy, and I have no doubt that they all instinctively knew the difference between good and evil. In my days of practice in Govan I used to be greatly surprised how very kind and generous such ignorant, unhappy and neglected people could be to one another.

Less than 2000 years ago, a very short time, really, in the history of man's evolution, Jesus of Nazareth lived in Palestine. This is the part of the world from which most of man's knowledge and understanding of spiritual things has come. Man's spiritual knowledge has increased through the ages, just as his knowledge of the physical world has increased. Gradually man's idea of God seemed to change. The Psalmist said, 'The Lord is my Shepherd'. The prophet Hosea spoke of God's forgiveness and love for His children.

The idea of God which Jesus gave to the world transcended anything that had gone before. We have even yet not realised the full significance of his message. He spoke many wonderful words which have changed the whole history of the world and which men have studied and argued about ever since.

It is significant that this man Jesus, to whom this idea about God came, spent most of his life as a simple peasant and carpenter. When he could no longer keep his thoughts to himself and felt that he must tell the message that had come to him, he went about the simple people among whom he lived, telling them his message by word of mouth. He lived according to the message which he spoke. He went about doing good and comforting all those who needed comfort. He was always especially concerned about the sick and suffering.

One thing which Jesus of Nazareth said many times during his ministry on earth was that he was the Son of God. He said also that we were God's children, and that God had infinite love for each one of us. Man is growing up fast in recent years if he is learning to control his own evolution. Surely if we are growing up, we should begin to help with our Father's business. This may sound rather like Humanism, but I am not a Humanist. I know that we would lose the way very soon if we lost our faith in God.

The road along which mankind has to travel is not an easy one. Sometimes it goes through pleasant places, but more often it is rough and stony and always seems to be going uphill. After many years' observation and close study of human nature, I have come to understand that this is the best road and in fact the only road along which God's children can travel.

Afterword by Alec Glen's Sons

How will new generations respond to this story of order and disorder, in which two world wars occur, and life is depicted at times as a struggle between good and evil?

The final act of Bridie's last play, *Baikie Charivari* (1952), deals with the possibility of war with hydrogen bombs and germ warfare and the modern predicament of being caught between two solid blocks of fanatics. Bridie gives his hero these words:

'I know order and I know disorder.
Order I have forever loved and ensured.
Here and there I have imposed order upon this eel-pit of a world.
My order could move within itself, orderly,
Propagate and increase in peace.
This is the order of two dead stones –
Two dead, flat stones, pieces of machinery
I will not lie down and be crushed by these horrible stones.'

In the scientific world, order and disorder are governed by the Second Law of Thermodynamics which, put simply, tells us that free energy is required to bring about a reduction in disorder, or entropy.★ Serious work is being done to extend this principle to the study of disorder arising from conflict in the world, but there are gaps. How is the energy to be directed? Furthermore, the Second Law also tells us that, in a closed system, increasing order in one part will result in greater disorder elsewhere. We do not yet know if the universe is a closed system.

The problems of order and disorder remain and there we leave it, with the closing exchange from the play in which the De'il is asked:

'Can I wait for time?'
'I dinna ken.'

Iain Glen and Alastair Glen
Dalnavert and Glasgow, 2012

★Free energy change = the change in initial energy state – the change in entropy or disorder; or Delta G = Delta H – T Delta S. (The Gibbs equation for a closed system.)

Index